# Gender, Development, and Globalization

# Gender, Development, and Globalization

## Economics as if All People Mattered

### Lourdes Benería

Routledge
New York & London

Published in 2003 by
Routledge
29 West 35th Street
New York, New York 10001
www.routledge-ny.com

Published in Great Britain by
Routledge
22 New Fetter Lane
London EC4P 4EE
www.routledge.co.uk

Routledge is an imprint of the Taylor & Francis Group.
Printed in the United States of America on acid-free paper.

10  9  8  7  6  5  4  3  2

Library of Congress Cataloging-in-Publication Data

Benería, Lourdes.
    Gender, development, and globalization : economics as if all people mattered / by Lourdes Benería.
        p. cm.
    Includes bibliographical references.
    ISBN 0-415-92706-4 — ISBN 0-415-92707-2 (pbk.)
        1. Feminist economics. 2. Women in development. 3. Globalization.
I. Title.

HQ1381 .B46 2003
330'.082—dc21

                                                              2002036622

# Contents

# Acknowledgments

As with most books, these chapters are a reflection of a collective project and it would be difficult to thank all those who, in different ways, have contributed to it. I am most grateful to the group of friends working on gender and development with whom I have collaborated on a variety of projects over the years: Isabella Bakker, Radhika Balakrishnan, Savitri Bisnath, Gunseli Berik, Nilufer Çagatay, Diane Elson, Shelley Feldman, Maria Floro, Caren Grown, Amy Lind, Martha MacDonald, Brenny Mendoza, Martha Roldan, Luis Santiago, Gita Sen, and Jennifer Tiffany. Many thanks also to other friends and colleagues who have been most helpful in a variety of ways: Juan Arbona, Cristina Carrasco, Martha Chen and other members of WIEGO, Marianne Ferber, Sakiko Fukuda-Parr and fellow researchers at UNDP's Human Development Report, William Goldsmith, Sherry Gorelick, Noeleen Heyzer, Aileen Allen and other friends at UNIFEM, Renana Jhabvala, Naila Kabeer, Arthur MacEwan, Philip McMichael, Julie Nelson, Porus Olpadwala, Katharine Rankin, Amartya Sen, Gale Summerfield, and Verena Stolcke. I have also learned much from my many Latin American friends and colleagues who over the years have helped me understand the realities of that vast and always fascinating continent. I am appreciative for the fellowships received for writing from the John D. and Kathrine D. MacArthur Foundation and the Woodrow Wilson International Center for Scholars in Washington. Many thanks also to the Radcliffe Institute for Advanced Study, which provided a forum to discuss parts of these chapters when I was a fellow at the Institute, and to Paula Rayman and Françoise Carré for inviting me to participate. At Routledge, I want to thank my editor Eric Nelson as well as Ben McCanna and Nikki Hirschman. Last but not least, I must thank those who helped me with research and technical work at various stages, particularly Ana Arroyo, Len Ktach, Wooyong Hyun, Marjorie Miles, and the group of students at Cornell's Department of City and Regional Planning who worked with the interviews in Cortland, New York, that provided information for chapter 4.

# Introduction

The chapters in this book reflect the conviction that women's issues cannot be isolated and separated from the socioeconomic and cultural contexts in which they are immersed. As an economist, I have grounded my research, teaching, and action in the material world that shapes the roots of our feminist concerns. The book's two main objectives are, first, to examine the ways in which gender has been integrated in economics as a central category of analysis and, second, to examine various aspects in development and the global economy that illustrate the ways in which they interact with the social construction of gender, gender in equality, and human welfare. Discovering the role and condition of women in development began by considering the lacunae in the field. Over the years, confronting the absence of women's experience in economics in general and in development in particular, feminists have moved beyond critiques of androcentric models to the creation of alternative policies for women and for development.

These chapters are the product of my involvement in this process for almost a quarter century. In 1977, early in the spring semester, I was encouraged to apply for a job to coordinate the International Labour Organization's (ILO) Programme on Rural Women from Geneva, Switzerland. Since the fall of 1975, I had been teaching economics at Rutgers University after finishing graduate school with a concentration on labor economics and development. My own written work on women had been limited to a paper on women in Spain during the 1940–72 period of

Franco's dictatorship. In graduate school I had taken courses in economic development, and had mostly concentrated on Latin America, but my knowledge of the developing world had not been accompanied with any first-hand experience in Third World countries. With some hesitation, I decided to apply for the job, and we moved to Geneva, Switzerland, in May 1977. The program I was to coordinate was part of the ILO's World Employment Programme, with a clear mandate to concentrate on the Third World and rural women. Although I did not realize it at the time, I had embarked on an experience that would change my understanding of the world and the orientation of my work; a much more direct contact with the Third World widened my intellectual horizons and deepened my encounter with other cultures (as well as my own). This book includes many illustrations of the work that followed.

Once at the ILO, I soon found that my training in economics was insufficient to deal with the work of a program addressing the problems of rural women. As an economist, I had acquired theoretical and conceptual tools that turned out to be too narrowly defined and not interdisciplinary enough to work on issues affecting the large majority of the world's rural women around whom the Programme was organized. The most relevant, but not very abundant, literature on the subject at the time came from fields other than economics, such as anthropology and sociology. There were a few exceptions, such as the work of Danish economist Ester Boserup—who in 1970 published her pioneer book *Woman's Role in Economic Development*—and the initial writings of the new contributors to the field of what we now call "gender and development." To a great extent, the influence of their work—which began to appear during the second half of the 1970s—along with that of other social scientists, is reflected in the pages of this book.

Very soon, I became aware of the need for an interdisciplinary approach to the Programme's activities. The questions that were emerging as relevant to these activities were diverse and multifaceted, influenced by the cultural and socioeconomic conditions in which women were immersed across countries and regions. Economistic approaches to the Programme's organization and activities would clearly have been too narrow. While it was important, for example, to focus on economic factors in the process of development in order to contextualize questions of poverty, growth, and opportunities among rural women, other factors such as patriarchal norms, traditions, institutions, and values affecting women's lives were also key to understanding their condition and subordination. Likewise, it was not enough to look at labor market factors to understand women's incorporation in the labor force; other aspects of this process needed to be taken into consideration, such as the limitations placed on women by cultural practices affecting gender constructions, women's and men's work and women's mobility. Each of these factors had to be taken into consideration. This was obvious for the overall work of the Programme; it also changed my own work and ways of seeing in fundamental ways.

Given that the unfolding feminist work at the time emphasized the need for interdisciplinary approaches, much help could come from the growing interest in women's issues that emanated from the still-young international women's movement. The first world conference of the United Nations (UN) Decade of Women had taken place in Mexico City in 1975. In November of 1977, a conference at the University of Sussex, England, organized by a group of English women under the umbrella of their "subordination of women" (SOW) project, gave me a first opportunity to attend a pioneer gathering of international women focusing on a variety of development themes that reflected many of the initial steps toward the unfolding of feminist approaches to development.[1] We were just beginning to understand the ways in which development processes had been far from gender neutral over the years. The papers and discussions at the conference raised new questions about gender inequality and the subordination of women across countries and cultures. Within the predominant theoretical paradigms of the 1970s, new questions arose on the "naturalness" of gender divisions and the factors affecting women's lives and ability to function under different economic and social systems. At the same time, old questions—such as population control and the role of women in reproduction and production, the gender division of labor, the control of women's sexuality, and others—were analyzed under new, feminist lenses. Many new questions and unexplored areas of research and action emerged as a result. It was clear that the amount of work ahead was enormous, and the challenges both overwhelming and exciting.

This book is a reflection of some of the avenues followed and of the progress made in the analysis of gender and development issues since the 1970s. Grounded in the discipline of economics but nourished by interdisciplinary work, it reflects the conviction that feminist analysis is key and relevant to understanding basic questions of human development. While focusing on general questions having to do with issues not normally associated (often mistakenly) with feminist analysis, the book uses the notion of gender as a central organizing category to discuss selected topics in international development and the global economy. More specifically, it makes use of the lens provided by feminism, and of feminist economics in particular, to highlight the extent to which a gender perspective can enrich our understanding of many areas of economics and international development—including the formation of global markets, economic restructuring, labor market informalization, the feminization of the labor force, and the changing patterns of gender constructions. In many ways, the book is a product of the collective, rich, and passionate work that has involved many women and some men during more than three decades.

Although this book deals with a small proportion of this enormous effort, it also provides an illustration of the unfolding of this new field as well as of the transformation of knowledge—with implications for policy and action—along the lines described by philosopher Elizabeth Minnich (1990). Discussing the question of how traditional analysis that excluded women resulted in partial knowledge, Minnich points out that knowledge is not only a human construct but suggests a "deferred meaning" within, and between, its own texts/discourses, its own cross-references. She adds that whatever is actually included in these constructs in fact plays "against what is absent, denied, suppressed" (p. 148). In this typical fashion, the field of development had largely ignored women as actors and subjects—even as passive recipients—in the economic and social processes that have affected their lives. Women's concerns and interests had most often been *absent, denied, suppressed* in official discourses, as well as in policy and action.

The 1970s was a decade of what we might call post-Boserup discovery: we had learned that, from colonial times on, the historical processes that had been given the name of "development" had had a differential impact on men and women, but much more knowledge and details were needed to fully understand them. Various studies contributed to our knowledge of the ways in which this gender differentiation manifested itself. Since then, this work has expanded enormously, and in different directions, encompassing all disciplines and areas of action. In retrospect, we have learned a great deal and much has changed for women (and men) since that time— the chapters in this book contain many illustrations of this process. Unfortunately, however, many problems remain—and some even have intensified or appeared new. Despite a great deal of work and many successes, there is much room for disappointment in what the past three decades have accomplished in terms of improving the lives of all people and, more specifically, the lives of women. One of the arguments of this book is that, although women have made tremendous progress toward gender equality and many inroads at all levels of society, the results have been uneven, in many ways insufficient, and often contradictory.

From a development perspective, the past two decades have been discouraging. The onslaught of neoliberal policies across the globe since the late 1970s brought a new era in which market-oriented criteria—even market fundamentalism—have taken over in setting goals and development objectives. Many Third World countries have witnessed a deterioration of living conditions for a majority of their population, with increased financial instability, economic insecurity, and social tensions. To be sure, globalized markets have brought new prosperity and growth to a variety of sectors and regions. Markets have generated new sources of accumulation and unprecedented wealth, but within the context of growing inequalities, both within and between countries. Within the Organization for Economic Co-operation and Development(OECD), for example, earnings inequalities during the 1980s increased the most in the United Kingdom and the United States, and the least in the Scandinavian countries (UNDP 1999). In Latin America during the 1990s, the historically very high degree of income concentration did not diminish even in countries that achieved some growth. To illustrate with the important case of Mexico—a country that has been viewed as a leader in Latin American trends—a recent study shows that economic liberalization and globalization have resulted in an increasing "economic, social and territorial polarization" (Dussel Peters 2000). At the global level, the United Nations Development Programme (UNDP) estimates for 1998 showed that the assets of the three richest people were more than the combined GNP of all least developed countries, while the assets of the 200 richest people were more than the combined income of 41 percent of the world's population.[2] In the same way, capital has become increasingly concentrated through mergers and acquisitions of megacorporations at the national and transnational level, raising many questions about the danger in the corresponding concentration of power and the real meanings of democracy. UNDP figures for 1997 show that top corporations had sales totaling more than the GDP of many countries (UNDP 1999).[3]

Yet, parallel to these trends, hegemonic discourses have emphasized the notion that neoliberal policies and expanding markets have been important mechanisms for the building of democracies, particularly in developing countries. The contradictory tendencies observed, especially when we differentiate between political and economic democracy, have by and large not been confronted. Referring to the Latin America region, president Dualde of Argentina has put it this very explicitly:

> The dream of economic growth, peace and democracy has been shattered. In its place, there is depression, populism and deteriorating personal security. Argentina itself has been caught in a vicious circle of repression, unemployment, falling living standards, social unrest and political paralysis.[4]

Despite these worrisome trends, world leaders and many development actors seem to ignore the likely consequences of growing social tensions. Instead of prioritizing policies to eliminate poverty and redistribute the new wealth and access to the resources generated by the new economy of flexible capitalism, redistribution has been left on the back burner, mostly confined to poverty alleviation programs, which focus on extreme poverty, not on the systemic factors generating it.[5] Hence, malaise and critiques of these global trends continues to mount. No wonder that the "end of history" and the notion of no alternative to the neoliberal world are now being questioned from a wide variety of quarters and political perspectives.

We have heard these criticisms on many occasions, often very loudly. As I write this the Group of Eight (G-8) summit in Genoa, Italy, in July 2001 has brought us the vivid images of the thousands of demonstrators in the city's streets, the killing of one protestor by the police, and the contradictory and disturbing picture of leaders from the world's most powerful "democracies" being surrounded by barricades and a fortress of security of medieval proportions. One can not help but ask whether they understand what is happening outside the fortress. U.S. President Bush's reply to the demonstrators was to preach free trade as the best tool for helping poor nations, thus reiterating the official U.S. position without any effort at listening to those who insist that free trade has *not* helped *them*. Immediately after the Genoa events, Bush has continued to display similar insensitivity to the need to foster a global dialogue about these issues. At the Roman Forum from which he spoke after the Genoa events, the President maintained his righteous candor by affirming, "I know what I believe" and "I believe what I believe is right."[6]

Britain's prime minister Tony Blair did no better. Reacting to the Genoa events before knowing how thuggish the Italian police had acted, Blair declared: "So these people can come and they can riot and protest on the street and throw petrol bombs at the police and then we, the democratic leaders, should conclude from that that we should never meet again."[7] France's conservative president Jacques Chirac's reaction was more open-minded: "One hundred thousand people don't get upset unless there is a problem in their hearts and spirits," he affirmed.[8] Likewise, France's prime minister, Lionel Jospin, reinforced this contrast with the Anglo-Saxon reactions: "While denouncing the violence to which a minority resort on the pretext of denouncing the ravages of globalization, France rejoices in the worldwide emergence of a citizen's movement, in much as it expresses the wish of the majority of mankind better to share the potential fruits of globalization."[9]

As these quotes illustrate, many world leaders do not seem to understand that concerns and even resentment about social inequalities, corruption, arrogance, and abuses of economic and political power are deep and widespread. Further, they can be found not only among the poor and developing countries. The passion of the demonstrators is about specific global issues such as trade, finance, and the environment; it springs from a sense of dignity, justice, equality, and fairness, which contrasts with the displays of power, lavishness, and top-down communication (or lack of it) emanating from the participants at these meetings. Rather than listening to the concerns of the activists, world leaders remain insensitive to the urgent need to understand those who experience life from a different perspective.

The conflict between activists and the development establishment was also symbolized by the 1980s and 1990s protests against the International Monetary Fund (IMF) and the World Bank—such as the Fifty Years is Enough campaign. One result was the World Bank's attempt to respond to the many critiques of its work through a reorganization of its programs—with mixed results, as will be discussed in chapter 2. Others are beginning to talk about a turning point in development thinking, but even this process soon will be aborted if it is not engaged in a true democratic dialogue that communicates from the bottom-up the needs felt at different levels of society and across countries. "Helping poor people"—an expression often found in the literature and in the attitudes of those involved with development work—should not be the goal. Instead of "helping," the objective should be to do away with poverty by enabling the poor to find their own solutions and by recognizing their right to be fully integrated in the collective processes of human development. This is particularly applicable to women; their economic, social, and political rights must be recognized and their voices heard without patriarchal constraints to gender equality.

To be sure, the effort of listening to these concerns encompasses much more than activism and politics. It begins with our conceptualizations and visions of society and social change. This is one of the basic arguments in this book which focuses on the connections between theory and practice, between the local and the global, and between development and the economics and politics of everyday life. Chapter 1 introduces the conceptual frameworks that contextualize the book, with a discussion on discourses of gender, development, and economics. Chapter 2 provides a historical overview of the gradual integration of women's issues and of gender analysis in the field of economics. Chapter 3 focuses on gender and globalization, first by presenting the notion of market constructions at the global level and, second, by analyzing the gender dimensions of market society. Chapter 4 reviews current trends in economic restructuring, labor market informalization, and the generation of precarious jobs, emphasizing the gender dimensions of such processes and their connection to persistent poverty and economic insecurity across nations. Chapter 5 focuses on the importance of unpaid work as an economic activity and presents the various aspects of the paid/unpaid labor debate and the two-decade old efforts at measuring unpaid work. Finally, chapter 6 summarizes themes and presents suggestions for policy and action. As indicated, there are parts in the book that have been published before; most have been revised in order to integrate them into the corresponding chapters.

## CHAPTER 1

# On Development, Gender, and Economics

*We have moved from seeing women as victims to seeing them as essential
to finding solutions to the world's problems*
—speaker at the UN Conference on Women, Beijing, China, 1995

*The cooler rational types may fill our textbooks,
but the world is richer*
—Amartya Sen, 1987

## Development at a Crossroads?

This chapter introduces the various analytical frameworks under which this book has been written, focusing mostly on "development" discourses, gender, and economics. I have written the word "development" in quotes to indicate that, as discussed below, there are problems with this notion as an organizing concept given the problematic history of development and "undevelopment" affecting many countries today. In some academic circles, the notion of "post-development" has appeared to indicate not only the lack of development afflicting many countries and regions; it also reflects a critical view of the ways in which most work on development has had an economistic bias. However, throughout the book I continue to use the term for lack of a more appropriate substitute and because it facilitates the links with the existing literature and work discussed. This section introduces various aspects of the development context that inform a good proportion of the theoretical and practical issues discussed in the book. It begins with the account of a specific event at a development conference, which I use to highlight some of the themes and problems discussed in the different chapters and to introduce institutional aspects that provide a reference for the discussion of development.

On June 21 to 23, 1999, I attended a conference in Paris titled "Governance, Equity, and Global Markets," organized by the World Bank and the French Ministry of the Economy, Finances, and Industry. Focusing mostly on development in Third World countries, this was the first World Bank conference of its kind in Europe. It was intended to indicate that Europe, as a whole, represented the Bank's largest shareholder and as such should play a corresponding role in the Bank's structure and activities; this has not been the case throughout the Bank's history. The conference reflected World Bank president James D. Wolfensohn's notion that the Bank needed new and radical approaches to deal with the challenge of development in the twenty-first century. As Wolfensohn stated in his opening speech, poverty in the world had been on the increase during the 1990s, taking on new and socially destructive forms and illustrated in a widening gap between the rich and poor. The answer to this problem, he pointed out, was no simple solution, but he emphasized that the most effective development strategies strike a balance between economic, social, financial, and environmental factors. The best strategies, Wolfensohn pointed out, begin and end with the dignity of each human being.

One could hardly disagree with these general remarks and objectives; the problem is how to make the strategies more specific at the theoretical and practical level—and then how to translate them into concrete and effective policies and action. A different issue is the extent to which the Bank itself can be criticized for failing to operationalize these objectives, or even for creating some of the problems as discussed.

In the same vein, French prime minister Lionel Jospin, also in attendance, emphasized in his conference opening speech, that development cannot be reduced to economic and financial aspects but must be considered as a whole. The process of equality in development, he pointed out, cannot be reduced to a universal model. Development strategies must be tailored to the history and social reality of each country, transforming it without destroying the fundamental values on which it is based. I mention this point for its striking contrast with the homogenizing tendencies that have been represented by the Washington Consensus during the past two decades—in which the market and capitalism, in particular, have been presented as the only path leading to world development and global economic interaction—and to "the end of history."

This consensus, based on market-driven capitalist development, led to the package of policies that has become very familiar since the early 1980s in high- and low-income countries. The list is well known: attacks on Keynesianism and critiques of government intervention in the economy, market deregulation, government budget, cuts and the dismantling of the welfare state, privatization of public industries, trade liberalization, and open doors to foreign investment and mergers leading to the increasing concentration of capital in large multinational corporations and resulting in a shift toward more globalized economies. In countries with high levels of foreign debt, these policies have been implemented under the umbrella of structural adjustment programs with the key purpose of dealing with the debt burden and debt payments. The consequences have been devastating for a large proportion of the population. Increasing economic inequalities and social polarization, even increasing poverty, have been the subject of much research and debate among development circles. I return to this topic throughout the book.

The World Bank and the IMF, together with the U.S. government, played an important role in shaping this Washington Consensus, but the contributing actors have been many. As the applause of the *The Economist* and *The Wall Street Journal* have often emphasized, "the free market revolution" spread "from the classrooms of Cambridge, Massachusetts" to other parts of the world, often through former students applying "economic theories of elite U.S. universities" to Latin America and other regions with very different historical contexts (*Wall Street Journal*, August 8, 1994). The writings in these publications have typified the notion that the Davos Man, representing the global economic and political elites across continents (see chapter 4), by embracing "the free-market spirit of recent years," would "bring peoples together more that force them apart" (*The Economist*, 1/14/95 and 2/1/97). Echoing the optimistic conventional wisdom among academic circles in economics, *The Economist* has often reflected the strong conviction that "free markets produce prosperity and growth" even though this means that "some people will get very rich, and that some firms [and individuals] will go spectacularly bust."

Since the Asian Crisis of 1997, in particular, the triumphalism of the Davos Man has been more subdued and tamed by the vociferous protests and demonstrations—from Seattle in 1999 to Prague 2000, Quebec 2001, and Genoa 2002, to the global tensions that have emerged around terrorism across countries and antiprivatization riots in Latin America. Many of these demonstrations are by now associated with the meetings of international organizations including the World Bank, and the annual Group of Seven (G-7) summit involving the leading high-income countries. The demonstrations express the growing popular conviction that the market needs regulation to avoid its own negative consequences. In the case of global financial markets, the call for reform has been widespread, even among those who have been important players in them (Soros 1998). The key question now is what sort of controls and what forms of governance will be established. The Paris Conference reflected this transitional situation from the Washington Concensus but from the perspective of the development establishment.

The panels and papers at the conference showed the difficulties of changing these institutions and their goals from within; they made explicit the contradictions between the goals expressed—at least in some of the papers—and the prevailing views of how to best achieve them. Listening to the discussions, one could hardly fail to be reminded of the French expression *plus ça change plus c'est la même chose.* The conventional discourse among most conference participants was quite overwhelming with its hegemonic weight. Yet, some of the papers presented and the discussions that followed did reflect a break from the Washington Consensus.[1] How this break could have an impact on the World Bank agendas and ultimately on development programs aiming at progressive social change was much more complicated.

A panel on the issue of foreign debt and debt relief reflected the conviction that debt forgiveness for the poorest countries was essential, even though a complete write-off was unlikely. A few days earlier on June 18, 1999 in Cologne, Germany, the G-7 representatives had agreed during their annual summit to cancel some $70 billion of debt owed by the world's poorest countries. Pending approval at the different country levels and subject to the debt-relief plan to be agreed at the annual IMF–World Bank meeting three months later, thirty-three countries were to benefit from this agreement if they met the conditions set by the plan. The agreement was presented as a significant step in the urgent need for debt relief for the poorest and most indebted countries, although it fell short of expectations—as subsequent efforts have continued to do. In many ways, the debt crisis has become the problem that does not go away, at least for many countries and not just for the poorest. As illustrated by the Argentinean crisis that precipitated the country's default in January 2002, problems associated with the debt continue to be a source of serious financial and economic instability and a reason on the part of the international community to question the development model associated with the neoliberal policies of the past two decades.

The heavy burden that the debt presents for many countries has been discussed widely during the past two decades; thus, the information that follows is provided solely to re-state general trends and present an illustration for the Latin American region. Table 1.1 shows that from 1980 to 1999 total external debt continued to increase for all Latin American countries despite almost two decades of structural adjustment and belt tightening. To be sure, expressed in relative terms, some improvements have been registered. Sixteen out of the twenty-five countries have seen their total debt/GNP ratio decrease considerably, although the largest countries registered a deterioration in this trend. Thus, it cannot be said that there were no improvements. As a visit to any Latin American capital illustrates, lavish

**Table 1.1** Changes in External Debt: Latin America, 1980–1999

| COUNTRY | TOTAL EXTERNAL DEBT (US$ MILLIONS OF CURRENT DOLLARS) | | | TOTAL DEBT TO GNP (%) | | | TOTAL DEBT SERVICE AS % OF EXPORTS | | | INTEREST PAYMENTS AS % OF EXPORTS | | |
|---|---|---|---|---|---|---|---|---|---|---|---|---|
| | 1980 | 1993 | 1999 | 1980 | 1993 | 1999 | 1980 | 1993 | 1999 | 1980 | 1993 | 1999 |
| Argentina | 27,157 | 74,473 | 147,981 | 35.6 | 28.6 | 54 | 37.3 | 46.0 | 69.6 | 20.8 | 25.3 | 28.6 |
| Bolivia | 2,702 | 4,213 | 6,157 | 93.4 | 61.9 | 76 | 35.0 | 59.4 | 31.8 | 21.1 | 16.0 | 11.5 |
| Brazil | 71,012 | 132,749 | 244,673 | 31.8 | 26.3 | 34 | 63.1 | 24.4 | 120.8 | 33.7 | 9.2 | 15.5 |
| Chile | 12,081 | 20,637 | 37,762 | 45.5 | 44.7 | 56 | 43.1 | 23.4 | 17.4 | 19.0 | 9.4 | 5.5 |
| Colombia | 6,941 | 17,173 | 34,538 | 20.9 | 32.3 | 41 | 16.0 | 29.4 | 43.2 | 11.6 | 10.1 | 11.8 |
| Costa Rica | 2,744 | 3,872 | 4,182 | 59.7 | 48.1 | 31 | 29.1 | 18.1 | 6.2 | 14.6 | 6.8 | 2.4 |
| Dominican Republic | 2,002 | 4,633 | 4,771 | 31.2 | 45.1 | 29 | 25.3 | 12.1 | — | 12.0 | 5.3 | — |
| Ecuador | 5,997 | 14,110 | 14,506 | 53.8 | 98.8 | 81 | 33.9 | 25.7 | 22.8 | 15.9 | 11.3 | 9.7 |
| El Salvador | 911 | 2,012 | 4,014 | 26.1 | 21.0 | 33 | 7.5 | 14.9 | 7.7 | 4.7 | 6.2 | 4.8 |
| Guatemala | 1,166 | — | 4,660 | 14.9 | 22.4 | 26 | 7.7 | 13.2 | 9.6 | 3.6 | 4.9 | 4.3 |
| Guayana | — | — | 1,527 | — | — | 246 | — | — | 15.0 | — | — | 6.8 |
| Haiti | 303 | — | 1,191 | 20.9 | — | 28 | — | — | — | — | — | 3.2 |
| Honduras | 1,472 | 3,865 | 5,333 | 60.6 | 101.2 | 102 | 21.4 | 31.5 | 13.4 | 12.4 | 13.1 | 7.5 |
| Jamaica | 1,904 | 4,279 | 3,913 | 78.0 | 103.5 | 60 | 19.0 | 20.1 | 18.6 | 10.8 | 8.4 | 6.4 |
| Mexico | 57,378 | 118,028 | 166,960 | 30.5 | 32.8 | 35 | 48.1 | 31.5 | 24.6 | 26.6 | 10.5 | 5.5 |
| Nicaragua | 2,192 | 10,445 | 6,986 | 108.5 | 695.4 | 341 | 22.3 | 29.1 | 27.6 | 13.4 | 15.9 | 15.5 |
| Panama | 2,975 | 6,802 | 6,837 | 81.8 | 101.6 | 77 | 6.3 | 3.1 | — | 3.3 | 1.2 | 9.4 |
| Paraguay | 955 | 1,599 | 2,514 | 20.7 | 20.4 | 32 | 18.6 | 14.9 | 8.5 | 8.5 | 4.6 | 5.5 |
| Peru | 9,386 | 20,328 | 32,284 | 47.6 | 46.1 | 64 | — | 58.7 | 26.2 | 19.9 | 23.8 | 17.6 |
| Trinidad & Tobago | 829 | 2,137 | 2,462 | 14.0 | 47.6 | 38 | 6.8 | — | 10.8 | 1.6 | — | 3.6 |
| Uruguay | 1,660 | 7,259 | 7,447 | 17.0 | 54.3 | 36 | 18.8 | 27.7 | 20.4 | 10.6 | 16.5 | 22.2 |
| Venezuela | 29,345 | 37,465 | 35,852 | 42.1 | 62.6 | 36 | 27.2 | 22.8 | 21.3 | 13.8 | 12.5 | 9.6 |

*Sources:* The World Bank, *2000/1: Attacking Poverty (09/2000)*, pp. 314–15.
The World Bank, *Global Development Finance 2001: Building Coalitions for Effective Development Finance*, pp. 145–47.

office buildings and shopping centers as well as privileged gated communities have appeared in prosperous locations. They reflect the benefits from their connections to the more prosperous sectors linked to modernization and globalization, such as the financial and export sectors.

The same mixed picture is illustrated by the figures on total debt service—that is, the annual interest that countries are required to pay, as a percentage of exports. These trends are not exclusive of Latin America; they have also been experienced by African and Asian countries. As illustrated in Table 1.2, between 1980 to 1999 many countries in these two regions also registered a considerable increase in the total debt to GNP ratio. The picture is mixed in terms of total debt service and interest payments as a percentage of exports which improved in fourteen out of the thirty eight countries included in the two tables.

The persistence of financial instability and continuous economic crisis in many countries has become a permanent feature of the social malaise and deep pessimism surrounding their inability to get out of this precarious situation under the prevalent economic model resulting from the Washington Consensus. This is why many authors have referred to a "crisis of development." Persistent poverty, economic insecurity, and growing inequalities feed the social tensions that have become a permanent burden for many areas. This is reflected in growing crime rates and insecurity, particularly in large urban centers of the South, corruption and drug-related problems, and the new waves of emigrants in areas that had traditionally attracted immigration, such as with the notorious case of Argentina.

The persistent problem of poverty has attracted increasing attention at the turn of the century. The World Bank's *World Development Report 2000/2001: Attacking Poverty* makes explicit the extent to which, at the beginning of the twenty-first century, "poverty remains a global problem of huge proportions" (p. vi):

> Of the world's 6 billion people, 2.8 billion—almost half—live on less than $2 a day, and 1.2 billion—a fifth—live on less than $1 a day, with 44 percent living in South Asia. . . . In rich countries fewer than 1 child in 100 does not reach its fifth birthday, while in poorer countries as many a fifth of children do not. (p. 3)

From a regional perspective, the report points out that poverty has decreased over the years in East Asia, despite an important setback as a result of the 1997 financial crisis. However, "in Latin America, South Asia, and Sub-Saharan Africa the numbers of poor people have been rising"(p. 3). Interestingly enough for a World Bank report, it takes poverty to mean "not only low income and consumption but also low achievement

**Table 1.2** Changes in External Debt: Selected African and Asian Countries, 1980–1999

| COUNTRY | TOTAL EXTERNAL DEBT (US$ MILLIONS OF CURRENT DOLLARS) | | | TOTAL DEBT TO GNP (%) | | | TOTAL DEBT SERVICE AS % OF EXPORTS | | | INTEREST PAYMENTS AS % OF EXPORTS | | |
|---|---|---|---|---|---|---|---|---|---|---|---|---|
| | 1980 | 1993 | 1999 | 1980 | 1993 | 1999 | 1980 | 1993 | 1999 | 1980 | 1993 | 1999 |
| Burkina Faso | 330 | 1,144 | 1,518 | 19.5 | 21.4 | 59 | 5.9 | 7.0 | — | 3.1 | 3.6 | — |
| Ghana | 1,398 | 4,590 | 6,928 | 31.6 | 47.6 | 91 | 13.1 | 22.8 | 20.1 | 4.4 | 9.0 | 4.8 |
| Kenya | 3,394 | 6,994 | 6,562 | 48.1 | 103.0 | 63 | 21.0 | 28.0 | 27.7 | 11.1 | 11.3 | 5.6 |
| Madagascar | 1,223 | 4,594 | 4,409 | 31.1 | 108.7 | 120 | 17.1 | 14.3 | 16.3 | 10.9 | 5.7 | 4.4 |
| Malawi | 821 | 1,821 | 2,751 | 72.1 | 42.6 | 155 | 27.7 | 22.3 | 17.9 | 16.7 | 8.4 | 5.0 |
| Mali | 732 | 2,650 | 3,183 | 45.4 | 58.8 | 124 | 5.1 | 4.5 | 11.5 | 2.3 | 1.8 | 4.0 |
| Mozambique | 0 | 5,264 | 6,959 | 0 | 339.4 | 187 | 0 | 20.6 | 28.0 | 0 | 12.0 | 11.2 |
| Rwanda | 190 | 910 | 1,292 | 16.3 | 28.8 | 66 | 4.2 | 5.0 | 41.5 | 2.8 | 2.8 | 10.7 |
| Senegal | 1,473 | 3,768 | 3,705 | 50.5 | 46.7 | 78 | 28.7 | 8.4 | 9.3 | 10.5 | 2.9 | 5.5 |
| Tanzania | 2,972 | 7,522 | 7,968 | — | 248.7 | 91 | 25.9 | 20.6 | 11.8 | 12.7 | 9.5 | 3.0 |
| Uganda | 702 | 3,056 | 4,077 | 55.7 | 55.7 | 64 | 17.3 | 143.6 | 23.1 | 3.7 | 25.6 | 5.3 |
| Zambia | 3,261 | 6,788 | 5,853 | 90.7 | 160.8 | 195 | 25.3 | 32.8 | 38.1 | 8.7 | 14.8 | 23.3 |
| Bangladesh | 4,053 | 13,879 | 17,534 | 33.4 | 31.1 | 37 | 23.2 | 13.5 | 10.4 | 6.4 | 4.3 | 3.0 |
| India | 20,582 | 91,781 | 94,393 | 11.9 | 29.1 | 21 | 9.3 | 28.0 | 15.6 | 4.2 | 14.8 | 9.9 |
| Indonesia | 20,944 | 89,539 | 150,096 | 28.0 | 58.5 | 113 | 13.9 | 31.8 | 37.9 | 6.5 | 11.0 | 13.8 |
| Nepal | 205 | 2,009 | 2,970 | 10.4 | 25.6 | 58 | 3.2 | 9.0 | 7.0 | 2.1 | 3.6 | 2.6 |

Sources: The World Bank, 2000/1: Attacking Poverty (09/2000), pp. 314–15.
The World Bank, Global Development Finance 2001: Building Coalitions for Effective Development Finance, pp. 145–47.

in education, health, nutrition, and other areas of human development," and "it expands this definition to include powerlessness and voicelessness, and vulnerability and fear" (p. v).

This view of poverty represents an important leap forward, away from more narrow definitions that reduce it to some strictly economic measurement. The report, through Wolfensohn's voice, promises to take up this challenge with "passion and professionalism" and it indeed represents an informative and interesting document, including a strategy for action, that involves the contribution of well-known authors in the development field. The report also clearly acknowledges the problem of "an unequal world," referring to disparities between rich and poor countries as well as between social groups separated by "rigid sociopolitical hierarchies which constitute powerful social barriers explicitly aimed at preserving the status quo of the better off" (p. 123). Similarly, it shows how race and gender discrimination can be "psychologically devastating" in addition to being a source of material deprivation.

I am using this rather atypical World Bank report to show that the Bank under president Wolfensohn has tried to respond to some of the strong criticisms of the Bretton Woods institutions voiced especially since the 1980s. The Bank has taken on world poverty as a central issue in some of its programs and activities. This raises the question of whether a document like the 2000/2001 report represents a turning point in the Bank's development thinking and practice. Can the Bank's efforts make a difference for poverty elimination? It is not difficult to be skeptical. To be sure, the analysis, as well as the suggestions included in the report's strategy for action, represent a change in the Bank's traditionally more narrow focus on growth and efficiency as the best approach for the elimination of poverty. But the production of the report itself underlines the difficulties of reforming these institutions from within. The report's leading economist, Ravi Kanbur, resigned over a dispute around the report's argument that the market by itself might not be able to eliminate poverty—thereby implying that some sort of government intervention could be necessary for the lagging sectors. Most accounts of his resignation attributed it to the pressure exercised by Larry Summers, former chief economist of the World Bank and U.S. Treasury Department Secretary during the Clinton administration, and currently Harvard University's president.

Symbolically enough, the limits to the possibilities for change within the Bank regarding its discourse on poverty had been reached, and the power of the U.S. government over the institution had been exposed. Kanbur's resignation followed the firing a year earlier, also under Summers' pressure, of Joe Stiglitz, now Nobel prize winner and former chief economist of the World Bank. Stiglitz' criticisms of the Bank and particularly of the IMF are

well known and focus on their incompetent diagnosis of problems and their application of one-size-fits-all policies.[2] Both incidents reflect the difficulties encountered when real issues linked to powerlessness, voicelessness, vulnerability, and fear are seriously confronted.

## A Panel on "Gender Economics"

My contribution to the Paris conference was to participate in a panel entitled "gender economics." All participants in the panel were women, with the exception of one male commentator. By contrast, women were virtually absent from the other conference panels, with few exceptions, although many women attended the two-day event. The predominant male presence among speakers was a strong reminder of a traditionally male-dominated development establishment, somewhat of a setback for those of us who in recent years have grown accustomed to a greater presence of women in a variety of international circles, including many UN agencies. It did not even reflect the growing weight given to gender issues at the World Bank itself during the past decade.

Our panel had a small audience of men and women and the discussion was shared among the audience and panelists. It was difficult to avoid the feeling of marginalization of gender issues at the conference, a concern that was voiced. The problem is well known: gender is considered a "special subject" quite apart from the more general and central conference topics. The presence of some token event to discuss gender is normally due to pressure generated by a few committed women, perhaps with the help of a few men. The overall result is the absence of a real dialogue about important issues, with women often speaking mostly among themselves. Other panels at the conference easily could have integrated a gender perspective—in particular those panels that focused on labor markets, poverty, social protection, and debt-related discussions. This would have placed gender issues as more central in several of the related panels. This is not to underestimate the importance of the panel in which we participated. As one of the French women who played a key role in the conference organization pointed out, "it was a success that anything related to women was included."

The panel dealt with key issues centered around gender equality, generating a lively debate, particularly on the relationship between social policy, unpaid work, and fertility rates. A key argument on the subject of gender equity and European demographics made by one of the papers, was that the very low fertility rates currently registered in the Southern European countries were due to the absence of social services to replace domestic work and facilitate the participation of women in the labor market

(Majnoni D'Intignano 2000). Without these services, women find it difficult to combine paid work and family responsibilities, opting to have fewer children, which has resulted in the lowest fertility rates in the world.[3] The Northern European countries, the paper argues, experienced higher fertility levels during the 1980s as a result of policies that facilitated women's incorporation in the paid labor force—even though, at least in Sweden, budget cuts in the 1990s resulted again in a reduction of its rate from 2 to 1.6 children for every woman.

The discussion that followed this paper focused on the differences between the various European models of provision of social services and their significance for women's ability to participate in the labor force. It also emphasized the difficulties of projecting conclusions from European experiences on to Third World countries whose levels of social spending have not developed to the same degree; in addition, these countries have suffered large setbacks in the provision of social services during the past two decades. While many European countries, as well as Japan, are concerned with fertility rates below demographic replacement levels, pronatalist policies in developing countries, to the extent that they exist, often result from more traditional attitudes toward birth control, including religious beliefs, rather than from concern about low fertility rates. Finally, low fertility rates are linked to factors other than the availability of services replacing reproductive work, such as high unemployment and labor market insecurity among the young.

I am dwelling on this discussion of European demographics to point out that gender deserves central attention in any discussion of economic and social development. No one would deny the major significance of demographic change for development and policymaking, including its impact on the gender division of labor, household composition, gender relations, and the changing structure of the labor force. To relegate it to a segregated panel is to perpetuate the underestimation of the significance of gender for many of the issues discussed and to cripple our understanding of the dynamics of development and social change. Most women, and many male social scientists, have understood this message, but many economists seem to remain insensitive to the issue. This despite prominent exceptions like Nobel laureate Amartya Sen, who for more than a decade has shown a high level of familiarity with the literature on gender and development to which he has contributed significantly. He and others like him have understood the key role played by women in the development process. As stated in his work on India, with coauthor Jean Drèze, "the agency of women as a force for change is one of the most neglected aspects of the development literature" (Drèze and Sen 1995: 178).

The centrality of gender to economic and social change has also been understood by many among those involved in development agencies and international organizations. The United Nations has played a pioneering role in taking up women's issues, creating units specifically focusing on these issues, such as the Division for the Advancement of Women (DAW) and United Nations Development Fund for Women (UNIFEM), and setting up gender-related programs in its different agencies. Perhaps the UN's most internationally and domestically visible effort during the past decades has been the organization of the world conferences on women—from Mexico in 1975, Copenhagen in 1980, Nairobi in 1985, to Beijing in 1995—which have served as a powerful mechanism to discuss women's concerns and to set agendas at a world level. In addition, gender issues have played an important role in other world conferences organized by UN agencies, such as in the case of the 1994 Cairo conference on population in which women and gender-related debates played a key role in the deliberations and adoption of documents. By now all agencies have incorporated gender analysis and programs in some form related to their specific area of work. The effort has been referred to as "gender mainstreaming" and it has required both an increased representation of women at all levels and greater integration of gender issues in their activities. The same can be said for other institutions working on development and international fields such as nongovernmental organizations (NGOs), many specifically organized by and for women. They are part of the multiple international networks that have been very successful in specific areas such as those working on violence against women (Keck and Sikkink 1998).

Despite this progress in the inclusion of gender issues in international organizations, development agencies, and NGOs, several concerns and problems remain. First is the danger of instrumentalization of these issues, or their inclusion in program activities and projects for purposes that do not necessarily serve feminist goals or might even be in conflict with them. Feminists have often called attention to long-standing functionalist approaches to women's issues. The examples are numerous—from programs of population control whose objectives reflect not so much a concern for women's wellbeing as a way to use women to reach demographic goals, to short-term employment programs for women aimed at toning down the negative effects of male unemployment, rather than promoting women's long-term interests. The World Bank and other agencies have provided many examples of this functionalism, for instance by emphasizing the importance of women's education as a way of increasing productivity in the household and in the market, therefore contributing to economic growth. As argued in chapter 2 in more detail, feminists have often criticized this "efficiency approach," pointing out that, although important for women's advancement, the primary goal is not women's wellbeing (Beneria and Sen 1981; Moser 1993; Elson 1991). This is not to say that women should oppose such programs but to emphasize the need to make sure that their own needs and goals are not left out.[4] A different problem is that of cooptation and shifts in agendas to accomodate the requirements of donors.

Within academic circles, criticism of the work carried out by international agencies on behalf of women has appeared frequently (Tinker 1990). Different reasons for these critiques can be pointed out. First, academic concerns and practical work, either in development organizations or in the field, often evolve without sufficient links with each other. Lack of information on the part of academia about the work done in the agencies (and vice versa) and the usual contradictions between theory and practice create tensions that require a continuous dialogue not always put in practice sufficiently. Second, perhaps due to some arrogance on the part of those who see themselves as "theorists," we often see a sheer lack of understanding among some academics of the successes and failures of international organizations. Irene Tinker, in her classic article discussing the work of advocates, practitioners, and scholars working in the field of gender and development, pioneered the analysis of the differences as well as commonalities among these different groups, pointing out the advantages, shortcomings, and constraints facing them (Tinker 1990). Thus, academic work in the field has tended to be more theoretical, less focused on policy and action, and more conducive to setting ambitious goals since it does not have to deal with the limitations imposed by institutional frameworks and the practical constraints facing advocates and practitioners. This is important, but academic work needs to be empirically grounded in order to be relevant for policy and action. Hence, the need for a continuous interaction between the different constituencies working on development at the practical level. In the rest of this chapter, I turn to a discussion of the role played by the discipline of economics in development work and to a discussion of human development and the need for interdisciplinary approaches.

### Economics at a Crossroads?

It can be argued that the crisis in development thinking and practice is to a great extent a derivative of the problems rooted in the discipline of economics, which strongly impacts the path followed by the development establishment. It is nothing new to say that the discipline of economics is in need of mending. In their incisive 1995 book *The Crisis of Vision in Modern Economic Thought*, Heilbroner and Milberg identify one of the key problems of present-day mainstream economics as the disconnect between theory and reality and the contrast between the discipline's increasingly obsessive focus on technical "precision" and "rigor" and its inability to respond to society's needs—or at least to the needs of a large proportion of the population. Amartya Sen (1987), expressing a similar concern, has argued that modern mainstream economics has gradually become focused on its "engineering" aspects, separating itself from the ethical concerns that were manifest in the initial stages of the discipline. In this process, he points out, "the nature of modern economics has been substantially impoverished" (p. 7).

For Heilbroner and Milberg, this process has resulted in the widespread belief that economic analysis can exist as some kind of socially disembodied study. The result is the "extraordinary combination of arrogance and innocence" (p. 6) with which mainstream economics approaches important issues such as unemployment and poverty, the erosion of real income and health benefits for specific social groups, and other matters of vital importance to society. They argue that this "extraordinary indifference" to social needs can be traced from the core assumption that "forces located within the 'individual' constitute the conceptual core of economics." That is, the emphasis on individual needs and choices, not on collective needs and social goals, is central to the mainstream. This argument is supported by the authors' account of the history of economic thought, evolving from the socially embedded theory of the classical economists to the narrower concerns of marginalism and the more recent rational expectations school—with Keynesianism, through its strong focus on the real world, representing a mid-twentieth century revolution, and a parenthesis in economic thought.

Ironically, the evolution of economic thought in recent decades has remained immune to the postmodern critiques of universalist approaches to theory and practice. Economists are well known for their tendency to isolate themselves in the narrowness of their own models; thus they have been quite oblivious to the critiques that, although not always directly, challenged their methodologies, assumptions, and generalizations. For example, in an era in which categories were destabilized and stripped of their earlier assumptions of "naturalness," new theorizing in mainstream economics went in the opposite direction—for example by relying on universal categories rather than acknowledging their nature as social constructs. To use one example provided by Heilbroner and Milberg, the so-called New Classicism—one of the incarnations of rational expectations theory—represents, in their words

> a denial of sociality not only of governments but of all economic agents and the markets in which they interact. *Individual preferences and technology are considered "natural"*—that is, outside the

workings of the economy itself—and thus any changes in them are also natural. They are taken as given to the economic problem. (p. 83, emphasis added)

Thus, by assuming that individual preferences are "natural," instead of influenced by a variety of exogenous factors, many economists have remained oblivious to the need to understand the social construction of the categories used in the social sciences and of the social dynamics that affect their interaction. If this seems surprising, we may not be surprised that disagreement and confusion is widespread within the discipline, despite the many appearances to the contrary. Doubts and confusion regarding the relevance of economic theory and its associated empirical work can be found among economists on all sides of the political spectrum, including mainstream economists. Heilbroner and Milberg, for example, quote Lawrence Summers as referring to the "scientific illusion" in modern macroeconomics and concluding that, "In the end, I am not sure these theoretical exercises teach us anything at all about the world we live in." Similarly, Summers—a mainstream economist with experience in the real world of politics—has expressed doubts on the reliance on econometrics for empirical work, pointing out that "econometric results are rarely an important input to theory creation or the evolution of professional opinion generally" (p. 93). From a different perspective, Donald (now feminist economist Diedre) McCloskey (1993) has referred to the strong reliance of the profession on econometric models as a result of "a masculinist methodology" in the discipline that tends to emphasize the technical and quantitative over the human and social components.

For Heilbroner and Milberg, the retreat of modern economics from the policy arena "is the single most important result of the crisis of vision in the discipline since Keynesianism was driven from center stage" (p. 96). Increasing dissatisfaction with the state of the profession is also being expressed in more collective ways, for example through professional groups such as the Post-Autistic Economics Movement in Europe—representing students and faculty particularly from France and the United Kingdom—and through proposals to reform the discipline and its teachings. One such proposal from the Association for Evolutionary Economics (AFEE), signed by a list of students, researchers, and academics from twenty-two nations, has called for a transformed field, one that would include a broader conception of human behavior, recognition of culture, consideration of history, a new theory of knowledge in the discipline, empirical grounding, expanded methods, and an interdisciplinary dialogue.[5]

These are among the most prominent problems in the teaching and practice of economics. Critically minded students, as the statement points out, face an unhappy choice between abandoning their interests in order to progress within the profession or abandoning economics altogether for disciplines more hospitable to reflection and critical thinking. In the field of development economics, much dissatisfaction has been expressed with the monolithic, "one size fits all" approach that has paralleled the predominance of neoliberal policies. Some have called it the TINA ("there is no alternative") approach associated with the Washington Consensus.

I have dwelt on Heilbroner and Milberg's analysis because, although focusing mainly on a significant contribution to the deconstruction of mainstream economics, it also presents an opportunity to point out what feminism adds to their critique. They emphasize the notion that mainstream economic analysis is embedded in the specific social order called capitalism and that it has become inextricably entangled with capitalisim in such a way that it serves the ideological function of claiming its universality. In the author's own words:

> The failure of mainstream economics to recognize the insistent presence of this underlying [capitalist] order, with its class structure, its socially determined imperatives, its technologies and organizations, and its privileges and rights, derives from its preconceptual basis in a natural rather than a social construction of economic society. (p. 113)

This critique of mainstream economics is rather incomplete from a feminist perspective. It is indeed the case that mainstream analysis is embedded in capitalism and has become a key apologist of its associated institutions and practices. However, from a feminist perspective, capitalism is not the only underlying order to be concerned about. Patriarchal forms, gender inequality, and women's oppression can be intrinsically embedded in different forms of capitalist institutions, but they also exist in other economic and social formations. Gender-related hierarchies have often been reconstituted with institutional and systemic changes. This implies that any alternative analysis needs to incorporate the full range of factors that explain oppression, inequalities, and discriminatory practices tied to gender socialization and women's position in society. The same can be said for other hierarchical or class-based constructions/divisions such as those associated with race and ethnicity, colonial, and postcolonial tensions, and North-South divisions. Although these constructions are part of the underlying capitalist structures referred to in the above quote, they need to be acknowledged as having their own dynamic as well. One of the lessons we have learned from post-structuralist analysis is that oppressive structures and patriarchal relations are not universal and static; they are based on a multiplicity of factors that can shift continuously and be contested, and therefore may be changed through action and policy.

Similarly, the alternative vision presented by Heilbroner and Milberg for the direction in which economic thought must move falls short of incorporating what we might call a feminist vision. They call for an enlarged and central role of the public sector in formulating guidance "into the workings of capitalism itself." This requires a transformation in the nature of economic analysis with the purpose of inferring the best policy to attain an end result. Feminists have been skeptical about alternative visions that do not include in an integral and clear way the priorities of women and other marginalized social groups. Feminism, in its varied expressions, has worked through very decentralized forms of action, mostly following a bottom-up approach that might or might not reach the public sector. As a result, there is a wide range of feminist answers to the problems associated with capitalism. At one extreme we have those who, like Dierdre McCloskey, go as far as to say that capitalism, the market, and bourgeois virtues have been good for mankind and for women. In her own words, "A free exchange may not be a loving gift, but it's nicer than male violence, which is often the alternative method of allocation."[6] Many feminist economists, on the other hand, are critical of the way capitalist institutions and the market tend to generate inequalities based on gender, and they do not think that the alternative to male violence is necessarily the free and unregulated market.[7]

These feminist critiques range from the earlier Marxist and socialist positions to more contemporary liberal and left approaches. Most of them are aware of the fact that alternative institutions do no guarantee the elimination of gender subordination. One of the basic commonalties among the different expressions of modern feminism has been the importance of reaching a new social contract with deep and honest democratic processes involving the constant interaction and visions of all social groups. Branches of feminism might differ on the necessary combination of capitalist, socialist, or other institutions, or in what formulae to combine state and market. This can be a matter of negotiation and scrutiny responding to social conditions, human agency and the bargaining power of different groups. However, what has characterized the feminist approach is its decentralized, multifaceted, and bottom-up effort to finding alternative models. In this sense, Heilbroner and Milberg's vision is insufficient.

## Human Development

This book's emphasis on "human" rather than "economic" development reflects an agreement with a vision of development beyond its material aspects, even though recognizing that these are important for the elimination of poverty and the attainment of acceptable living standards for all countries and social groups. Particularly since 1990, the notion of human development has been promoted mainly through the UNDP's annual *Human Development Report*, which has emphasized that the concept "has moved to the center of the global development debate" (UNDP 1992: 12). Strongly influenced by the work of Amartya Sen, the first (1990) report defined this concept as "a process of enlarging people's choices" (p. 10), including the ability to enjoy long, healthy, and creative lives:

> The process of development should at least create a conducive environment for people, individually and collectively, to develop their full potential and to have a reasonable chance of leading productive and creative lives according with their needs and interests. (p. 1)

Along these lines, the most critical choices associated with human development are identified as those linked to the need "to lead a long and healthy life, to be educated, and to enjoy a decent standard of living." But additional choices include "political freedom, guaranteed human rights, and self respect—what Adam Smith called the ability to mix with others without being "ashamed of being in public" (p. 10).

This focus on "choices" has been criticized as having a Western bias for its emphasis on, presumably, *individual* choices. However, the quote illustrates that it can be understood as including collective choices as well. As defined in the 1990 report, and heavily influenced by the work of Amartya Sen, human development encompasses both the notion of human capabilities, such as health and knowledge, and the use of these capabilities in people's lives. The objective is the provision of conditions that enable human potential to unfold for everyone. However, individual entitlements and human capabilities can result from the capacity of society to enlarge collective choices as well. This is, of course, not a new idea. The report itself points out that the notion that societies must be judged by the extent they provide "human good" goes back "at least to Aristotle" (p. 9). Although acknowledging that income and wealth are important factors in enlarging people's choices, income and wealth are viewed as the means to reach the larger objectives of human good, not an end in themselves. Despite widespread agreement with this view, we have a world in which policy and action are driven by powerful forces that continue to respond and give priority to the hegemony of economistic approaches to development and to the interests of economic elites.

One typical expression of this tendency to measure progress in economic terms is the still-frequent use of conventional economic indicators that can hardly capture the complexities of the human good. The deficiencies of measuring development in terms of GNP per capita or other conventional indices such as the number of cars or telephones per 100 inhabitants are all familiar, not just because they represent averages and therefore they tell us nothing about inequalities in their distribution, but also because they are insufficient to capture the wholeness of human development. In addition, and as the UNDP reports have pointed out, the extent to which economic growth and human development are linked is far from clear, particularly for a large proportion of the world's population. Barbara Harriss-White (2001) for example, has shown how higher income among middle class families in India can result in lower sex ratios—that is, diminishing survival possibilities for girls. A similar point has been made by Drèze and Sen (1995), who have pointed out that economic development does not automatically result in improving conditions for women while progress in women's lives can take place without a clear connection to economic development.

For these reasons, the 1990 Human Development Report introduced the now well-known human development index, or HDI, with the purpose of using indicators less dependent on exclusively economic variables and more appropriate for evaluating human development. The index is based on country data combining life expectancy, adult literacy rates, enrollment ratios in primary, secondary and higher education, and real GDP per capita. Table 1.3 shows the HDI rank for 1999 and the sets of inputs from which the index has been estimated for a selected group of countries. To be sure, income, life expectancy, literacy rates, and other educational measures represent an incomplete set of variables to evaluate human development.[8] However, the HDR must be seen as an important pioneer effort that can be expanded to include other dimensions of human development.

One of the dimensions has to do with gender equality. It is obvious that each of the relevant variables used in defining the concept has clear gender implications that might vary across countries and cultures. Philosopher Martha Nussbaum (2001) has elaborated the significance of the capabilities approach for women. First, contrasting it with a rights approach, Nussbaum argues that a focus on capabilities allows us to look at "what people are actually able to do and to be—in a way informed by an intuitive idea of a life that is worthy of the dignity of the human being . . . for each and every person" (pp. 4–5). Second, she points out that this approach is especially relevant for women, given that women's capabilities are often undeveloped or not given priority. This raises the question of whether gender-sensitive indicators of human development can be elaborated. For this purpose, the 1995 Human Development Report expanded its work on human development indicators to include two country-based indices: the gender-related development

**Table 1.3**  Components of the Gender-Related Development Index (GDI), 1999

| HDI RANK | LIFE EXPECTANCY AT BIRTH (YEARS) 1999 | | ADULT LITERACY RATE (% AGE 15 AND ABOVE) 1999 | | COMBINED PRIMARY, SECONDARY, AND TERTIARY GROSS ENROLLMENT RATIO 1999[a] | | ESTIMATED EARNED INCOME (PPP US$) 1999 | |
|---|---|---|---|---|---|---|---|---|
| | FEMALE | MALE | FEMALE | MALE | FEMALE | MALE | FEMALE | MALE |
| 1. Norway | 81.3 | 75.4 | d | d | 99 | 95 | 22,037 | 34,960 |
| 2. Australia | 81.7 | 76.0 | d | d | 118 | 114 | 19,721 | 29,469 |
| 6. United States | 79.7 | 73.9 | d | d | 99 | 91 | 24,302 | 39,655 |
| 9. Japan | 84.1 | 77.3 | d | d | 81 | 83 | 15,187 | 35,018 |
| 13. France | 82.3 | 74.5 | d | d | 96 | 93 | 17,525 | 28,554 |
| 21. Spain | 81.9 | 74.8 | 96.7 | 98.5 | 99 | 91 | 10,741 | 25,747 |
| 51. Mexico | 75.8 | 69.8 | 89.1 | 93.1 | 70 | 71 | 4,486 | 12,184 |
| 68. Saudi Arabia | 72.7 | 70.3 | 65.9 | 83.5 | 60 | 62 | 2,715 | 17,857 |
| 69. Brazil | 71.8 | 63.9 | 84.9 | 84.8 | 80 | 79 | 4,067 | 10,077 |
| 94. South Africa | 56.2 | 51.6 | 84.2 | 85.7 | 96 | 89 | 5,473 | 12,452 |
| 112. Morocco | 69.1 | 65.4 | 35.1 | 61.1 | 46 | 58 | 1,930 | 4,903 |
| 115. India | 63.3 | 62.4 | 44.5 | 67.8 | 49 | 62 | 1,195 | 3,236 |
| 145. Senegal | 54.8 | 51.1 | 26.7 | 46.4 | 31 | 40 | 996 | 1,844 |

*Source:* UNDP, *Human Development Report 2001*, Table 21, 210–13.

[a] Preliminary UNESCO estimates, subject to further revision.

[d] For purposes of calculating the GDI a value of 99.0 percent was applied.

index (GDI)—based on gender differences in life expectancy, earned income, illiteracy, and enrollment—and the gender empowerment measure (GEM) based on the proportion of women among parliament seats, administrators, and managers, as well as professional and technical workers.

To illustrate the significance of introducing the GDI index in the ranking of development, Table 1.4 shows the extent to which the GDI index for each country differs from that of the corresponding HDI. For Norway, Australia, and Spain, for example, the HDI rank for 1999 was not affected by the inclusion of the gender-related index. By contrast, Japan's rank declined by 2, Saudi Arabia's by 7, while the rest of the countries in the table improve their rank with their GDI. To be sure, as with the HDI, these gender-related indices fall short of capturing important aspects of gender equality and gender-aware development. They are imperfect ways to measure the extent to which women's lives benefit from development. Here, too, an extensive literature has emerged on the methodological and technical difficulties associated with these indices.[9] At a more general level, questions can be raised about the imperfections and insufficiency of quantitative measurements to evaluate human development. Indices can not, for example, capture a dynamic sense of empowerment at the level of individuals, households, and communities. However, this does not erase the importance of designing quantitative measures that can be used for comparative

**Table 1.4**  Human Development Index (HDI) and Gender-Related Development Index (GDI), 1999

| HDI RANK | GDI RANK | HDI RANK MINUS GDI RANK |
|---|---|---|
| 1. Norway | 1 | 0 |
| 2. Australia | 2 | 0 |
| 6. United States | 4 | 2 |
| 9. Japan | 11 | −2 |
| 13. France | 10 | 3 |
| 21. Spain | 21 | 0 |
| 51. Mexico | 49 | 2 |
| 68. Saudi Arabia | 75 | −7 |
| 69. Brazil | 64 | 5 |
| 94. South Africa | 85 | 9 |
| 112. Morocco | 101 | 11 |
| 115. India | 105 | 10 |
| 145. Senegal | 130 | 15 |

*Source:* UNDP, *Human Development Report 2001*, Table 21, 210–13.

analysis—cross-country and over time. The availability of indices, even if imperfect, can provide insights into gender equality and directions for further improvements.

A vision of development based on "an intuitive idea of a life that is worthy of the dignity of the human being . . . for each and every person" is much in tune with the basic objectives of feminist economics. As outlined in chapter 2, feminist economists in particular have emphasized the importance of constructing a discipline with objectives linked to provisioning and wellbeing, in contrast with the conventional emphasis on growth and accumulation.

A different issue, already mentioned, is the use of the notion of development as an organizing concept, given the historical record and the problematic experience of development in many countries and the critiques of the ways in which it has been used and misused throughout the years. A variety of authors have addressed this question, emphasizing the extent to which the conventional notions of development and underdevelopment constitute a Western invention with roots in the post–World War II period. In his influential book, *Encountering Development,* Arturo Escobar has traced the birth of the "discourse of development" to U.S. president Harry Truman's 1949 inaugural address in which he introduced "a program of development based on the concept of democratic fair dealing . . ."—giving rise to what Escobar calls "a historically produced discourse," which he documents with specific examples in order to deconstruct it. Different aspects of this discourse, Escobar argues, include the problematization of poverty—in the sense of constructing it in relation to the prevailing conditions in high income countries—the birth and growth of "development experts," and the professionalization and institutionalization of development through the inclusion of development studies into Western universities. He adds to the list the proliferation of international organizations focusing on development and developing countries' problems, which have fostered a conception of social life that privileges modernization over traditional forms of social organization. In particular, the emergence of development economics and the corresponding proliferation of experts associated with it contributed to what Escobar calls "the development of development economics" and the growth of "economics as culture," which see "life in general through the lens of production" (p. 60).

Escobar's analysis resonates among many of us who are familiar with the processes he describes. Given that multiple aspects of development have tended to perpetuate North-South differences rather than eliminate them, it is no surprise that the concept itself has been subject to scrutiny. An analysis of long-term trends in world income distribution among countries shows that the gap between rich and poor countries has been widening. According to UNDP estimates, this gap was about 3 to 1 in 1820; it increased gradually to 11 to 1 in 1913, 35 to 1 in 1950, 44 to 1 in 1973 and 72 to 1 in 1992 (UNDP 1999). For many developing countries, it is difficult to be optimistic about the prospects offered by current trends.

The case of Argentina might be extreme but is a good example that is far from unique. The extent to which the responsibility of its default, the largest in history, can be placed on development organizations and experts will be a subject of debate for a long time to come. Yet the high degree of influence on the part of the IMF and other key players linked to the Washington Consensus in setting the country's monetary and financial policy can not be denied. As Joseph Stiglitz has stated on many occasions, the IMF might work hard to shift the blame, pointing to allegations of corruption and claims that Argentina did not pursue the needed measures. The point is not to deny that the country needed reforms but to argue that following the IMF advice made matters worse."[10]

Argentina might be an extreme case but other countries are suffering similar problems. This disturbing trend seems to make no impact on world leaders unwilling to question the development policies that have predominated during the past three decades. Often their response is to point to the growth of some areas and regions where economic development has concentrated while benefiting a select few. The official and prevailing discourse seems to prevent the establishment from seeing the grim reality of those whose lives are becoming increasingly more vulnerable. Chapter 4 focuses on some of the paths that this type of development implies for a large proportion of the population affected by the informalization of labor markets that generate precarious jobs and high levels of unemployment. The following quote about the precariousness of life among marginalized workers in Lima, Peru, typifies the problem:

> Jobs come and go from one day to the other. Roofs are held in place with stones, and four poles wrapped in plastic serve as open-air outhouses.[11]

This description could apply to life in many other cities and countries across the developing world where, for a large proportion of the population, the predominant development model has not been generating "a life that is worthy of the dignity of the human being . . . for each and every person."

With the unfolding of the field of gender and development and of the enormous amount of work that women have contributed to the project of improving people's lives, it is hard to avoid the question of whether these processes have made a difference for development thinking and practice, and for women in particular. This book argues that much has changed and that progress has taken place at many levels. Yet the malaise surrounding development remains loud and clear, raising questions about the extent to which women and feminist analysis could make a stronger and more positive contribution to finding solutions to this impasse, not just for women but for humankind. To paraphrase the quote heading this chapter, we have moved from seeing women as victims to seeing them as essential to finding solutions to the world's problems. The danger is that, as women's participation in market society and public life continues to increase, much of the initial impetus of the women's movement and its objectives might get lost in individual advancement for a limited number of beneficiaries rather than achieving collective progress for all women and their families. To be sure, we must be aware that the goals and voices from the women's movements worldwide have, to some extent at least, been silenced by the onslaught of neoliberal policies. As Verónica Montesinos (2001) has argued for the case of Latin America, the hegemonic pressures and influence of these policies and of the leading role of economists that have inspired them has represented a serious setback for some of the advances that women made during the past two decades. So, far at least, this hegemony has not been sufficiently challenged and, she argues, "the dialogue between feminists and non-feminist critics of mainstream economics [for the purpose of finding alternatives] is still incipient" (p. 191).

## Bridging the Disciplines: On Words and Things

A human development approach to development requires the integration of policies taking into consideration both economic and noneconomic factors. This raises the question of how to overcome economism and how to incorporate this goal in feminist work. This section discusses some of the issues associated with the postmodern attempt to provide new theoretical formulations within the different disciplines and within feminism.

During the past fifteen years, a good proportion of academic disciplines in the social sciences and the humanities witnessed a profound transformation—some have called it a paradigm shift away from "the material" and toward the analysis of "meaning" brought about by postmodern and poststructuralist currents. In this sense, some authors referred to "the material" as representing "things" analyzed in the social sciences—in contrast with the analysis of "words" and of "meaning" which are the subject of study in the literary fields and the humanities. To many, these currents represented a devastating critique of the assumptions on which an important body of theory in the social sciences had been previously built. The deconstruction of static and seemingly immovable concepts on which earlier universalistic theories were based challenged the priority given to the analysis of material reality over that of discourses. In the words of Michele Barrett (1999), "the relative status of things and words has become a central one in contemporary social theory and philosophy . . ." (p. 18). In many ways, the priority shifted toward a more humanistic emphasis, although not without tensions and without affecting the various academic fields in different ways. Old paradigms were questioned and deconstructed in search of their hidden meanings while old definitions and concepts were rejected and theories destabilized. In particular, theoretical universalism was rejected for its essentialist vision of the real world and its inability to capture "difference" and the subtleties of increasingly more dynamic, and often contradictory, social (and economic) forms.

As a result, in some of the disciplines, analyses of meaning were given priority over analyses of causality and "search for the origins" of social phenomena. Hence, the emphasis on words, texts, discourse, language, deconstruction, rhetoric, and social constructions rather than on things, the material, and the focus on economic structures and systems. Although some disciplines were more affected than others, most of them were touched in some form. Economics—the discipline on which this book is primarily grounded despite its interdisciplinary character—has not been significantly affected by these currents among the social sciences; yet it has not remained untouched. As illustrated by the work of authors dealing with the rhetoric of economics (McCloskey 1990 and 1993; Milberg 1993) and by the work of many feminist economists (see chapter 2), the influence of these currents has also been felt, even if to a smaller degree than in other social sciences. As McCloskey (1990) puts it, economic "models" are a form of storytelling not always subject to the logic of rationality: ". . . until the storytelling in economics and in other sciences is recognized we are going to find it hard to be reasonable" (p. 9). However, the large majority of economists continue to be committed to, in McCloskey's words, the practice of "scientific autism." They pursue their work while ignoring the need to deal with epistemological questions that would lead them to ask about the meanings (social, human—in addition to economic) of their work.

Feminist analysis, in general, was strongly affected by the "turn to culture" in the disciplines. To quote Michele Barrett (1999) again, "The social sciences have lost their purchase within feminism and the rising star lies within the arts, humanities and philosophy" (p. 21). Written in the early 1990s, this statement may seem somewhat dated at present, but it does reflect prevalent tendencies of more than a decade within academic and, to a lesser extent, nonacademic feminism. In the United States, for example, a close look at many women's studies programs and their faculty affiliation, course distribution, research, and other activities shows the extent to which, even in the early 2000s, these programs took this cultural turn; their leading and most dynamic contributions during the period have come from disciplines such as literary studies, philosophy, history, sexuality studies, and anthropology. Women's studies were nourished by a largely interdisciplinary feminist theory, with a strong postmodern influence that grew in a variety of directions during the 1990s.[12]

As a result of the critiques of universalism, postmodern work emphasized issues of identity, difference, citizenship, and agency, resulting in the proliferation of what Nancy Fraser (1997) has called "fronts of struggle" having to do with "recognition" of social groups or social expressions and assertions of difference and representation—including gender as well as subjectivity, race, ethnicity, sexuality, North-South diversity, and other forms of social differentiation. The effort has been a most dynamic source of analytical power, political struggles, and social change and we have learned a great deal from the interesting contributions resulting from these currents. New areas of academic inquiry have enriched our understanding, for example, of identity politics, sexuality and gender, symbolic representations/intersections of gender and race, the multiple levels of an analysis of the body, postcolonial realities, and many others.

Interestingly, these tendencies have run parallel, on the material side of everyday life, to the resurgence of neoliberalism across countries and to the globalization of markets and of social and cultural life—generating rapid changes that need to be understood and acted upon. Yet a good proportion of postmodern analyses has tended to neglect the dynamics of political economy thus deemphasizing important areas of social concern having to do with the material and, more concretely, the economic. The result has been, in Nancy Fraser's terms, "a general decoupling of the cultural politics of recognition from the social politics of distribution" (Fraser 1997: 3). This generated a growing imbalance between the urgent need to understand economic reality—since distribution is about social sharing of things material—and the more predominant focus on "words," including issues of difference, subjectivity, and representation.

These tendencies have been a matter of concern for a variety of authors as well. For example, in their book on land and property rights in Latin America, Carmen Diana Deere and Magdalena León (2001), also echoing Fraser's work, point out that "the theoretical energy of feminists in Latin America as well as internationally has centered on . . . issues of recognition rather than redistribution" (Deere and León, 2001: 9). Thus, they insist in that the relationship between fundamental factors affecting women's lives, such as gender and property, has not been sufficiently explored and that attention to issues of redistribution, particularly of property, is fundamental for transforming gender relations and ending women's subordination . . ." (p. 9).

At the same time, much progress has taken place in women's participation in many spheres of public life. However, this, as political scientist Jane

Jaquette (2001) has argued, "has produced forms of democratic participation that rarely challenge neoliberal economic logic or prevailing 'supply side' assumptions about who should have access to global resources" (p. 7). Consistent with the argument presented here, she adds that "the main trends in feminist theory are helping depoliticize economic issues" (p. 7) and reiterates that "feminists today too often eschew political economy, preferring politics as 'identity,' 'text' or 'performance'" (p. 24). To sum, the point is not to say that the turn to culture and the emphasis on identity, representation, and agency are not important and useful, but to argue that something has been missing in the process: they need to be linked to other sources of empowerment having to do with the socioeconomic aspects of people's lives.

The privileging of the politics of representation in feminist work over areas related to political economy took many directions, such as a much wider attention given to issues of representation, diversity, and citizenship than, for example, the understanding of how globalization has been affecting everyday life. To be sure, these trends have been registered in the North and the South. One of the results has been a shortage of women economists interested and able to deal with gender issues—in academia and in policy-making. To illustrate, a few years ago, I was invited to a seminar for prospective faculty at a newly launched gender and development masters program at a Latin American university. After an interesting and heated discussion on the effects of structural adjustment policies on households, and more specifically on women, one of the organizers pointed out that the new program did not have a faculty member who could take up teaching in this topic, which was viewed as key for the program. At that point, no local economist had been involved in the planning process, and it wasn't easy to identify one. The reality was that local women economists did not seem interested in gender analysis and shared the limitations of conventional economics while the local feminists lacked the necessary economics background needed for the program.

For similar reasons, it has been difficult to bring together economics and feminisim. One specific version of this problem has been the tendency to dichotomize and contrast "economic justice" and gender justice," often implying that the later represents a more "feminist" prespective. The conflict created by this dichotomy surfaced at some of the sessions organized during the Beijing + 5 meetings in New York City held in June 2000, a conflict that at times took the form of North-South tensions. Growing inequalities between the North and the South have reinforced the concern about the urgent economic problems facing women and men in developing countries, such as poverty, the consequences of HIV-AIDs, financial instability, and the effect of economic crises, natural disasters, and other setbacks in the process of development. These are viewed as economic justice questions. Northern feminist adgendas tended to be identified with gender justice issues such as those related to sexuality, identity, and citizenship.

While this dichotomy is useful to understand diversity within feminism, it tends to polarize and oversimplify the complex range of feminist conceptualizations and practical action, and it tends to trivialize the interconnectedness and wholeness of feminist visions. The connection between gender justice and economic justice, even if not always direct, is not difficult to trace. It is often poor women who are most affected by restricted reproductive rights and rich women who most benefit from increased representation and openings in the political arena. Similarly, the negative effects of poverty for women can be intensified as the result of unequal gender-related distribution of resources within the household. Likewise, domestic violence against women has been linked to problems of poverty and unemployment among men. Consequently, campaigns against domestic violence should focus both on the social construction of gender that shapes men's and women's attitudes and behavior and on the root economic justice aspects of the problem. In the same way, higher illiteracy rates among women can result from a combination of the biases constructed by gender socialization and from poverty and lack of access to resources. Hence, gender justice and economic justice are highly interconnected. To the extent that a dichotomy is made between them, the division is often artificial and misleading, leading to policies and practice focusing too narrowly on one or the other.

Among some academic and research circles, a similar polarization has been referred to by differentiating between "practical" and "strategic" gender interests. Maxine Molyneux (1985) first made this distinction in her analysis of women's participation and influence in the measures adopted by the Sandinistas in Nicaragua. Her objective was to distinguish between women's needs related to daily survival and other urgent problems facing them—the practical gender interests—and women's struggles for gender equality, which might require longer time to bear fruit—the strategic gender needs. She saw the practical gender needs as not necessarily "feminist" because they didn't necessarily confront sexism and gender asymmetries. In the long run, however, the more feminist goals of gender equality could be confronted though different means and channels. The distinction was used and elaborated by other authors (for instance, Moser 1993) and it has been used widely in the literature, perhaps because it has proven to be a useful way to analyze not only the different types of needs facing women but also their significance for feminist agendas (Lind 1990; Ferguson 2001). However, the distinction is problematic in the sense that it views struggles of daily survival and other material aspects of women's as nonfeminist because they do not confront gender relations and do not focus on gender equality. This, however, is a dubious assumption. There are many examples of women's struggles to meet the urgent needs of daily survival that, although not directly confronting gender inequality and raising feminist questions, end up being transformative and empowering for women.

As one example, the collective soup kitchens in Lima, Peru, during the economic crisis of the 1980s initially had the specific goal of organizing the provision of meals for groups of households living in different neighborhoods. Women took up the leadership in the collective efforts of organizing shopping, cooking, and other tasks associated with the provision of meals for a large numbers of households (see chapter 3). This seemed a typical case of dealing with practical gender needs (Barrig 1996; Lind 1990). Yet, the process led to confronting strategic gender needs as well. Women were empowered because they learned new skills as a result of having to manage such collective forms of provisioning, including the contacts with NGOs, government officials, and other institutions that in some form became involved with the soup kitchens. Case studies showed that, as a result, some tensions between men and women arose and gender relations were affected, thus implying that changes in strategic gender interests were at work. Examples of this type are abundant; they imply that, although these theoretical differentiations might be useful for analytical purposes, in fact they tend to blur the wholeness of their interconnections.

To sum, the polarization between economic and gender justice or between practical and strategic gender needs, even though conceptually useful to differentiate between the various concerns behind women's actions and goals, might ultimately be less helpful to understanding the complexities of women's lives and actions. In fact, this polarization can have a negative impact when some approaches and actions are viewed as "feminist" and others are not. The dichotomy is reminiscent of many of the debates that took place in the 1970s among those who emphasized feminist issues and those whose views were anchored in more structuralist thinking as a way of understanding women's issues.[13] With time, the two views developed into a more integrative approach (see chapter 2). The experience of the last quarter century has taught us that this integration, at the theoretical and practical level, is possible, athough often difficult.

A related implication is the importance of integrating key areas of work aimed at achieving gender equality with feminist goals contributing to progressive social change. The profound changes generated by globalization and its impact on economic and social life during the past decades have been taking place at an accelerating, almost frightening, speed. Within academic feminism, the increasing sophistication of its discourses has often not integrated well enough the significance of these transformations for feminism, leaving the analysis of "things" to the margin. Although this appears to be changing, we can not overestimate the importance of this project. One of the basic arguments in this book is that a major challenge for feminists is to understand the dynamics of the material world without neglecting the important lessons learned from the critical perspectives represented by the "turn to culture" in the disciplines. Without this understanding, it will be difficult to engage in some of the most challenging issues of our time.

This book is written within the framework of what has come to be called feminist economics. It is based predominantly on an analysis of the material, from a feminist perspective. As already suggested, feminist economics has developed parallel to some of the intellectual currents of the last two decades—questioning the wisdom of conventional economic thinking and critiquing its androcentric nature and essentialist assumptions about human nature and human behavior. As I will argue in chapter 2, the discipline of economics has had a rather long history of inclusion of women's issues, although not necessarily representing feminist concerns. Rather, within orthodox economics this inclusion represented what philosopher Sandra Harding (1987) called an "add women and stir" approach; while including analysis and information about women, it did not question gender-based power relations and left intact some of the basic assumptions behind the models. Unorthodox approaches such as Marxism also suffered from, in the words of Heidi Hartmann, an "unhappy marriage" with feminism. This is what has led Randy Albelda (1997) to state that "By and large the economics profession had done a poor job understanding the economic contributions of half of the world's people" (p. 166). Chapter 2 will elaborate on the process of integration of gender issues in the discipline.

## CHAPTER 7

# The Study of Women and Gender in Economics: An Overview

*The reason to study Economics is to avoid being duped by economists*
—Joan Robinson[1]

Chapter 1 mentioned the subject of feminist economics as a recent development in the process of integrating gender analysis in the field of economics. This chapter provides a more detailed historical account of the trajectory through which issues pertaining to women and gender have gradually been incorporated in the discipline. I argue that, in its initial formulations, this integration did not incorporate feminist questions in the sense of focusing on the dynamics of unequal gender relations; the inquiry was mostly addressed to strictly economic inequalities between men and women without much regard to the wider issues of gender relations and women's subordination. The influence of feminism became more visible since the 1970s and particularly since the early 1990s.

It is obvious that during the past thirty years, feminist scholarship has had a profound impact on many disciplines. It has raised difficult questions, often perceived as troubling, out of place, risky, and irritating. It has challenged definitions and expanded the boundaries of knowledge by confronting and dealing with previous exclusions of gendered issues from accepted knowledge. In the humanities and the softer social sciences, it has in many ways transformed research questions, the disciplines and the curriculum. It has also raised important challenges in economics and in the hard sciences. Given that it challenges old tenets, this has not been an easy task; in the words of philosopher Elizabeth Minnich (1990):

> The old errors and exclusions and hierarchies are by no means 'only'
> conceptual; they reveal and perpetuate the articulated hierarchy in
> intrapsychic, education, social, historical, and political relations that
> have very serious consequences indeed. (p. 160)

This "articulated hierarchy" is strong in the economics profession, which
privileges orthodox thinking and excludes heterodox alternatives through a
variety of forms—from the nature of graduate school programs to screen-
ing in economic journals and in selection of participants in policymaking
and other areas of work. The process includes a very narrow definition of
the field, without much opening to epistemological questions and interdisciplinary inquiry, and an emphasis on modeling and quantitative methods
of analysis. This includes the often exclusive association of "rigorous" work
with mathematical quantitative analysis. For these reasons, any opening
and transformation in the field is a difficult one: it addresses deeply
ingrained practices and it challenges deeply entrenched "ways of knowing,"
of theorizing, and of "doing science."

Although feminist analysis might finally be noticed in the profession, it
has proven to be the least open of the social sciences to the challenges raised
by feminism. This may sound surprising given that, first, there have been
many feminist economists whose voices have been heard during this period
and, second, the economics profession has dealt quite extensively with
women-related issues. Yet these efforts had not made much of an impact on
economic analysis in a fundamental way, in the sense that the use of gender
as a category of analysis could transform the discipline itself by altering
some of its basic and often androcentric assumptions—as has happened,
for example, in history, philosophy, anthropology, psychology, and the literary and artistic fields. In this sense, as argued in this chapter, a turning
point in the profession of economics can be situated in the late 1980s and
early 1990s, even though the process has been a gradual one and has built
upon previous efforts since the 1960s and 1970s. The transformation has
not been an easy task; mainstream economics is accustomed to being hegemonic and finds it difficult to admit the importance of gender as a central
category of analysis with an impact on the construction of economic
knowledge. As McCloskey has humorously pointed out with regards to
neoclassical economists:

> They are a motorcycle gang among economists, strutting about the
> camp with clattering matrices and rigorously fixed points, sheathed in
> leather, repelling affection. They are not going to like being told that
> they should become more feminine. (Ferber and Nelson 1993: 76)

In what follows, I briefly review the gradual incorporation of women-
related issues in the literature and of gender as a category of economic
analysis. First, I review alternative approaches used in the integration of

women and gender in economics, beginning with the hegemonic paradigm of neoclassical economics and including Marxian and institutional approaches. I discuss the notion of gender as a central category of analysis and as the core of more recent feminist work in the profession. I then review the efforts to integrate gender in macroeconomics since the 1980s, mainly through two avenues: the inclusion of unpaid work in national income accounts (a topic elaborated in chapter 3) and the shift of analysis from micro to macro issues, particularly from the perspective of the gender and development literature and including the more recent work on gender and trade/finance. Finally, I discuss the contributions to economic analysis made from different aspects of the work on gender and development since the 1970s. To be sure, this chapter is not a comprehensive review of the field of gender and economics; rather, it provides a historical overview of the integration of women's issues and feminist work in the profession, elaborating on some of the themes introduced in the previous chapter.

## Mainstream Models

Economic analysis has a history of inclusion of women's issues ranging from the scrutiny, during the 1930s, of the reasons for the existence of wage differentials between men and women to the work on household production and time allocation during the 1960s and 1970s. In the United States, earlier work since the establishment of economics as a profession was more scattered and has been explored by various authors (Pujol 1992; Albelda 1997). The 1930s "equal pay controversy" in Britain, carried out mostly by male economists with the notable exception of Joan Robinson, had as a purpose the understanding of the reasons behind male/female wage differentials. Wage inequality was a topic that had already been discussed in 1918 by Millicent Fawcett, an English feminist, and which attracted names such as F. Y. Edgeworth, A. C. Pigou, J. R. Hicks, and R. F. Harrod, among others (Madden 1972). The controversy focused on wage determination under imperfect competition, an emphasis which, as Janice Madden (1972) has pointed out, was replaced by the assumption of perfect competition in the neoclassical models of discrimination during the post–World War II period. Both periods shared an interest in the analysis of inequalities between men and women by focusing mostly on the dynamics of the market rather than on the role that gender discrimination and unequal power relations play in it. The notion of the social construction of gender and its links with economic analysis had yet to be born.

In the 1950s, neoclassical economics pioneered the work toward a better understanding of the reasons behind the labor force participation of women. The work of Jacob Mincer and other labor economists began with the interest in explaining why women's participation in the labor force was increasing at a time of rising family income (normally assumed to be negatively correlated with labor supply). That is, what needed to be explained was why women were entering the labor force in larger numbers at a time when families were financially better off. The answer to that apparent puzzle was explained through the "substitution effect" generated by the increasing opportunity costs of staying at home; the raise in wages fostered by the economic growth of the period had created an economic incentive for women to engage in paid work rather than to stay at home. The substitution effect, it was argued, was greater than the income effect inducing women to stay home, thus resulting in an incentive for women to participate in the paid labor force. It is interesting to recall that this was the decade that inspired Betty Friedan's *Feminine Mystique*, detailing the multiple problems facing women staying at home in America's increasing suburban society. Friedan's description of women's oppression and of housewives' frustrations was in contrast with the strictly economic analysis of opportunity costs in Mincer's model and it was symbolic of the task ahead if the feminist questions raised by Friedan were to be taken up by economic analysis; much more than narrow economistic explanations were needed.

Mincer's work, and that of other economists who followed, represented a transition toward an increasing interest in using economic analysis to understand the sphere of the household. It was an important step in the inclusion of women's work in mainstream economics. This process was intensified in the 1960s with the work of Gary Becker and other human capital theorists that built the New Household Economics. Their approach was characterized by the application of market-oriented concepts and models to household production. Time allocation analysis was used to explain the sexual division of labor at home and the decisions of household members to engage in paid market work. Asymmetries in the division of labor and inequalities in the distribution of domestic work were explained through individual choices made under the assumptions of utility maximization. These choices were assumed to be made within the framework of a harmonious household making individual decisions, although they affected collective household dynamics. This type of analysis opened up new theoretical and empirical inquiry into other issues such as the economics of marriage and choices around labor supply, the number of desired children, and fertility rates.

With the emergence of the women's movement, the majority of economists focusing on women's issues continued to use either existing neoclassical models or some more critical variations of mainstream economics. The first was taken up mostly through microeconomic analysis, with the New Household Economics playing a central role and expanding this approach in different directions. This effort included the emergence of new themes in the analysis, such as the application of Gary Becker's work on racial discrimination to gender discrimination, the use of human capital theory to understand gender differentials in educational attainment and choices in schooling and education, research on earnings and wage differentials, job training for men and women, and the determinants of wages and unemployment (Benham 1974; Lloyd 1975; Blau 1976; Beller 1979; Lloyd and Niemi 1979). Perhaps to a lesser extent, it also took up macroeconomic policy issues, for example regarding the gender dimensions of social security, training programs, and welfare policy, among others. Using different tools of analysis, a small proportion of this work applied the theory of comparative advantage developed in international trade theory to the economics of marriage (Santos 1975).

Methodologically, these neoclassical models essentially followed Harding's "add women and stir" approach. Although informative and with an emphasis on mathematical and quantitative analysis, these models had limitations from a feminist perspective. "Trapped" within the constraints set up by the orthodox analytical framework and the basic assumptions of neoclassical models, it was not conducive to ask, let alone answer, the kind of questions that the women's movement had generated about gender socialization, inequality, and asymmetric power relations, for example. As repeatedly pointed out, the assumption of a harmonious household was not helpful to understanding conflicting interests and relations of domination/subordination among family members (Bruce and Dwyer 1988); and the assumption of joint utility maximization requiring the aggregation of individual tastes and preferences among family members was problematic (Folbre 1988).

Similarly, the application of the theory of comparative advantage and of human capital models to the analysis of specialization in home or market work and to the analysis of marriage was inherently static: it took as given the initial allocation of resources among household members, such as the gendered skills whose acquisition and distribution feminists were questioning. It also neglected the process by which this allocation takes place and did not problematize the resulting differences in autonomy, power, and ability to maximize the individual well-being of different household members. For these reasons, this analysis was not transformative in the sense of a) questioning orthodox models for their androcentrism; b) incorporating noneconomic factors relevant to the social construction of gender; and c) pointing to feminist solutions—in addition to economic solutions—for the questions examined.

The hegemony of the New Household Economics within the profession continued through the 1980s, as symbolized by the central role played by Gary Becker's *A Treatise on the Family* (1981) in neoclassical writings on the household. Faithful to the Chicago School of Economics and building on exclusively economic explanations, Nobel Prize–winner Becker brought the analysis further in terms of building quantitative models of the division of labor in households and families, which he saw as "determined partly by biological differences and partly by different experiences and different investment in human behavior" (p. 14). This partially sociobiological approach to explaining women's place in the household and the labor market represented a sharp contrast with the constructivist approaches emanating from feminist theory and from empirical and theoretical work in the social sciences and among feminist economists. Although a new edition of his book was published in 1991, there was little indication that Becker had paid any attention to his feminist critics (Bruce and Dweyer 1988; Folbre 1988). Neoclassical economists writing on the economics of the family have mostly continued to ignore gender analysis and feminist concerns in their work (Cigno 1994; Polacheck 1995).

Despite these trends within the profession, feminist concerns were often present in the work of women economists who raised many questions about the narrowness of the standard models and criticized them for their assumptions about preferences, differences in individual ability to make choices, and the role of the market in preventing optimal solutions for everyone (Ferber and Birnbaum 1977; Sawhill 1977). Using mainstream tools of analysis, new models were constructed to explain gender inequality in the labor market (Bergmann 1974). The critiques of neoclassical work and the realization of its shortcoming became more apparent during the 1980s, especially with an emphasis on the negative consequences that the traditional division of labor had for women. For example, after describing the simple neoclassical model of the traditional family—"with the man as the breadwinner and the woman as the homemaker"—Blau and Ferber (1986) concluded that "Growing recognition of the drawbacks of the traditional division of responsibilities between husband and wife may be one of the factors that has contributed to the decline in the proportion of families following this pattern" (p. 57). Part of these "drawbacks" had to do with the opportunity costs of staying at home—economic considerations. But here is where Friedan's noneconomic factors discussed in her *Feminine Mystique* become highly relevant—and the need for transcending the narrowness of the neoclassical model apparent. The drawbacks of staying at home had to do also with gender socialization resulting, for example, in male domination and women's low level of autonomy and self-confidence; hence, a more holistic analysis was needed.

*Alternative Approaches*

Beginning in the 1970s, and in some cases earlier, alternative routes to neoclassical models were followed mostly by feminists who used either a Marxian or an institutional framework (or both). In particular, the Marxian focus on exploitation, inequality, and systemic tendency for capitalism and market forces to generate social hierarchies and class inequalities seemed to be more conducive than the neoclassical framework to answering the questions raised by feminists. It also seemed more open to interdisciplinary approaches and more appropriate to analyze social relations and power inequalities between men and women. Thus, the domestic labor debate of the late 1960s and early 1970s focused on the nature of domestic labor and its functions within the economic system as the source of maintenance and reproduction of the labor force. More specifically, the debate focused on the ways in which unpaid domestic work contributes to lowering the costs of maintenance and reproduction of the present and future generations of workers; it also applied the notion of unequal exchange to the traditional division of labor within the household (Himmelweit and Mohun 1977). The debate was useful to legitimate feminist questions within the Marxian paradigm but it failed to identify and analyze implicit gender relations behind domestic work and the household division of labor and to address more specific questions about gender inequality and reproduction. Feminist critics of the debate also pointed out the limitations of the traditional Marxist conception of accumulation, which ignored the role of reproductive labor in the process (Molyneux 1979; Benería 1979; MacKintosh 1978). These critiques expressed concern with the structuralist approaches of the Marxian tradition, even when, methodologically, the critiques themselves were close to that tradition.

A similar approach was applied to the role of rural women's work in subsistence economies with male labor in the "modern" capitalist sector of developing countries. As in the case of domestic work, this literature emphasized women's concentration in unpaid productive and reproductive activities in situations where men were engaged in wage labor, either locally or as migrant workers (Deere 1976). The analysis underlined the crucial contribution of women's unpaid work to social reproduction and to making possible lower wages for male labor engaged in the capitalist sector, in addition to providing a source of cheap female labor for that sector. Similar to the domestic labor debate, this effort legitimated the introduction of gender issues within an orthodox Marxian framework in development economics; and similar to the New Household Economics, it represented a new application of economic analysis to the previously ignored areas of unpaid work. However, given their essentially androcentric questions, these structuralist analyses were unable to incorporate an understanding of the dynamics of gender relations and of their complexity within the household and in subsistence economies.

Feminists dealt with this problem: first, by pointing out the shortcomings of orthodox Marxism, second, by integrating Marxian categories within a feminist framework (Hartmann 1979 and 1981; Folbre 1982). Folbre, for example, discussed the extent to which the concept of exploitation can be applied to work carried out at the domestic level. Her analysis raised interesting questions about home production and its comparability with market work, a topic that, as elaborated in chapter 3, has been further explored by the large body of work on accounting for unpaid activities, although not necessarily following a Marxian framework. At a wider level of analysis, this framework was also used in debates about more systemic issues, such as the connections between capitalism and patriarchy, reproduction and production, and between patriarchy, the household, and the labor market (Hartmann 1976a and 1976b; Benería 1979).

In the United States, if not elsewhere, one of the problems of using a Marxian framework was that it was relegated to the margins of the economics profession. As such, it developed with little interaction and insufficient dialogue with other feminist economists. More important, perhaps, the postmodern critique of "grand theories" and their tendency to essentialize what is not universal paralyzed its further development and potential impact. It is interesting to note that, although postmodern critiques of grand theory apply equally to orthodox economics, the latter has remained much less sensitive to it, even if not totally immune (as pointed out in chapter 1).

Institutional economics provided another avenue for feminist analysis. During the 1970s and early 1980s, labor economists in the United States combined Marxian and institutional approaches to the analysis of labor market structures and of how they were related to labor stratification and to class, racial, and gender inequalities (Edwards et al. 1973; Gordon et al. 1982). This allowed them to discuss the historical and contemporary processes of labor market segregation, segmentation, and discrimination that implied a critique of the competitive labor market model and to construct an alternative approach to the understanding of wage inequalities and other differential labor market outcomes according to worker traits and characteristics. Segmentation theory had many implications for an analysis of gender inequality (Reich et al. 1980). But, here too, it did not incorporate gender as an integral part of the model; at least initially, women were "added on" to the analysis as a way of describing their location and conditions of participation in the labor market rather than as a way of explaining why segmentation was gendered (Benería 1987). Feminists, however, made use of this approach by drawing the connections between labor market segmentation and sex segregation and by emphasizing how both were linked with socialization processes outside the workplace where they were reproduced and transformed (Hartmann 1976b; Strober 1984). Other contributions from institutional economics have emphasized the notion that social processes are not governed by universal laws and do not have universal meanings, hence the importance of placing feminist analysis within cultural and historical contexts, including changing institutions in order to "explain women's disadvantages" (Jennings 1993).

An important contribution toward the construction of alternative models was introduced with Amartya Sen's bargaining model, whose notion of "cooperative conflicts" captured household dynamics in a much more realistic way. Although household bargaining dynamics had been discussed by feminists (Benería and Roldán 1987), Sen's application of game theory to the household and his view of the family as a site of cooperative conflicts was an innovative contribution and a step forward from the harmonious rational choice model. Based on a critique of neoclassical models on the basis that they could not explain the systematically inferior position of women in many societies, Sen's (1990) model underlined the notion that "conflicts of interest between men and women are unlike other conflicts, such as class conflicts"—that is, gender conflicts exist across class and different social characteristics. His emphasis was on understanding the possibilities for cooperation and conflict that result from the conditions in which men and women are immersed and which derive from their differing bargaining power. This led toward an understanding of the factors that could increase women's bargaining power and women's agency, in addition to women's well-being. Given the complexity of the family, Sen's argument was also an improvement over the view of the household "as a locus of conflict" found in earlier feminist analysis. In addition, Sen's model was much less imbued with Western individualistic biases and was formulated more closely in connection with the literature dealing with gender and development.

Sen's formulation, even though subject to feminist critiques for not focusing directly on gender relations, was conducive to analyzing questions about the factors behind women's subordination, powerlessness, and low bargaining power; as such, it has subsequently been used by other economists with a more specific feminist lens (Seiz 1991; Agarwal 1992; Duggan 1994; Kabeer 2000). Agarwal (1992), for example, elaborated on Sen's approach, focusing more directly on intrahousehold gender relations. Her rich analysis of factors shaping bargaining power was informed by empirical information mostly from work on India. In her analysis, the factors affecting women's fallback positions and relative bargaining strength include social perceptions and norms, self-perceptions, altruism and self-interest—together with other external factors, such as the market, the community and the state, subject to transformation through policy and action. Similarly, Kabeer (2000) has used a bargaining approach to analyze women's choice and negotiations with patriarchal conjugal contracts, including renegotiations around purdah in different geographical settings.

*Gender as a Central Category of Analysis*
During the 1980s and 1990s, the approaches followed by feminists in general and feminist economists in particular tended to converge for a variety of reasons, at least in the United States. Three main reasons for this convergence can be pointed out.

First, a significant shift to the politics of the right during the 1980s threatened to do away with many of the gains made since the emergence of the women's movement. The threat of a backlash affected women of different persuasions and provided a common cause for political struggle and intellectual pursuits. The result was a partial erasure of political boundaries between the different feminist approaches, which set the basis for an increasing dialogue between them and for a degree of convergence around feminist theory. Interestingly enough, this happened at a time of emphasis on "difference" within feminism, focusing on the importance of distinguishing between the varied experiences of women from different social, racial, sexual, and cultural backgrounds, a process that was intensified with the postmodern emphasis on identity politics and representation. To a great extent, in the academy and elsewhere, the emphasis on difference was equally relevant to all theoretical approaches, thereby providing another basis for convergence among them. Within economics, this tendency toward convergence materialized in the creation of the International Association of Feminist Economics (IAFFE) in 1992, an organization in which economists and other social scientists of different persuasions created a forum for pursuing debates on feminist economics and the discussion of common goals.

Second, the theoretical shift away from structural approaches and toward the use of gender as a central category of analysis was a key factor in the development of new theoretical formulations. The notion of gender as a social construct, constantly shaped and reconstituted, implied a rejection of essentialism in feminist work and destabilized categories and previously assumed connections between structure and the socioeconomic conditions affecting men and women. At the same time, "gender" was not a substitute for "women." Instead, it was a way of underlying the notion that "information about women is necessarily information about men" (Scott 1986). In Scott's own words:

> The core of the definition rests on an integral connection between two propositions: gender is a constitutive element of social relationships based on perceived differences between the sexes, and gender is a primary of signifying relationships of power. (p. 1067)

As a constitutive element of social relationships based on perceived differences between the sexes, Scott described four interrelated elements involving gender: culturally available symbols, normative concepts that set forth interpretations of gender meanings, kinship systems, and subjective identity. The all-encompassing nature of these elements led her to state that "gender is everywhere." The power of these conceptualizations affected the different approaches to feminist analysis and contributed to the partial erasure of differences among them—analytically and at the practical level.

Unfortunately, Scott also emphasized the notion that gender becomes a way of denoting "cultural constructions," thereby bypassing the role of material constructions. As emphasized in chapter 1, this perspective contributed to the neglect of the economic dimensions in feminist theory. Indeed, gender is everywhere, including in the all-important and often dry landscapes of the material world of economics and its structural connections.

The intellectual currents of postmodernism resulted in the tremendous growth of feminist theory during the 1980s and 1990s. The power of gender as an analytical category was combined with the critiques of positivism and of the grand theory that had characterized earlier feminist approaches. The postmodern critique undermined stable categories of analysis and opened up new questions about the most effective ways of theorizing and doing research. I have suggested in chapter 1 that, although postmodernism had its most significant impact on the humanities and literary fields, it also strongly influenced the social sciences. Within economics, even if it had a more marginal effect, the literature on the rhetoric of economics was an illustration of its impact, as can be found in the work of economists Deirdre McCloskey, Arjo Klamer, William Milberg, Jack Amariglio, and others. Their work was an indication of the shift of emphasis from an analysis of causality, so prevalent in economics, to that of meaning. McCloskey's work on the rhetoric of economics, for example, continues to be an important effort to analyze the "official methodology of economics" as a modernist discourse with an excessive faith in the power of mathematics and quantitative methods. Their impact on feminist economists facilitated the formulation of new questions about the discourse of economics and its androcentric biases, raising new and fundamental questions about its nature and basic assumptions, as discussed below.

*Feminist Economics*

The feminist influence on economic analysis grew gradually during the 1970s and 1980s, and particularly since the early 1990s, symbolized by the birth and increasing presence in the profession of the IAFFE and its journal, *Feminist Economics*. It was also symbolized by the publication and success of *Beyond Economic Man* (Ferber and Nelson 1993) which had the "integrative" subtitle *Feminist Theory and Economics*, indicating its interdisciplinary nature and feminist character but also its focus on the discipline. Since that time, much has been written on the subject.[2] Feminist economics has continued to pose challenging questions to the profession—what Albelda has called "disturbances in the field"—and to present alternatives to traditional analysis. It has moved in various directions that include historical, theoretical, and empirical analysis. Without being exhaustive, the following areas of concentration represent illustrations of the work being carried out.

First, a large body of the literature has focused on the *social construction of economics* as a discipline. In particular, the emphasis has been on the deconstruction of orthodox economics, particularly in its neoclassical version, and on its implicit biases—in general and from a feminist perspective. This effort has included a critique of the ways in which the market and market society is assumed to function, hiding, in Diana Strassmann's terms, "a distinctly androcentric and Western perspective on selfhood and individual agency" (Strassmann 1993). This type of critique has been accompanied by an open debate on the nature of markets and the ways in which they foster, as well as limit, the goals and actions of individuals and communities. The debate has shown that feminist economics involves a healthy variety of viewpoints and approaches ranging from a defense of the market as a source of material growth and individual freedom to a variety of critiques based on its inability to accomplish these goals for everyone.[3]

As elaborated below, one of these critiques focuses on the assumptions of economic rationality and maximizing behavior as the behavioral norm on which mainstream economics has been built. Chapter 3 returns to this topic, including the extent to which differences can exist between men and women as well as between different individuals and cultures. Feminist economists have questioned basic tenets in the discipline, such as the rhetorical force of the pursuit of efficiency. They have critically discussed the concept of efficiency itself and its central place in economic analysis, on the basis that: a) Pareto optimality assumes that "measures of economic well-being can be collapsed into a single metric," and b) "distributional issues must remain outside the scope of economic science" (Barker 1995: 35). Similarly, feminist economists have questioned the "disciplinary authority" through which the mainstream profession has imposed its views about what constitutes economic analysis, identifying it with a specific approach:

> By proscribing what can count as economics, this identification [with mainstream economics] constrains the pattern of acceptable disagreement in a way that silences serious challenges to the primacy of self-interested individualism and contractual exchange. (Strassmann 1993: 55)

Further, feminist economists have deconstructed other basic tenets in the profession such as the way in which the tale of Robinson Crusoe, so often used in economics textbooks as the quintessential economic man, strikes a responsive chord in the imagination of many economists. He is the prototype of *homo economicus*, self-sufficient but concealing and using the labor of others. As Ulla Grapard (1995) has argued very incisively, this powerful image does not reveal relationships of power and unequal exchange, ignoring elements of domination and exploitation while avoiding "the ethical burden of addressing the disturbing issues of race and gender in our narratives" (p. 33).

Second, and more specifically, feminist economists have *questioned the central emphasis placed on choice as the focus of mainstream analysis, contrasting it with an emphasis on provisioning* for individual and collective well-being as the central alternative objective of economics. Along these lines, Julie Nelson (1993) has pointed out that what is needed is a definition of economics that focuses on the provisioning of human life rather than simply on rational choices between alternatives. To be sure, feminists are not unique in raising this question. They have joined the chorus of other voices speaking from different perspectives. Kenneth Boulding, for example, has stated that "modern economics has gone wholly towards the view of economic life as society organized by exchange, and has largely lost the sense of being a process of provisioning of the human race, or even of the whole biosphere" (quoted in Nelson 1993: 23). As mentioned in chapter 1, other authors have written about the "extraordinary indifference" of conventional economics vis a vis pressing social issues such as poverty, health care needs, deteriorating social conditions for a proportion of the population, and similar issues (Heilbroner and Milberg 1995). However, feminist economists have added a new dimension to these criticisms, emphasizing the importance of unpaid work, "caring labor," and the care economy for the provisioning of human welfare.

By focusing on the important role of women in provisioning and human welfare and on their traditional concentration in unpaid work, feminist economists have made an important contribution to rethinking economics. They have also highlighted the nature and functions of unpaid work and have contributed to raising the problem of undercounting women's work in national labor statistics and national income accounts, underlying the significance of unpaid activities for social reproduction and the functioning of the economy. Questions about unpaid work originally focused on domestic labor, around which much was written in the earlier years of the feminist movement. Since the 1980s, the issue of invisibility and measurement of women's activities has been taken up at the international level and an extensive body of work has emanated from it (see chapter 5). At the theoretical and practical level, feminist economists have focused on caring labor as a central issue, defining it as that "undertaken out of affection or a sense of responsibility for other people, with no expectation of immediate pecuniary reward" (Folbre 1995b and 2000). Based on the crucial significance of the ways in which childcare is provided for understanding how women are treated across countries, this issue has been key in feminist theory as well as in activist circles. Equally important has been the analysis of family policy in which many feminist economists have been involved theoretically and practically.[4]

Third, feminist analysis has been important in *pointing out the biases of many tenets behind conventional microeconomic models,* such as their individualistic and androcentric assumptions in consumption and time allocation theory. A significant part of this critique has centered on the notion that these models are based on the assumption of economic rationality in the behavior of economic actors, therefore excluding the influence of any form of emotional attachment involved in individual choices. As Paula England (1993) has pointed out, three of the basic assumptions in neoclassical economic theory—namely, the impossibility of interpersonal utility comparisons, the exogeneity and static tastes in economic models, and the rational/selfish behavior informing individual decisions—flow from a "separate self model" of human nature:

> [This model] . . . presumes that humans are autonomous, impervious to social influence, and lack sufficient emotional connection to each other to make empathy possible. (England 1993: 38)

The fact is that these assumptions do not hold in many instances and are foreign to the predominant ways in which humans, and women in particular, interact through ways that imply emotional connection with others rather than separation from them. The assumption of a "connected" or "relational" self, England argues, implies the possibility of interpersonal utility comparisons, as well as a better understanding of the social construction of tastes and their continuous change. It also implies a type of human behavior based on empathy, altruism, and care for others, rather than exclusively on economic rationality and the selfishness assumed in conventional models. This type of behavior is likely to generate a tendency to cooperate rather than to compete with others, searching for collective rather than individualistic solutions. The implications of this analysis for economic theory are far reaching. They suggest that existing models are either unrealistic or incomplete in terms of how many people behave.

Equally important have been the feminist critiques of neoclassical models such as in the case, already mentioned, of the New Household Economics and its underlying theory of the family, à la Gary Becker, on the basis that they are "fatally simplistic," "irrelevant," or "misleading" in understanding women's problems (Bergmann 1995). Bergmann's critique points out that the New Household Economics, whose approach is typified by Becker's analysis, depict institutions as benign and individuals as able to reach their goals through the market, therefore leading to the conclusion that government intervention is useless and might even be harmful. But this isn't necessarily so, adds Bergmann, pointing to many instances in which government intervention is needed. The list of feminist economists agreeing with this type of critique is large. Rather than presenting ways to challenge the traditional division of labor by which men "specialize" in paid work and women in domestic or other unpaid work, these models take as given a set of assumed (static) gender characteristics—such as that women are better than men at cooking and child care while men are better at market work—in order to explain and justify the traditional, gender-biased division of labor and corresponding inequalities within and outside the household. On the contrary, feminists begin questioning gender socialization and gender stereotypes in order to change these outcomes, thus rejecting gender-based assumptions in theoretical models.

Fourth, beyond the more traditional analysis of discrimination and occupational segregation, the analysis of *women's employment in relation to the provision of equality of opportunity* has been central to feminist economics in the labor market and its outcomes. Various areas of research have taken up this task. One includes the analyses of women's labor force participation and employment policies, family policy, and other factors affecting women's incorporation in the paid labor force (Strober 1984; Blau and Ferber 1986; Power and Rosenberg 1995; Trzcinski 2000; Rubery et al. 2001). This includes the understanding of working time regimes, the differences related to class, race, ethnicity, and sexuality, and the analysis of labor market hierarchies related to gender discrimination and segregation.[5] An important contribution of this literature is the conclusion that the position of women in any given society is less governed by the existing legislation on equality of opportunity than by institutional factors such as active labor market policies, the allocation of time in paid and unpaid work, social security, welfare rights, and the institutional regime of pay determination (Laufer 1998; Rubery et al. 1998; Bruegel and Perrons 1998). A related area of work refers to welfare policy and welfare reform. In the case of the United Sates, debates around this issue have produced an extensive literature on work/family legislation and on the problems facing women and families at the low-wage level of the labor market (Blank 1994; Bergmann 2000; Albelda 2001). Finally, feminist economists have engaged in debates about other types of policy initiatives such as the promotion of minimum income schemes in different countries (Lavinas 1996; McKay 2001) and questions related to social security policy and its different impact on men and women (MacDonald 1998; Bergmann 2000).

Taken together, these different aspects in the literature on women's work show that feminist economists have mapped out an agenda beyond the more conventional analysis of human capital and market forces to press for equality of opportunity while emphasizing the importance of factors such as reproductive rights, family policy, the care economy, and antidiscriminatory policies that go beyond the more traditional forms of discrimination such as wage and occupational segregation, which have also been extensively analyzed.

Fifth, feminist economists have been involved in *interdisciplinary analysis* through their use of feminist theory—which cuts across disciplines—

and by incorporating the literature and concerns derived from other fields of inquiry into their work, engaging directly with debates generated in other disciplines. To illustrate, Frances Woolley (2000) has discussed John Rawls' *A Theory of Justice*, which analyzes the problem of justice between generations by focusing on fathers and sons. Woolley has brought mothers into the Rawlsian social contract, which presumes altruism in the family and selfishness in the market place à la Becker. By introducing *both* parents into Rawls' model of transference of resources from one generation to the next, Woolley highlights the importance of the interaction between parent's choices, pointing out the significance of gender roles and of intrafamily distribution of resources in the process. In doing so, she opens up new avenues for a feminist analysis of the family with regard to intergenerational choices.

This interdisciplinary dialogue, even if not always present, can be detected in journals such as *Feminist Economics* and other publications in which noneconomists have contributed through a variety of subjects as well (Peterson and Lewis 1999). To illustrate, philosopher Sandra Harding (1995) has joined the debate on objectivity in economics, pointing out that models of scientific knowledge that are viewed as "objective," including the social sciences, often "express and serve the projects only of dominant institutions" from which women have been excluded (p. 8). Her argument resonates loudly among feminist economists and other social scientists who have engaged in this debate.

The gender and development field offers many illustrations of interdisciplinary work, particularly resulting from the fact that the process of development is multidimensional and holistic. This tendency can be found among individual authors as well as in many cases of coauthorship involving economists and other social scientists. Feminist economists who have worked on questions of rural women have often relied on the contributions of anthropologists to understand, for example, the complexities and cultural differences in land distribution as well as the norms and traditions affecting property rights and the access to resources in different societies (Agarwal 1994; Deere and León 2001). Similarly, the problem of "missing women," referring to the low female/male ratios observed traditionally in many areas, particularly in Asian countries such as Pakistan, Bangladesh, India, and China, has benefited from an interdisciplinary approach that can help explain its multiple levels—anthropological, social, cultural, and economic (Drèze and Sen 1989; Balakrishnan 1994).

To be sure, feminist economists in the development field have also focused on more narrow and specialized economic analysis that helps them establish a dialogue with male economists. These topics are discussed in more detail in the sections that follow.

Lastly, feminist economics has produced an abundant literature on the *gender and development field* and in the area of *international labor, gender, and globalization*. Most of the areas of concentration described so far have had a component focusing on developing countries, but this field includes a more specific focus on development. From the initial emphasis during the 1970s on microeconomic issues dealing, for example, with rural women, the gender division of labor, and labor markets across countries and regions, the 1980s and 1990s saw an innovative expansion of this work into new areas of gender analysis, from macroeconomics to the environment, and from gender and trade issues to women's rights and access to resources, including property rights and education. The field includes also a rich array of contributions focusing on families and households—both as sites of production and social reproduction across countries and cultures. The rest of this chapter, as well as other chapters in the book, present more detailed discussions of the field.

To sum, the success of the work carried out under the umbrella of "feminist economics" is twofold. On the one hand, it addresses the social construction and economic bases of women's subordination, with important implications for our understanding of the factors generating the various forms of gender inequality and hierarchical power relations, and for policy and action. It also addresses questions of women's interests and needs. On the other hand, it challenges some fundamental tenets and basic assumptions in the discipline of economics, either joining other critiques from different perspectives or representing unique feminist contributions. In this sense, feminist economics transcends the more explicit feminist project by questioning the very nature of economic analysis and its objectives, and it performs an important critical role for the profession as a whole.

## Macroeconomics and Austerity Programs

I have mentioned that the publication in 1970 of Boserup's book *Woman's Role in Economic Development* made clear that the process of development had not been gender neutral. This seems obvious now, but many of us might have forgotten what an impact her thesis made at the time. Boserup's contributions were numerous and have been widely discussed since then by economists and other social scientists (Benería and Sen 1981; Harriss-White 1998 and 2002; Tinker 2002). From the perspective of feminist economics, her work represented a turning point in the development literature, with many consequences for policy and action. Although her analysis did not clearly have a clear feminist content, her recognition of women's role in economic development emphasized the ways in which development processes had been gendered and how modernization had marginalized women. This led her to argue for the integration of women in development, a notion that has been discussed repeatedly during the past three decades.

The significant amount of research carried out since then has built upon Boserup's book and moved beyond it. During the 1970s, a good proportion of the work on women and development concentrated on the "discovery" of gender dimensions in the previously genderless development literature. Boserup's analysis was shaped by its acceptance of modernization theory. The feminist literature that followed focused both on a critique of modernization theory and on the deepening of our understanding of how development processes affected women and gender divisions across countries and cultures. From 1970 to 1985, economists and other social scientists made an important contribution to the field, mostly concentrating on studies at the micro level and dealing with many of the issues discussed above.

By the time of the 1985 UN Decade of Women conference in Nairobi, feminists had begun to pay more attention to policy and macroeconomic issues. For example, they began to discuss the gender dimensions in structural adjustment programs, environmental degradation, and technological change. Likewise, during the 1980s and 1990s, processes such as those linked to economic restructuring, the virtual dismantling of the welfare state in many countries, the feminization and informalization of labor markets, and the effects of globalization of production and trade liberalization provided further evidence of the importance of gender-sensitive analysis at a more macro level. The Beijing Platform of Action from the Fourth UN Conference on Women in 1995 made an explicit reference to the need to review and modify macroeconomic objectives and social policies with the full participation of women and taking into consideration the objectives of the platform. Neoliberal policies provided feminists many opportunities to analyze their effects from a gender perspective in many countries, for example regarding the effects of government budget cuts on welfare and the deconstruction of domestic budgets (Bakker 1994). Similarly, development policies and the structural adjustment packages of the 1980s and 1990s raised a variety of questions regarding gender biases in macroeconomics and, as a result, set the stage for further integrating gender in macroeconomic models. More recently, work on the gender dimensions of international trade and finance has also emerged. The next section concentrates more explicitly on these areas in which progress toward engendering economic analysis has been made since the 1990s.

The foreign debt crisis that brewed during the late 1970s and early 1980s in many developing countries surfaced to the general public on August 15, 1982, when Mexico announced its inability to meet debt payments and the adoption of its first rescue package of structural adjustment policies (SAPs). The package followed what became the typical World Bank-IMF model inspired in the set of neoliberal policies associated with the Washington Consensus, including the participation of international commercial banks and the help of governments from high income countries, with the United States taking a strong lead. Throughout the 1980s, many other countries in Latin America and Africa followed the Mexican model, and the same can be said for the Eastern European countries during the post–1989 period.[6] During the 1990s similar austerity programs were adopted by countries that faced financial crises: Mexico in 1994, the countries affected by the Asian crisis in 1997, Russia in 1998, and again Argentina in many occasions through 2002. All of these countries were subject to strong austerity measures representing minor variations of the SAPs model. Since the mid-1990s, austerity programs ceased to be referred to as structural adjustment policies, perhaps because SAPs had become very controversial and contested terrain, despite the fact that they continued to be adopted in different countries.

Soon after structural adjustment politicies began to be implemented, it became clear that the burden of adjustment was not equally distributed among the population. Studies have shown that many countries registered an increase in poverty levels, income inequality, and social polarization—one of the factors at the root of the well-recognized poverty problems discussed in chapter 1. During the initial period of SAPs, the virtual absence of social policies, coupled with cuts in social services, left the family household as the only refuge where the negative effects of adjustment resulting, for example, from higher levels of unemployment and deep budget cuts, were dealt with on a daily basis. Over the years, studies documented the social costs of adjustment affecting a large proportion of the population (Cornia et al. 1987; ECA 1989; Commonwealth Secretariat 1989; ECLAC 1990 and 1995).

Former World Bank chief economist and Nobel Prize-winner Joe Stiglitz has denounced on many occasions the ways in which these policies have tended to create problems of corruption through privatization, and to open the door to "hot money" speculation that results from capital market liberalization, thus generating destabilizing capital flows. He coined the expression "IMF riots," a phenomena often registered in countries experiencing pressures on household budgets caused by market-based pricing introduced with SAPs. This tends to raise the price of basic goods such as food, water, and cooking gas and to materialize into various forms of social unrest. Within this framework, trade is viewed as the basic form of poverty reduction, assuming that markets are the best form of eradicating it.

In addition to the impact on the whole population, studies focusing on the gender dimensions of adjustment have documented the ways in which the burden of adjustment has not been gender neutral, resulting in a new area of inquiry focusing on gender and macroeconomics. These studies have illustrated the ways in which women are affected both as members of specific social groups and as a result of the division of labor in and outside of the household. Mostly based on case studies and country-level analysis, this literature has shown that there are both household and market effects reflecting the gender dimensions of the costs of adjustment. Household effects include the intensification of women's domestic work, the interruption of children's education (of girls in particular) and increases in time inputs either to obtain basic services or to self-provision them. Market effects range from the increase in women's labor force participation to changes in the nature and conditions of their employment—for example, in terms of the informalization of work that will be examined in chapter 4. These are in addition to other costs—much less tangible and more difficult to measure—such as the increase in individual stress and domestic violence. Although some of these studies began in the late 1980s, the literature on the subject expanded during the 1990s and has resulted in a body of work with important theoretical and policy implications.[7]

In retrospect, we may ask about what we can conclude from this literature on gender, macroeconomics, and structural adjustment. The list of observations that follow is an attempt to summarize some of the implications that incorporate a good proportion of the key arguments discussed.

First, austerity programs have basically assumed that those who are negatively affected can endure the hardships and absorb the costs of adjustment on their own. As Diane Elson (1992) argued, macroeconomic policies have assumed an almost infinite capacity, on the part of those affected, to deal with whatever problems are generated by these policies. The limit to this capacity is obviously reached when people cannot survive, but the literature has actually illustrated the tremendous endurance of people at the high cost of pain, suffering, and depletion of human and nonhuman resources. Since the early 1990s, and based on the realization that SAPs were causing greater social stress than originally expected, the packages adopted included some form of palliative for "the most vulnerable"—such as with the case of the social investment funds that were created mainly in the early 1990s, many of which targeted employment programs for women. These efforts were sporadic, ad hoc measures aimed at palliating the most extreme cases of distress and poverty, and at preventing social tensions. From a gender perspective, they often tended to treat women as dependents and receiving the funds' benefits through the male heads of families (Benería and Mendoza 1995). As such, they were inadequate measures to deal with the *roots* of poverty.

Second, adjustment packages have focused on the market and the sphere of paid production while ignoring unpaid economic activities and the sphere of reproduction. Empirical studies have shown that the shifts in resource allocation and the increases in productivity assumed to take place through structural adjustment programs represented a transfer of costs from the market to the household: "the hidden 'equilibrating factor' is the household's, and particularly women's ability to absorb the shocks of stabi-lization programs, through more work and 'making do' on limited incomes" (Elson 1993: 241). Given that poor families have been most affected by these shifts, the literature has shown that there is both a gender and a class dimension to the adjustment process.

Third, a conclusion emphasized in the literature is that macroeconomic theory and policy, far from being neutral according to gender and other social characteristics, can be biased and requires compensating measures to deal with the unequal distribution of the burden of adjustment. Yet, auster-ity programs most often have been insensitive and even mistaken in dealing with the needs of women. For example, during the 1998 crisis in Brazil, the World Bank recommended the adoption of an employment program for women to compensate for the loss of male jobs that would result from the austerity plan adopted; at the same time, the package required the imple-mentation of budget cuts that curtailed daycare programs, hence, implying that the plan viewed women's incorporation in the paid labor force as a temporary measure and without regard to women's long-term interests and needs regarding daycare (Benería and Rosenberg 1999).

Fourth, one problem associated with orthodox macro models is that the complexity of gender divisions is often lost through the high level of aggre-gation used. This explains, for instance, why some evaluations of SAPs car-ried out in various African countries during the early 1990s, were overly optimistic about the effects of adjustment on the poor and paid little atten-tion, at least initially, to the heterogeneity among the poor and to gender differences.[8] Their exclusive focus on macro data and quantitative analysis using social accounting matrix (SAM) estimates did not allow for an under-standing of the gender dynamics generated at the micro level. In this sense, case studies and anthropological research have been more illuminating in terms of showing the ways in which austerity measures affect people's lives and generate gender-related asymmetries in the distribution of the burden of adjustment. For example, in an anthropological study about the effects of structural adjustment on gender relations in Zambia during the 1980s, Geisler and Hansen (1994) showed that one year after liberalization of mar-kets, entire villages abandoned maize production (which required fertil-izer) in favor of Soya beans (which did not) as a result of increases in the price of fertilizer. Traditionally, income from beans was considered to be women's income but, after the shift in crops, men began to claim it and con-flicts over income from beans increased. Contrary to conventional wisdom, married women were particularly vulnerable due to the fact that:

> while wives have no claim to husband's earnings, husbands make *culturally legitimated claims* on their wives' time, work, and in some cases income. (p. 96, emphasis mine)

This is precisely the type of gender dynamics that many macro level studies and static quantitative analysis do not capture. In this sense, qualitative information at the local level can add insightful information about the ways in which adjustment policies affect people's lives. This is not to say that the use of macro models is not appropriate but to point out that they need to be complemented with more desagregated level of analysis documenting the ways in which the effects of adjustment are lived and absorbed by households and communities. This includes the understanding of noneconomic factors such as traditions affecting the division of labor and cultural practices.

Feminist economists have also used large data sets to document the gender effects of adjustment. For example, Floro and Shaffer (1998), in a comparative study of the Philippines and Zambia, showed that global integration of labor markets generated some employment opportunities of women in the Philippines. This was not the case in Zambia, as a result of many factors constraining labor mobility, and where "new labor markets entrants, many of whom are women, cannot find jobs and are forced to create their own employment in the informal sector or to contribute instead to the growing pool of unemployed and discouraged workers" (p. 80). Yet, despite the authors' successful effort to take gender into consideration, their analysis would also have benefited from using more qualitative information to complement the quantitative findings.

Finally, austerity programs have mostly ignored structural factors that shape the ways in which they affect people's lives and gender-related impacts. Nora Lustig has provided a suggestive summary of these factors:[9]

> Among the structural factors are the distribution of income and wealth, tenancy relationship to the land, the type and degree of specialization in foreign trade, the density of chains of production, the degree of concentration in markets, control of the means of production by distinct types of actors (the private sector, the state, or transnational capital), the functioning of financial intermediaries and penetration of technical advance, as well as sociopolitical factors associated with the extent of organization of the working class and other influential sectors of the population, the geographical and sectoral distribution of the population and its level of skills.

Each of these factors can be thought of as having a gender dimension which can be captured through a more desegregated level of information than that which is normally used in orthodox models. The objective is the incorporation of sources of gender differentiation, such as intra-household income flows and gendered labor market outcomes, in order to design appropriate policies. To this end, micro studies are again essential for engendering macroeconomics; we cannot entirely understand markets without being aware of how families and households function and how they evolve over time, in the same way that macro models need to understand how markets function or fail to do so. This type of work can be found among recent contributions to the literature.[10]

To sum, we have learned much about the gender dimensions of adjustment from past experiences in many countries. The challenge is also to translate this knowledge into practical policies, a topic discussed in the next section.

## Alternative Macro Policies and Feminist Research

Since the 1980s, the notion that there is no alternative—some have called it TINA—to neoliberal policies and, more specifically, to the one-size-fits-all adjustment packages and austerity programs inspired in the Washington Consensus, prevailed in national and international circles. The break of the Consensus has led to the search for alternatives, so far not necessarily representing a radical shift but rather implying a higher degree of attention paid to poverty alleviation (rather than eradication) and to social policies. The World Bank's *World Development Report 2000/2001* is an illustration of the new approach at the level of mainstream economic institutions. At the same time, individual researchers and institutions have engaged in debates about the world's persistent poverty without the institutional constraints of mainstream approaches. In view of these debates and of the literature discussed so far, we can ask to what extent gender-aware analysis has contributed to the search for alternative macro policy models. This section presents a summary of possible answers to these questions. Let's begin with basic general objectives, as expressed by UNIFEM's executive director, Noeleen Heyzer, who, in her preface to *Progress of the World's Women 2000*, has eloquently summarized a set of objectives:

> Women want a world in which inequality based on gender, class, caste and ethnicity is absent from every country and from the relationship among countries. Women want a world where fulfillment of basic needs becomes basic rights and where poverty and all forms of violence are eliminated. Where women's unpaid work of nurturing, caring and weaving the fabric of community will be valued and shared equally by men. Where each person will have the opportunity to develop her or his full potential and creativity. Where progress for women is recognized as progress for all. (p. 6)

Although the sources of inequality mentioned in this quote could be expanded for example to explicitly include race, nationality, sexual preference, and others, it is very clear regarding its commitment to women and to gender and other forms of equality. The quote also tends to essentialize women in a world in which there are class and growing inequalities among them. Thus, the difficult question is how to translate these general principles into policy and action. The literature on gender and macroeconomics discussed so far provides some guidance in the search for alternative models of adjustment. The following list summarizes some of the implications derived from this body of work.

- Alternative policies should not assume that people have an infinite capacity to bear the costs of adjustment. Instead, they should aim at preventing human hardships and avoiding class, gender, ethnic, and other biases in the burden of adjustment. The insensitivity toward these issues on the part of policymakers has been notorious. The accumulated social tensions have led to the breakdown of the Washington Consensus and to the current debates on poverty and social policy. After two decades of adjustment, and as chapter 1 shows for the Latin American region, some countries can point to improvement in macroeconomic indicators, such as lower inflation rates, increases in foreign investment, high level of exports, and positive, even if moderate, growth rates. Yet persistent financial crises and development problems continue to raise the spectrum of enormous hardships. In the case of Argentina, its adherence to orthodox neoliberal policies did not prevent the country's financial default, with high costs for the average citizen, including the middle class. Likewise, trade liberalization policies, global migration, relocation of production, and other factors generating global and national tensions have created problems of adjustment for individuals, households, and communities, calling for a clear understanding of who are the winners and losers in the process. If we are to put people at the center of development, the question of who bears the burden of adjustment must be taken seriously.

- In the same way, alternative policies should take into consideration the *hidden costs* of adjustment documented by a variety of studies, such as the deterioration of infrastructure, discontinuities, and interruptions in schooling of children—and of girls in particular—with the corresponding long-term losses in future productivity, deterioration of the environment, educational achievement, and other hidden costs such as the intensification of domestic work. Adjustment policies have also had other social costs such as increases in crime and violence and in urban insecurity. As early as 1987, UNICEF's pioneer study of the costs of adjustment called attention to the need for adjustment policies "with a human face" (Cornia et al. 1987). This challenge is still before us.

- Adjustment policies need to be accompanied by two types of social policy, one focusing on short-term compensatory measures and the other addressing long-term planning. The first is necessary to deal with the most urgent needs and with the negative effects of adjustment facing individuals, households, and communities. In the late 1980s and early 1990s, as already pointed out, measures of this sort were addressed with the creation of social investment funds (SIFs), which focused on the poorest population groups. However, SIFs often neglected gender differences and, to a great extent, were designed to avoid social tensions rather than to provide long-term solutions (Benería and Mendoza 1995). The second type of measures include longer-term social policies addressing empowering and distributive goals and focusing, for example, on the gender dimensions of property rights and income-generating policies, changes in the division of labor in paid and unpaid production, educational and retraining programs to prepare women for the requirements of technological change, productivity increases in the nonpaid sectors of the economy, and the creation of networks empowering women.

• One basic objective of macro models should be a clear recognition of the links between productive and reproductive activities. The implementation of SAPs has often accentuated and made more obvious the nature of these links by showing, among others a) the increasing importance of women's income-earning activities as male earnings decline, b) the intensification of domestic work as household budgets shrink, c) the difficulties encountered by women in terms of access to markets, and d) time input effects of budget cuts and of privatization of social services. As argued in chapter 3, feminist scholarship has emphasized the importance of accounting for time and resources spent on unpaid work, including reproductive activities; it has pointed out the special needs of female-headed households (Benería 1992; Floro 1994) and, in the study by Geisler and Hansen, mentioned earlier, the specific problems of wives. These are crucial issues if we are to view macro models as a means to designing policies for the provisioning of needs and maximizing social welfare rather than just a means of setting the prices right or maximizing efficiency and economic growth.

• In contrast with the emphasis of mainstream economics on markets and choice, micro and meso studies have provided much evidence about the *lack of choice* facing individuals and women in particular, and about the limited horizons and possibilities associated with poverty and with patriarchal norms and traditions. Thus, alternative models should not assume that people face a wide range of choices associated with their "maximizing behavior," as orthodox models tend to assume. To the contrary, and as Rebecca Blank (1993) has so eloquently stated, the assumption of an empowered individual in economic models does not leave room for the fact that people might "feel dominated, repressed, passive, stuck, ill, unsure about his or her abilities, or unaware of alternatives" (p. 141). Women's ability to enter the labor market, for example, is often hampered by tradition and sexist norms and institutions, which, as Douglass North (1994) has argued, are humanly devised constraints that structure human interaction and affect the way markets work. To the extent possible, these noneconomic constraints need to be incorporated into macro models and feed economic policy:

> Neoclassical theory is simply an inappropriate tool to ana-
> lyze and prescribe policies that will induce development. It is
> concerned with the operation of markets, not with how
> markets develop. How can one prescribe policies when
> one doesn't understand how economies develop? (North
> 1994: 359)

• Finally, it is important to take into consideration how feminist concerns, in some cases, might interact with macro objectives. For example, an emphasis on demand-side policies opens up the possibility to take actions that can help achieve the objectives mentioned in this chapter. Antidiscriminatory policies based on the enforcement of equal pay for equal work laws, employment schemes addressed to women, or investment policies fostering export promotion in predominantly female industries are examples of such policies. If properly applied, these measures can achieve both macroeconomic goals and feminist objectives, pointing out the possible compatibility between the two.

### Gender, Trade, and Finance

An even more recent effort to integrate gender in economics has taken place in the areas of gender and trade as well as gender and finance. This effort has been a natural outcome of the increasing interest in understanding the ways in which globalization and liberalization of trade and finance generate processes that are differentiated according to gender. Although this type of work has just begun, it includes both theoretical considerations as well as empirical work, including specific case studies, which are useful for a feminist understanding of these processes, as well as for policy and action. A growing literature on the subject is beginning to throw light on the ways in which gender is an important analytical category in trade policy (Wood 1991; Fontana, Joekes, and Masika 1998; Fontana and Wood 2000;

example, have explored a new conceptual framework to analyze how the economic and social effects of financial liberalization and financial crises work through household borrowing and access to various assets. They show how intrahousehold gender relations are intertwined with credit-market processes and financial structures. These processes shape household financial fragility (or strength) and the ways in which households respond to crisis, for example, through an increase in women's employment and affecting women's relative bargaining power. The final effects, they argue, can be different and contradictory, depending on specific factors such as dependency on cash-flow and the degree of control over assets. Their model suggests that "much of the social and human cost of financial crisis may lie beneath the statistical surface: financial crises may alter gender relations through household adjustments which have profound implications not just for economic outcomes but for the social reproduction of households" (p. 1279).

A new avenue of work on gender and finance has to do with the debates on the international financial architecture, including an analysis of alternative proposals for reforms of institutions like the IMF and the World Bank. (Aslanbeigui and Summerfield 2000). This work has barely begun, and the need here is twofold. On the one hand, it is important for women and men with feminist concerns to participate in the ongoing debates so as to get their views heard within the relevant circles. On the other hand, more theoretical and empirical work is necessary, along the lines set out by Dymski and Floro, in order to incorporate it in the debates and negotiations.

### Additional Contributions

In addition to the areas of research and action mentioned so far and contributing to the integration of gender in economics, the field of gender and development has paved other avenues that are part of this effort. Briefly, and without being exhaustive, this section highlights three significant areas of work.

First, the field has made a variety of *conceptual and methodological contributions* in development economics, either as critiques of existing development theories or as an effort to engender existing development work. In addition to the critique of development, feminists have engaged in debates about development policies that have taken place among international circles. In the 1970s a feminist perspective on the variants of the basic needs approach to development provided an evaluation of its contributions, pointing out that it was an initial step forward in recognizing women's work burden (Palmer 1977). At the same time, this evaluation emphasized that the approach needed to go further in "opening up" the household in order to understand the ways in which it was part of production and exchange affecting families and communities and underlying asymmetric gender relations. Over the years, much work has been added to this initial effort and to the reconceptualizations and theoretical work leading to

Kucera 2001; Bisnath 2002; Çagatay 2002). The set of issues anal
from a focus on North-South trade and its impact on female labc
ufacturing to the construction of models that capture the effect.
on women and men, both at the level of the labor market and at h
including country-specific empirical analysis.

Foreign trade can have a variety of impacts on the wages and
women and men, their paid and unpaid work, and their leisure time, tl
ating gender-related income and consumption effects. The existing lite
on the subject is far from conclusive about this impact. For example, <
the initial concerns regarding the effects of trade liberalization wa;
increasing integration of low-wage countries in the global economy w
have negative employment effects on high-income countries. A pionee
study by Wood (1991) actually did not find such a negative effect. Howe
this finding has been challenged by Kucera and Milberg (2000), who sh
that, in a sample of industrialized OECD countries and for the 1987 to 1ϟ
period, trade liberalization reduced female employment in manufacturiı
relative to male employment. To be sure, more empirical studies of this typ
are needed before generalizations can be made. Needless to say, these effort
have resulted from the realization that trade is a gender issue affecting people's lives. While there was a time when trade negotiations were barely noticed
by the average citizen, since the 1990s, in particular, we have seen an increasing attention paid to trade issues—due to the realization of their importance
for the economics and politics of globalization and of everyday life.

Among international organizations, UNIFEM has promoted work on
gender and trade, particularly at the regional level, for example by promoting women's participation in regional trade agreements (Allen and Benería
2001). This work has also been taken up at a more activist level, with an
effort to increase the understanding of the gender effects of trade and the
significance of trade negotiations upon a wider public. Similarly, WIDE
(2001) has worked on a gender analysis of trade agreements between the
European Union (EU) and Latin America (with focus on Mercosur and
Mexico). An International Gender and Trade Network with links in many
countries in the North and South and including all regions has been functioning since the mid-1990s. Combining research and activism, this group's
presence has been felt in events such as WTO meetings and other international activities dealing with gender and trade.

The work toward a gender analysis of finance is even more recent. Again,
it has been inspired by the realization that the importance of this sector at
the national and global levels requires a better understanding of how men
and women might have different links with this sector, with implications
for gender relations and gender inequality. In particular, the Asian crisis
and subsequent financial turmoil raised many questions in this respect and
provided an incentive for this pioneer work. Floro and Dymski (2000), for

gender-aware development economics and including a feminist evaluation of existing development models (Elson 1999). At the methodological level, progress has been made in projects permitting greater sophistication in data and information gathering, including the generation of statistical series and survey data that can be used to obtain a variety of indicators with a focus on gender. In addition to the human development indices published by UNDP and mentioned in chapter 1, UNIFEM, DAW, the ILO, and the World Bank, among others, have also contributed to this effort.

Second, a large body of literature has appeared in the *area of family, welfare, and development* from the perspective of experiences in developing countries. This work constitutes an interesting complement to the work on this area examined earlier in this chapter. A good proportion of this work provides insightful critiques of neoclassical models of the family, particularly since they are based on the richness of information resulting from cross-cultural empirical realities. At the general level, these critiques point out the unrealistic and simplistic assumptions of the models that do not reflect the variety of ways in which families and households function across countries and cultures. More specifically, they point out the inability of these models to capture the inequalities and conflicts that constitute an integral part of gender relations within households. Yet the analysis of inequalities and conflicts are key to understanding how households function. As Sen (1983) noted, "Evidence of inequality within the family is widespread across the world, but in the poorer countries sex bias can be very strong even in such elementary matters as survival, nutrition, health and literacy." Neoclassical models fail to capture these inequalities, as well as the complexity of contributing factors, therefore they are unable to understand the tensions in gender relations that they generate. In her analysis of agricultural households in Africa, Jeanne Koopman (1991) illustrates the extent to which the assumption of an undifferentiated unit of production and consumption results in "a distorted image of the rural household." The existence of men's and women's "separate productive enterprises within households" imply that assumptions of shared preferences and of pooled resources misrepresent processes of production and consumption in African agricultural households. Thus, policy interventions need to be designed accordingly. Empirical work of this type has added rich information illustrating the various ways in which households function under different institutional settings and cultural forms across the continents.

An underlying theme in this work provides an important contribution to the critique of the myth of the "harmonious household" assumed in conventional models. Writing about rural households in Third World countries, Katz (1991), for example, has argued that these models fail to account for the conflict and negotiation inherent in household units. As an alternative, she introduces a bargaining model in which gender-based differentials in the access to key economic and noneconomic resources "conditions the formation of household economic goals, the allocation of labor and income to competing uses, and the welfare outcomes of household economic activities for all household members" (p. 399). This type of analysis is an illustration of how Sen's notion of cooperative conflicts and bargaining model can be combined with a more explicit feminist view of gender relations and gender inequality. The result has been a more "politicized" and "feminist" conceptualization of the household, one centered around the dynamics of unequal gender relations and linked to institutional and structural factors that affect intrahousehold distribution of resources and the social construction of gender. In this sense, the notion of cooperative conflicts in bargaining models transcends the dichotomies associated with some of the most prevalent views of the family, namely: a) the neoclassical view of a harmonious unit; b) the orthodox Marxian view of the family as a source of unity and survival for the working class; and c) the earlier feminist view that focuses on the family as a locus of conflict and struggle.

Finally, the gender and development literature has generated an extensive body of work on *policy and action* as well as on *institutional, economic, social, and political change*. To be sure, these are questions that do not fit squarely into conventional economics because they are also linked to political and interdisciplinary concerns. However, they have been important in the engendering of development economics. A key question has been how social change is conceptualized and operationalized. At one level, there has been much work in the area of development practice. Project implementation has been an important element in Women in Development (WID) circles and international organizations, given their strong involvement at the practical level of assistance and financial aid to developing countries. A large proportion of these projects take place without questioning existing institutions—that is, they are designed to improve the conditions of women within a limited framework of social and political change. As such, they are constrained by the conditions imposed through the institutional setup within which they operate. Myra Buvinic's classic 1986 article about the misbehavior of income-generating projects in the Third World analyzes some of the problems associated with their implementation. In particular, she points out how economic objectives have tended to turn into welfare interventions in their implementation. These problems underline the projects' limited transformative power for women suffering not only from the prevalence of interventions with a welfarist approach but also reducing women to passive recipients of aid instead of improving their capacity for survival, autonomy, and self-sufficiency.

Obviously, the appearance of this type of difficulty does not mean that positive change for women cannot take place without basic institutional changes. The field of gender and development has provided many illustrations of gender-related transformative changes within a given sociopolitical development model (see below). Thus, it is important to differentiate between the type of change taking place within a given sociopolitical development model and the more fundamental transformations represented by systemic shifts, such as the transition from a capitalist to a socialist regime or vice-versa. The gender and development literature has also taken up the analysis of these transformations (Wiegersma 1991; Agarwal 1994; Meurs 1998; Moghadam 2000; Deere and León 2001). Taken together, this literature suggests several basic points:

- Within a given socioeconomic development model, an awareness of gender differences can generate various effects in terms of the impact of state policies on women. To illustrate, Deere and León's analysis of agrarian reforms in Latin America distinguishes between two periods. In the initial generation of reforms, women *de facto* did not have equal access to the redistribution of assets; most of these reforms benefited men primarily, largely because "households" were designated as the beneficiaries of land redistribution under the assumption that men and women share the distributed assets and can benefit equally. More recently, however, neoliberal agrarian legislation has done away with the concept of male household head as the focus of state land-distribution and titling efforts. Deere and León argue that this had been "one of the principal mechanisms of exclusion of women as direct beneficiaries in the agrarian reforms of previous decades" (p. 332). Influenced by feminist discourses and women's agency, the second stage of reforms has shown that state action has provided, at least in some countries, a formal equality in men's and women's land rights, thus showing the importance of taking women's interests more directly into consideration.

- Here it is important to differentiate between access and control over resources since, for women, access to property does not guarantee control over it. This will depend on traditions, norms, and social constructions that shape the nature of gender relations, bargaining power, and contestation around access and control over resources. In this sense, it is crucial that policy and state action facilitate women's agency and protect their interests.

- Women's organizations and collective actions have proven to be crucial for the promotion of social and institutional change responsive to women's short- and long-term needs and goals, while at the same time creating the conditions of more egalitarian gender relations. In Latin America during the 1980s, women's organizations played a crucial role in urban struggles around survival strategies and urban growth (Lind 1990). In many cases, this pointed to the importance of women's organizations that were independent from men, so that they could represent unambiguously women's special interests. For example, Gillian Hart's 1992 study of farm households in Malaysia showed the importance of poor women to form their own organizations to defend their interests separately from men. A very different example is provided by India's Self-Employed Women's Association (SEWA) which over the years has defended the interests of home-based workers by organizing workers that in the past had been seen as unorganizeable.

• The literature illustrates the importance of taking into consideration the need to combine two types of policy and action for feminist and progressive social change. On the one hand, a focus on the transformation of gender relations with policies that will enhance gender equality. Here, policy and action can rely on a wide range of possibilities—from educational policies to the many dimensions of cultural transformation, identity politics, and gender constructions. On the other hand, more structural policies aimed at socioeconomic change and the promotion of development models capable of incorporating progressive social change are an integral part of this transformation. Both types of policy are not mutually exclusive; on the contrary, they can complement each other and are interconnected. The gender and development field has made a significant contribution toward visualizing and implementing "imagined communities" that incorporate these goals.

CHAPTER 3

# Markets, Globalization, and Gender

*Throughout much of the development world,*
*globalization is seen, not as a term describing objective reality,*
*but as an ideology of predatory capitalism*

—Kofi Annan, 1998[1]

Since the 1980s, the process of accelerated globalization that we have witnessed has been a powerful source of change—driving national economies, deepening their international connections, and affecting many aspects of social, political, and cultural life. Globalization has become a common buzz word meaning different things to different people while the international "antiglobalization" movement suffers from a misnomer given that it is not so much "anti," per se, as against the prevailing model and its negative consequences. Despite debates about whether the extent to which the current degree of globalization is higher than in other historical periods, few of us doubt the powerful forces at work toward the formation of "global villages." The strong reactions and contestations that have followed from it are a reflection of the importance that it has taken in people's lives across countries.

From an economic perspective, basic features of globalization are the transformations linked to ever-expanding markets, intensified by the rapid technological changes in communications and transportation that transcend national boundaries, and shrinking space. Multiple processes of globalization are reflected in the various avenues through which they take place: the growth of global corporations and global mergers and their increasing weight in global politics; the formation of "virtual firms" and the relocation of production across the globe; the formation of global social movements and transnational networks; higher levels of labor mobility and international migration; trade and financial liberalization and the formation of regional trade organizations such as common markets and free trade zones. The expansion and deepening of markets has taken place within the context of the neoliberal model of development, which during the past quarter century has returned to the laissez-faire discourse and practice that characterized nineteenth century capitalism. A basic argument presented in this chapter is that, despite its different framework, the global expansion of the past quarter century presents similarities with the earlier expansion of markets during the nineteenth century. This expansion and its globalized nature have involved both high and low income countries, including those in transition to market economies from centralized planning to globalized capitalism.

This chapter includes two quite distinct but interrelated parts. Part I focuses on the construction of global markets during the late twentieth century. Beginning with Karl Polanyi's book *The Great Transformation. The Political and Economic Origins of Our Time*, I discuss his analysis of the self-regulated market and the profound changes in human behavior associated with its functioning. I then examine the extent to which Polanyi's notion of "market society" and his notion of the market as a social construction during the nineteenth and early twentieth centuries in Europe can be applied to the more recent formation of global markets in late twentieth century. Part II deals with the significance of gender for the analysis of markets and asks the question of whether globalization has implications for the construction of feminist models of economic analysis and social change; I attempt to "engender" Polanyi's work by arguing that the construction and growth of markets has gender dimensions, and by pointing out that there is a tension between the assumptions of economic rationality associated with market behavior and the real-life experiences and desires of women and men. I then focus on questions of gender and global markets and summarize some of the themes that have emerged from the abundant body of literature on this subject since the 1970s. Next is a discussion of the extent to which women's values and choices are likely to be influenced by their increasing participation in market society. Finally, I argue that the predominant assumptions in orthodox neoclassical models need to be expanded or replaced by alternative "transformative models" of human behavior that include feminist visions.

# Part I—
# The Social Construction of Markets

## The Self-Regulated Market

Polanyi's *The Great Transformation* was first published in 1944. It is an analysis of the construction and growth of the self-regulated market and of laissez-faire capitalism during the Industrial Revolution up to the early part of the twentieth century in Europe. Within this context, the "great transformation" alluded to by Polanyi referred to the many efforts leading to the "taming" of the market and advocated by those who saw its negative consequences. It was represented by what he calls the "collectivist countermovement," which, beginning in late nineteenth century and continuing through the twentieth, advocated "social and national protectionism" as a reaction against "the weaknesses and perils inherent in a self-regulating market" (p. 145). In this sense, there are commonalities and links between Polanyi's work and Marx's nineteenth century critique of capitalism. However, Polanyi's emphasis was not based on class-related conceptualizations. He thought that popular Marxism had led to "a crude theory of social development" and was based on "a narrow class theory"(p. 151). Although in many ways the two authors complemented each other, Polanyi underestimated the ability of class-related factors to explain long-run social processes. His main emphasis was on understanding markets and market society, while Marx centered his analysis on the functioning of capitalism as an economic system. While Polanyi envisioned the functioning of markets that could be "disciplined" by values and norms different from those prevalent under market society (his expression to refer to the functioning of markets under capitalism), Marx envisioned the replacement of markets and of capitalism by communism.

Polanyi's analysis centered on the profound change in human behavior represented by market-oriented choices and decisions in which gain replaced subsistence as the center of economic activity. Gain and profit, Polanyi argues, had never before played such an important role in human activity. Critical of Adam Smith's suggestion that the social division of labor depended upon the existence of markets and "upon man's propensity to barter, truck and exchange one thing for another" (p. 43), Polanyi argued instead that the division of labor in earlier societies had depended on "differences inherent in the facts of sex, geography, and individual endowment"(p. 44). Production and distribution in many earlier societies, Polanyi explains, were ensured through reciprocity and redistribution—two principles not currently associated with economics as a discipline. These principles were part of an economic system that was "a mere function of social organization"—that is, at the service of social life. Instead, capitalism evolved in the opposite direction, leading to a situation in which it became the economic system that determines social organization, its goals and outcomes. Commenting on Smith, Polanyi argues that ". . . no misreading of the past ever proved to be more prophetic of the future . . ." (p. 43) in the sense that, one hundred years after Adam Smith wrote about man's propensity to barter, truck, and exchange, this propensity became the norm—theoretically and practically—of industrial capitalist/market society. Although Polanyi is not always persuasive in terms of whether the pursuit of economic gain is a result of market society, its fundamental role in a market economy, and in the theoretical models that sustain it, is clearly central.

For Polanyi, a crucial point in this gradual transformation toward the predominance of "the economic" was the step "which makes isolated markets into a [self-regulated] market economy." One of his central points is that, contrary to conventional wisdom, this change was not "the natural outcome of the spreading of markets" (p. 57). On the contrary, Polanyi argues, the market economy was socially constructed and accompanied by a profound change in the organization of society itself. Thus, the construction of a laissez-faire market economy required "an enormous increase in continuous, centrally organized and controlled interventionism," such as in the form of legislative initiatives, including—in England—the "complexity of the provisions in the innumerable enclosures laws" and the "bureaucratic control involved in the administration of the New Poor Laws" (p. 140). Polanyi mentions also the enormous increase in the administrative functions of the state newly endowed with a central bureaucracy, the strengthening of private property, and the enforcement of contracts in market exchange and other transactions:

> The gearing of markets into a self-regulating system of tremendous power was not the result of any inherent tendency of markets towards excrescence, but rather the effect of highly artificial stimulants administered to the body social in order to meet a situation which was created by the no less artificial phenomenon of the machine. (p. 57)

Likewise, Polanyi describes the formation of a competitive national labor market in eighteenth and nineteenth century England as the result of a series of policies that dislocated labor and forced the new laboring classes to work for low wages. Here Polanyi's analysis could be complemented with the Marxian vision of proletarianization through which the large proportion of the population loses ownership and control of the means of production and capital becomes increasingly concentrated. Polanyi raises the seemingly contradictory notion of laissez-faire liberalism as "the product of deliberate state action," including "a conscious and often violent intervention on the part of the government . . ." (p. 250). As he points out, "all these strongholds of government interference were erected with a view to the organizing of some simple [market] freedom."

In contrast, Polanyi contends that the "collectivist counter-movement" or "great transformation"—the subsequent great variety of (re)actions taken against some of the negative consequences of the expanding market—started spontaneously as the critiques of capitalism led to political organizing and a variety of citizens' actions. Many of these actions were defensive on the part of different social groups. The left movements and social planning of the twentieth century were a product of this transformation, and the welfare states that emerged one of its important outcomes. Polanyi saw the origins of this transformation not as reflecting "any preference for socialism or nationalism" but as "the broader range of the vital social interests affected by the expanding market mechanism" (p. 145). In fact, Polanyi argues, economic liberals themselves often advocated restrictions on laissez-faire, such as with "well-defined cases of theoretical and practical importance" like the principle of association of labor and the formation of trade unions, trade protection, and others. Thus, if the great variety of spontaneous reactions and interventions to counteract the market—including those advocated by the different socialist movements—are called "planning," Polanyi's argument emphasizes that while "laissez-faire was planned, planning was not" (p. 141).

For Polanyi, the 1920s "saw the prestige of economic liberalism at its height," with the emphasis on "sound budgets and sound currencies" justifying whatever social costs had to be paid for their attainment. His analysis, in fact, seems to echo contemporary processes linked to neoliberal policies and to contemporary problems of foreign debt and structural adjustment policies:

> The repayment of foreign loans and the return to stable currencies were recognized as the touchstones of rationality in politics; and no private suffering, no infringement of sovereignty, was deemed too great a sacrifice for the recovery of monetary integrity. (p. 142)

However, Polanyi also argues that the 1930s "lived to see the absolutes of the twenties called in question," with international debts repudiated and the tenets of economic liberalism disregarded "by the wealthiest and most respectable" (p. 142).

The profound change represented by the gradual construction of a market society strongly influenced human behavior, leading toward the prevalence of rational economic man, the selfish individual in pursue of his own desires through the market. Polanyi emphasizes that "a market economy can only exist in a market society"—that is, it can only exist if it is accompanied with the appropriate changes in norms and behavior that enables the market to function. Economic rationality is based on the expectation that human beings behave in such a way as to pursue maximum gains; as emphasized in any course in introductory economics, while the entrepreneur seeks to maximize profit, the employee seeks to attain the highest earnings possible, and the consumer the maximum utility. At the theoretical level, Adam Smith linked the selfish pursuit of individual gain to the maximization of the wealth of nations through the invisible hand of the market and, in so doing, he saw no contradiction between the two. The orthodox tradition in economics has continued to rely on this basic link without questioning the consequences of its corresponding institutions and norms on human behavior and social goals.

In that tradition, and as feminist economists have often pointed out, the assumption of rational economic man has been a basic tenet embodied in neoclassical economic theory. Economic rationality is assumed to be the norm in human behavior and the way to ensure the proper function of the competitive market. This is expected to result in the most efficient allocation of resources and the maximization of production at the lowest possible costs. Feminist economists have also pointed out that this excludes behavior based on other types of motivation such as altruism, empathy for others, love and compassion, the pursuit of art and beauty for their own sake, reciprocity, and care. Selfless behavior is viewed as belonging to the nonmarket sector, such as within the family.[2] To be sure, in recent times there has been an effort among economists to revise the neoclassical models in the direction of incorporating what Nancy Folbre (1994) has called Imperfectly Rational, Somewhat Economic Persons or institutions. These agents pursue their self-interest in ways not neatly adjusting to clear-cut definitions of economic rationality and "selfishness," often leading, for example, to complex mixtures of behavior—from solidarity to competition or from altruism to selfishness—that are difficult to model even if they are more realistic. However, as Folbre points out, these revisionist models undermine any claims about the inherent efficiency of a market economy. They are also important in elaborating alternatives to the assumption that economic rationality is the norm in human behavior, thus reinforcing one of Polanyi's basic objectives. Likewise, a growing number of experiments regarding individual preferences show that individuals respond to a variety of factors other than self-interest. We will return to this issue below.

## The Construction of National and Global Markets

*Capitalism without bankruptcy is like Christianity without hell*[3]

Many parallels can be traced between the social construction of national markets analyzed by Polanyi for nineteenth century Europe and the expansion and deepening of both national and transnational markets across the globe during the past quarter century. To be sure, a debate exists about the extent to which globalization represents a new historical trend or a repetition of past experiences. Various authors, for example, have pointed out that some of the current indicators of the degree of globalization are similar to those reached in earlier historical periods, such as during the early part of the twentieth century leading up to World War I. Yet the intensification of integrative processes during the past thirty years—for example in terms of increasingly rapid flows of goods, communications, and all types of cultural exchange among countries and regions—has been unprecedented. The financial sector has led in the degree to which its markets have transcended national boundaries. Likewise, trade liberalization and the internationalization of production have accelerated the global integration of markets in goods and services. At the social and cultural level, the melting pot of cultures has affected everyday life across the globe, resulting in the intensification of multicultural currents but also in tensions across cultures. Thus, despite the strong forces leading toward the convergence of market societies, we have witnessed deep misgivings about the significance and consequences of such trends. The most common example provided is the refusal on the part of different groups in Islamic societies to accept what they view as the imposition of Western values and norms, many of which are transmitted through channels associated with global markets. Similar reactions can be found elsewhere as well.

At the national level, these processes have been facilitated by numerous efforts on the part of governments that have played an active role in the globalization of domestic economies and of their social, political, and cultural life. This time, however, the construction of global markets has taken place, in particular, under the umbrella of interventions on the part of international forces beyond national boundaries. This is the case with the regional formation of free trade areas and common markets and the growth and increasing power of multinational corporations. To these we must add the role of international organizations such as the World Bank and the IMF and the interventions of dominant foreign governments and other international actors in determining policy. The following list provides examples of such dynamics from an economic perspective.

- First, the role of the nation state in enacting deregulation schemes in financial, goods, and labor markets has been instrumental in the gradual erosion of economic borders across countries. Although the degree of deregulation varies by economic sector, markets, and countries, the tendency to "free" the market from intervention became an integral part of economic policy throughout. During the final decades of the twentieth century, these policies created tensions and opposition on the part of social groups that lost relative power and previously won benefits, as in the case of trade unions and labor in general. For this and other reasons, interventions to deal with this opposition required a strong hand—à la Polanyi—on the part of the state. The deep cuts in the social services provided by the welfare state in high-income countries and the dismantling of many of these services in former centrally planned economies provided many examples of how state actions along these lines have eroded a variety of historically won rights and privileges for large sectors of the population (Standing 1999; Moghadam 1993; Tilly et al. 1995). During the 1980s and 1990s, examples of opposition and challenges to these trends were numerous, both in low and high income countries.[4] The so-called antiglobalization movement represents a more recent and repeated expression of discontent with global proportions. Despite this strong opposition at many levels, and subject to the ups and downs linked to changes in national governments, states have pursued a neoliberal agenda leading toward a higher degree of globalization.

• Second, the formation of transnational entities and regional trade areas such as the European Union, North American Free Trade Agreement (NAFTA) and Mercosur have been instrumental in promoting the globalization of markets, responding to the initiatives and interests of social actors likely to benefit from such projects.[5] To be sure, globalization has been channeled through the action of individual governments as the main agents in international negotiation. For example, the Uruguay Round of trade negotiations that led to the replacement of General Agreement on Tariffs and Trade (GATT) by World Trade Organization (WTO) in 1995 resulted in the most global of existing international bodies. Under the leadership of the United States and the G-7, the creation of the WTO represented a substantial acceleration in trade liberalization across the globe and the integration of new sectors into liberalization schemes—such as intellectual property rights and services not previously included in GATT. Unlike its predecessor, the WTO has independent jurisdiction beyond national legislation and its rules on trade, patents, and intellectual property rights are binding on all members. The continuing tensions that have emerged, particularly visible in the WTO Seattle meeting in 1999, have reflected many questions about the extent to which the organization is serving the interests of developing countries (Kohr 2000). Despite these tensions, and the maintenance of protectionist measures in the United States and other high-income countries, the march toward further trade liberalization has been led particularly by the United States, not only through WTO channels but also through other emerging international organizations such as the FTAA (Free Trade of the Americas Association).

• Third, policies designed at the national level and leading to a higher degree of globalization of domestic economies have often been inspired, and at times dictated, from the outside. The structural adjustment policies adopted by numerous countries since the early 1980s provided a typical example. While affecting, in particular, countries dealing with debt repayment problems, SAPs represented a profound shift with respect to the expansion and deepening of the market in the countries affected. Their Washington Consensus-inspired measures of deep economic restructuring and belt tightening followed agreements between national governments, creditor countries, commercial banks, and international organizations such as the IMF and the World Bank, which imposed, and continue to do so, harsh conditionalities for negotiating new loans and terms of payment. Conditions included the well-known efforts to set up the right environment for the expansion of markets, including government budget cuts, privatization programs, deregulation of markets, trade liberalization, the easing of controls on foreign investment, and shifts from import substitution to export promotion development models. Many of these measures resulted in a much higher degree of integration of these countries into the global economy. They also fostered the liberalization of the financial sector, the opening of doors to global capital, and the enforcement of rules and regulations for the smooth functioning of the market à la Polanyi—such as the strengthening of property rights, enterprise reform, and decentralization policies aimed at "liberating" the private sector from government intervention in the economy.[6]

To be sure, these policies increased the economic freedom of many actors involved in the functioning of markets. However, they also involved the use of a strong hand on the part of national governments and international institutions to build the neoliberal model of late twentieth century. This hand responded to the interests of national and global elites, rather than to the wishes of most citizens, and the policies became instruments to lock in the rules associated with (globalized) markets and the "new economy" of late capitalism. To invoke Polanyi, they were the product of deliberate state intervention—often carried out in the name of market freedoms—imposed from the top down and without a truly democratic process of discussion and decisionmaking among all affected parties. As the *Wall Street Journal* put it for the case of Argentina, "[T]he reforms were largely accomplished by the political will of a presidential strongman who invoked executive decrees over 1,000 times" (O'Grady 1997). In Latin America, the only country that consulted its citizens about privatization was Uruguay, and the vote was negative. Many of the measures were also applied in most of the countries of the former Soviet Union. In this case, the shock therapy of structural adjustment has taken place simultaneously with the profound changes in economic and social relations and institutions represented by the transition from central planning to market economies.

During the 1980s and 1990s, the expansion of markets, associated also with the intensification of processes of "modernization" across the globe, was accompanied with triumphalist (re)statements and affirmations of hegemonic discourses emphasizing the norms and behavior associated with economic rationality and with the assumption that the invisible hand of the market is a better form for organizing the economy and society than any type of state intervention. This discourse can easily be seen as part of the process of constructing markets à la Polanyi. We have witnessed this process in different forms, ranging from the strong emphasis on productivity, efficiency, and financial rewards, to shifts in values and attitudes—typified by the yuppies in the 1980s and by the investment bankers of the 1990s. The result has been a new emphasis on individualism and competitive behavior, together with an apparent tolerance and even acceptance of social inequalities and greed.[7] The weekly *The Economist* associated this set of factors with the emergence of the Davos Man who, according to a 1997 editorial, replaced the Chatham House Man in its influence in the global marketplace.[8] The Davos Man, the editorial pointed out, included businessmen, bankers, officials, and intellectuals who "hold university degrees, work with words and numbers, speak some English and share beliefs in individualism, market economics and democracy. They control many of the world's governments, and the bulk of its economic and military capabilities." The Davos Man does not "butter up the politicians; it is the other way around . . . finding it boring to shake the hand of an obscure prime minister." Instead, the editorial pointed out, he prefers to meet the Bill Gates of the world.

Written as a critique of Samuel Huntington's thesis in his book *The Clash of Civilizations and the Remaking of the World Order*, this praise of Davos Man was also an ode to the global and more contemporary version of economic man:

> Some people find Davos Man hard to take: there is something uncultured about all the money-grubbing and managerialism. But it is part of the beauty of Davos Man that, by and large, he does not give a fig for culture as the Huntingtons of the world define it. He will attend a piano recital, but does not mind whether an idea, a technique or a market is (in Mr. Huntington's complex scheme) Sinic, Hindu, Islamic or Orthodox. ( *The Economist*, 2/1/97: 18)

Thus, at least in 1997, *The Economist* expected that the Davos Man, through the magic powers of the market and its homogenizing tendencies, was more likely to bring people and cultures together than force them apart. In the United States at least, the assumption that "everybody was eating MacDonalds, wearing Nike sneakers, buying in WalMart and being very happy learning the English language" seemed to be part of conventional wisdom.[9]

In many ways, the Davos Man represented the rational economic man in its incarnation through contemporary global elites, and the triumphalism of the period could not predict the global tensions that emerged in the early part of the twenty-first century symbolized by the 9/11/01 events. In recent years, global protests at international gatherings—from Seattle to Quebec to Genoa—have toned down this triumphalist discourse. What *The Economist* did not originally recognize is that the commercialization of everyday life and of all sectors of the economy generates social dynamics that many individuals and cultures across the globe might find repulsive. In many ways we have witnessed, in Polanyi's terms, the tendency for society to become "an accessory to the economic system" rather than the other way around. A Colombian friend expressed her version of this phenomenon with complaints about her perception of market society: "now we are living to work, work and produce, not to enjoy life." As the article containing the quote heading this section suggests, an integral part of this discourse is the survival of the fittest: hence the view that bankruptcy is a necessary punishment for those who do not perform efficiently and according to the dictates of the market. The following quote from the article is quite explicit:

> Corporations are "failing" in record numbers, but many keep on going anyway. As a result, the feeble are not eliminated, the fat is not trimmed, and the region's long-term prospects suffer. (WuDunn 1998)

The hegemonic assumption in orthodox economics that the feeble must be eliminated rather than "transformed" or helped in order, for example, to prevent massive layoffs and human suffering, is thus not questioned—thereby reflecting the centrality given under capitalism to efficiency rather than to people and human development. Likewise, the possibility that, in this case, the Asian way may be a model for diminishing the social costs of the crisis while searching for long-term solutions is not considered by the hegemonic discourses feeding market fundamentalism.

The shift toward the predominance of such pro-market discourses during the past quarter century has been particularly dramatic in the transitional countries of the former Soviet Union. The abuses associated with the search for individual economic gain and rapid accumulation of wealth from the newly created markets has been criticized even by some who have been involved in the process (Soros 1998). The transition from centrally planned economies during the post–1989 era was typically carried out with a great deal of state intervention, often guided by state forces and teams of advisors from the capitalist world (Kotz 1995; Sachs 1991 and 1997; Haney 2000). Unlike Polanyi's description of market formations in earlier Europe, the transition has developed within the context of the globalized neoliberal model. In this sense, some of the transitional processes in these countries, particularly in responding to global forces, resemble those observed in the Third World.

# Part II—The Significance of Gender

## Gender and the Market

This section argues that Polanyi's analysis of the social construction of markets has important gender-related implications that he did not take into consideration. My central argument is that the links to the market have been historically different for men and women, with consequences for their preferences, choices, and behavior. Although Polanyi pointed out that in a market society all production is for sale, he failed to discuss the fact that, parallel to the deepening of market relations, a large proportion of the population engages in unpaid production that is only indirectly linked to the market. Women are disproportionately concentrated in this type of work, which includes agricultural family labor—particularly but not solely in subsistence economies—domestic work, and volunteer work. In contemporary societies, women by far perform the largest proportion of unpaid activities. According to UNDP's "rough estimates" at the global level for 1995, if unpaid activities were valued at prevailing wages, they would amount to $16 trillion or about 70 percent of total world output ($23 trillion). Of this $16 trillion, $11 trillion, or almost 69 percent, represent women's work (UNDP 1995). As will be argued in chapter 5, it is difficult to compare paid and unpaid work because, without the competitive pressures of the market, productivity levels might be very different. However, these estimates do provide a rough indication of the important contribution of unpaid women's work to human welfare.

Thus, to a large extent, men and women have been positioned differently with respect to both market transformations and the linkages between gender and nature (Merchant 1989). The literature has discussed extensively that while the market has been associated with public life and "maleness," women have been viewed as closer to nature and reproduction—generally in essentialist ways—instead of as a result of historical constructions. This view, in turn, has had an impact on the meanings of gender, a subject analyzed extensively in the feminist literature dealing with the construction of femininity and masculinity (Gilligan 1982; Butler 1993; McCloskey 1993; Gutmann 1996; Andrade and Herrera 2001). Similarly, it has affected our notions of the market itself (Strassmann 1993). In this sense, Polanyi's analysis needs to be expanded to incorporate gender dimensions.

The norms and behaviors associated with the market do not apply to the sphere of unpaid work, which produces goods and services for use rather than for exchange. To the extent that unpaid work is not equally subject to the competitive pressures of the market, it can respond to motivations other than gain, such as nurturing, love, and altruism, or to other norms of behavior such as duty and religious beliefs and practices. Without falling into essentialist arguments about men's and women's motivations and keeping in mind the multiple differences across countries and cultures, we can conclude from the literature that there are historically-constructed gender-related variations in norms, values, and behavior (England 1993; Nelson 1993; Seguino et al. 1996). Likewise, the literature has discussed extensively women's concentration in caring/nurturing work, either unpaid or paid, and women have concentrated in the service sector in large numbers, including paid and unpaid activities (Folbre 2000; Himmelweit 1995), even though changes are taking place globally in the nature and extent to their involvement (see below).

Although the above UNDP data show that the current predominance of women in unpaid work and that of men in paid activities is beyond dispute, engagement in nongainful activities is not exclusive domain of women, nor is market work exclusive of men. In earlier societies, the principles of reciprocity and distribution described by Polanyi did not necessarily function according to the rules of market rationality. Instead, tradition, religion, kin, community, and social status played an important role in setting up norms and affecting collective and individual values; many of these factors did not respond to market criteria. But nonmaximizing behavior can also be found in contemporary market societies. In subsistence economies, production is not geared to the market and family labor is motivated primarily by needs rather than gain. Likewise, in market economies, behavior following norms of solidarity and work/leisure choices not necessarily pursuing gain or following the dictates of efficiency, competition, and productivity has by far not disappeared. This is illustrated by the high levels of volunteer work referred to in chapter 5 or by those engaged by choice in creative and/or in poorly remunerated work. Volunteer work at the community level, for example, might be motivated by a sense of collective wellbeing, empathy for others, or political commitment; and artistic work is often associated with the pursuit of beauty and creativity, irrespective of its market value.

Feminist economists have emphasized the need to develop alternative models based on assumptions of human cooperation, empathy, and collective wellbeing (Ferber and Nelson 1993; Strober 1994; Folbre 1994; Himmelweit 2002). In so doing, they join other scholars who have also questioned neoclassical assumptions, pointing out that they are predicated upon the Hobbesian view of self-interested individuals. These authors argue that the numerous exceptions to this rule suggest that human behavior responds to a complex set of often contradictory tendencies (Marwell and Ames 1981; Frank et al. 1993; Rose-Ackerman 1996). Thus, neoclassical assumptions seem to contradict "real-life experiments in which collective action and empathetic, connected economic decision-making are observed" (Seguino et al. 1996).

A variety of studies have shown that this type of behavior is often found among women (Guyer 1980; Gilligan 1982; Benería and Roldán 1987; Folbre 2001). In a study comparing the behavior of economists and non-economists, Seguino, Stevens, and Lutz (1996) suggest that "social structures that shape our preferences may differ along gender lines, with women more likely to exhibit constitutive desires and empathetic or connected behavior in contributing to public goods than do males" (p. 15). And recent experiments with individual preferences have shown that many alternatives exist to the traditional self-interested model, with motivations responding, for example, to notions of altruism, fairness, and reciprocity (Croson 1999). In addition, other authors have emphasized the extent to which social codes and identities are constructed "at the deepest cognitive levels through social interaction," therefore questioning the validity of static assumptions about tastes and preferences behind conventional economic models that take them as given (Cornwall 1997). As product developers and advertising agencies well know, this implies that social codes and individual preferences are subject to social constructions and to exogenous interferences that result in dynamic and continuous change.

The claim on the part of feminist economists that models of free individual choice are not adequate to analyze issues of dependence/interdependence, tradition, and power (Ferber and Nelson 1993) is of particular relevance for cultures in which individualistic, market-oriented behavior is more the exception than the norm. Feminists have also pointed out that neoclassical analysis is based on a "separate self model," in which utility is viewed as subjective and unrelated to that of other people. As Paula England has argued, this is linked to the assumption that individual behavior is selfish since "emotional connection often creates empathy, altruism, and a subjective sense of social solidarity" (England 1993). Thus, to the extent that women tend to be more emotionally connected than men, particularly as a result of their role in child rearing and family care and as part of the prevalent gender ideology, the separate self model has an androcentric bias. Similarly, to the extent that this model typifies Western individualism, it also has a Western bias and is foreign to societies with more collective forms of action and decisionmaking. Orthodox economic analysis has had little to say about these alternative modes of behavior and their significance for different forms of social organization and for policy and action under alternative institutions.

A different question is whether women's behavior is changing as they enter the labor market in increasing numbers and as the feminization of the labor force is intensified with globalization. Before examining this question, the following section focuses on the observed trends linking gender with the dynamics of global markets.

## Gender and Globalization

Much is being written on the subject of gender and globalization. My emphasis here is on women's employment and on the global processes that are affecting it. The rapid formation of a female labor force across the globe during the past decades has, to a great extent, been tied in particular to the growth of the service sector and of low-cost manufacturing, even though these have not been the only sectors behind the feminization of the labor force. The links between gender and globalization should not be seen as responding only to structural and economic forces. They are also shaped by the interaction between these forces and the different ways through which gender constructions have been reconstituted during the past three decades. The feminist movement, in its quest for gender equality, has contributed to this trend on the supply side by emphasizing the need for women to search for greater financial autonomy, bargaining power, and control over their lives. But other tendencies have been at work, both on the supply and the demand side.

The trend toward increasing employment of women has represented a sharp contrast with Boserup's assertion that women had been marginalized in the industrialization processes of the 1950s and 1960s based on import-substitution strategies. Since the late 1970s, studies documented a preference for women workers in different sectors, particularly in export-oriented, labor-intensive industries relying on low-cost production for global markets. Globalization has intensified these trends over time. In its initial steps, the body of research that documented these trends tended to focus on the jobs created by transnational corporations in low-wage industrializing areas such as South East Asia. The emphasis was placed on the exploitation of women by multinational capital and its ability to take advantage of female stereotypes associated with women workers: docility, nimble fingers, youth, often of rural origins from developing countries, acceptance of low wages, and poor working conditions. As mentioned in chapter 2, this analysis reflected a "women as victims approach," which gradually was seen as simplistic and unable to deal with the complexities involved (Lim 1983; Pyle 1982; Elson and Pearson 1989). Lim, for example, noted that women's employment in multinational corporations did result in improvements in their lives, a subject discussed in more detail in chapter 4. Various authors began to point out the ways in which women were not passive victims of exploitative conditions and illustrated the multiplicity of factors that affected their incorporation in paid work and their active involvement in it (Ong 1987).

As a result, this initial period was gradually replaced by analyses of female employment that captured the complexities and the often contradictory effects involved (Elson and Pearson 1989). Studies since then have also focused on forms of female employment other that that provided by multinational capital—including its linkages with local capital through subcontracting and informal employment (Benería and Roldán 1987; Kabeer 2000). In contrast to the women-as-victims approach, the emphasis in many studies has been on illustrating the multiplicity of effects associated with women's participation in the labor force, including the gains resulting from women's increased autonomy and bargaining power as a result of employment. In Naila Kabeer's words, women's paid work has been associated with an increase in the "power to choose," even if within the many still existing constraints facing those she calls "weak winners" (Kabeer 2000). Likewise, it has resulted in women's ability to act and defend their interests and those of their family and community in the face of most adverse circumstances. This type of empirical work has taken place throughout a wide range of historical contexts, cultural practices, and gender constructions—leading also to more conceptual and theoretical work.

A significant proportion of studies of women's employment have continued to focus on low-wage production for export where female labor tends to concentrate. Such is the case with export-processing zones and informal employment in low-wage, labor-intensive manufacturing; the latter includes, for example, lower-tier subcontracting chains, micro-enterprises, and self-employment, and it is analyzed in more detail in chapter 5. Both rely on systems of flexible production that find in women's labor the most flexible supply, such as in the use of temporary contracts, part-time work, and unstable working conditions. These conditions are at the heart of low-cost production for global markets and are tied to the volatility of global capital's mobility in search of the lowest cost location. Women's high level of employment in export-processing zones (EPZs) is illustrated in tables 3.1 and 3.2, which provide figures for selected Asian, Central American, and Caribbean countries. Table 3.1 for example shows that in Sri Lanka for 1981 and 1992, the proportion of female labor in EPZs was as high as 86.3 percent and 84.8 percent, respectively. Similarly, table 3.2 shows that, in textiles and clothing, the proportion of women in the labor force in the selected Central American and Caribbean countries has reached above 60 percent in all countries included, and 95 percent in the case of Panama.

**Table 3.1**  Share of Female Employment in Export Processing Zones (EPZs) and Non-EPZs in Selected Asian Countries (Percent) Selected Years

|  | YEAR | ALL ECONOMY | EPZs | NON-EPZ-MANUFACTURING |
|---|---|---|---|---|
| Malaysia | 1980 | 33.4 | 75.0 | 35.6 |
|  | 1990 | 35.5 | 53.5 | 47.2 |
| Philippines | 1980 | 37.1 | 74.0 | N/A |
|  | 1994 | 36.5 | 73.9 | 45.2 |
| Korea, Republic of | 1987 | 40.4 | 77.0 | 41.7 |
|  | 1990 | 40.8 | 70.1 | 42.1 |
| Sri Lanka | 1981 | 36.0 | 86.3 | 29.8 |
|  | 1992 | 46.4 | 84.8 | 46.0 |

*Source:* United Nations 1999, Table II.1.

**Table 3.2**  Total Employment and Share of Women in Employment in EPZs in Selected Central American and Caribbean Countries

| COUNTRY | NUMBER OF FACTORIES | WORKERS IN TEXTILES AND CLOTHING (%) | TOTAL EMPLOYMENT | WOMEN IN TOTAL (%) |
|---|---|---|---|---|
| Costa Rica | 250 | 70 | 50,000 | 65 |
| Dominican Republic | 469 | 65 | 165,571 | 60 |
| El Salvador | 208 | 69 | 50,000 | 78 |
| Guatemala | 481 | 80 | 165,945 | 80 |
| Honduras | 155 | 95 | 61,162 | 78 |
| Nicaragua | 18 | 89 | 7,553 | 80 |
| Panama | 6 | 100 | 1,200 | 95 |

*Source:* United Nations 1999, Table II.1.

The service sector has also absorbed a large proportion of female employment, which can be subdivided in various categories:

• Expanding services associated with global markets tend to employ low-skill women in *pink-collar offices,* for example for data entry and data processing in mail order business, airlines and rail systems, credit card providers, and other financial services like banking and insurance. These activities can be highly concentrated like in the case of the Caribbean and in some Asian countries such as China, India, Malaysia, and the Philippines. Referring to the case of Barbados, Carla Freeman (2000) has written about this offshore clerical work in the Caribbean as resulting in "a convergence between realms of tradition and modernity, gender and class—where transnational capital and production, the Barbadian state, and young Afro-Caribbean women together fashion a new 'classification' of woman worker who, gendered producer and consumer, is fully enmeshed in global and local, economic and cultural processes" (p. 22). Women's employment has also expanded in the tourist sector across countries. Some estimates indicate that the proportion of women in these services is as high as in the export sector and almost completely female in the case of the Caribbean (United Nations 1999). Needless to say, employment in this sector tends to be seasonal and unstable, depending also on the ups and downs of international demand.

• Globalization has also facilitated international networks linked to *prostitution and related services.* Again, this is a sector for which reliable data is difficult to obtain. Nevertheless, existing estimates provide an indication of its size and significance for specific countries, even though the range of statistics varies widely according to the different sources. To illustrate, 1993 to 1994 estimates for the number of prostitutes ranged between 140,000 and 230,000 in Indonesia, between 400,000 and 500,000 in the Philippines, and between 200,000 and 300,000 for Thailand. The widest estimates correspond to Malaysia with a range between 43,000 and 600,000 (Lim 1998). In addition, the growing phenomenon of child prostitution, male and female, has also become a matter of growing concern, and here, too, the numbers vary widely according to the source.[10] An international debate has emerged around the extent to which sex workers chose this profession, and therefore should not be viewed as victims but in charge of their own circumstance and choices (Doezema and Kempadoo 1998). In any case, international prostitution raises difficult questions in terms of human rights and the means to prevent minors from being drawn into it. Sex tourism is one of the sectors where international migration and prostitution are linked. This is the case with the above Asian countries but it involves other regions as well (Ehrenreich and Hochschild 2002). It is here, too, where an analysis of the economic base of prostitution is crucial to understanding its different forms and manifestations through class-related labor market segmentation and working conditions. As Lim has pointed out, "policy makers have to deal with an industry that is highly organized and increasingly sophisticated and diversified, as well as having close linkages to the rest of the national and international economy" (p. 9). Policy and action with regard to prostitution is for the most part addressed to the prostitutes (mostly female) rather than to their clients (mostly male), and the poverty that feeds it the institutions linked to the industry.

- Increasing migration by women from low- to high-income countries during the past decade has been getting much international attention. Much has been written about the large number of *domestic and daycare workers* from developing countries, supplying their labor either to elite families or to middle-class families with working mothers. Pushed by poverty and the search for a better life— imagined or real—migrant married and unmarried women from the Philippines, Sri Lanka, Mexico, Ecuador, Peru, and other Latin American countries have been working in the United States, Canada, and the European Community, as well as Hong Kong and the Middle East. The numbers involved are not easy to estimate, given the informality and precariousness associated with this type of employment, hence the lack of hard data. Most of the information has been provided by journalistic research, reports, and case studies, but the importance of this phenomenon is beyond doubt (Ehrenreich and Hochschild 2002). The crisis of care in high-income countries with a high participation of women in the labor market is at the root of this phenomenon, which we are only beginning to understand in terms of its long-term consequences. Migrant women, finding international employment more easily than the men in their communities, often leave their family behind—including their own children. In her study of children from the Philippines left behind and cared by fathers, older siblings, and other family members, Salazar Parreñas has pointed out the negative consequences of the loss of maternal care and the changes that this generates in their lives. She concludes that the children of migrant Filipina domestic workers suffer from the extraction of care from the global South to the global North, a pattern affecting many countries.

The feminization of the labor force has taken place even in countries where women's participation in paid work was traditionally low and socially unacceptable. The speed at which this phenomenon has occurred has raised interesting questions about the processes through which traditions and gender constructions can be dismantled or reconstituted and adapted to economic change. This has produced an interesting body of literature that analyzes the tensions and contradictions involved in the process (Pyle 1983; Ong 1987; Feldman 1992 and 2001; Kabeer 2000).[11] In this respect, sociological and cultural studies have made a rich contribution—incorporating levels of analysis that combine the more strictly economic aspects of globalization and women's employment with a focus on changes in gender relations, social constructions in the division of labor, women's agency, and household-market connections. Some authors, for example, have analyzed the phenomenon of prostitution within the framework of the different religions while others have suggested a close link between prostitution and the survival circuits facilitated through global cities (Lim 1998; Sassen 1998).

We can ask whether we can generalize with regard to the gender effects of globalization and I suggest that at least the following two points can be made. First, the literature has emphasized the notion that globalization and the feminization of the labor force have been parallel to the processes of labor market deregulation and flexibilization registered across countries during the past three decades and as a result of neoliberal policies. This has affected both men and women, although not necessarily in the same ways. Feminization has been linked to the deterioration of working conditions and as part of the race to the bottom resulting from global competition (Standing 1989 and 1999). Although some have interpreted this view as blaming this deterioration to women's new roles in production, its most common interpretation emphasizes the key role of women's labor to deal with the pressures of international competition and global markets. However, although a large proportion of women's jobs are located at the lower echelons of the labor hierarchy, the increasing economic polarization among women and North-South differences imply that some women have a relatively advantageous position in the global economy.

Second, generalizations about the effects of globalization on women must be approached with great caution since effects vary according to historical, socioeconomic, and other conditions. To illustrate, the variety of studies that over the years have analyzed the effects of export-oriented manufacturing in South East Asia since the 1970s have shown that the high level of female employment generated has in the long run resulted in improvements, even if far from spectacular, in women's earnings and a higher degree of gender equality (Lim 1983; Dollar and Gatti 1999; Seguino 2000). Yet, the Asian experience can not be applied to other countries. For instance, the maquiladora sector in the U.S.-Mexican border represents a model of export-oriented production that over the years has not resulted in gains for the large majority of women employed (Cravey 1998; Fussell 2000). Fussell's study for the case of Tijuana, Mexico, found that, in their drive to keep production costs low, multinational manufacturers have tapped into women's low-wage labor, "thereby taking advantage of women's labor market disadvantages and making a labor force willing to accept more 'flexible' terms of employment" (p. 59). Differences between these outcomes are due to varying factors having to do with labor availability (relatively limited in the case of the Asian countries and practically unlimited in the Mexican case), degrees of wage inequality, and the dynamics of the labor market with respect to male/female employment.[12]

As a result, a debate has been generated on the relationship between export-oriented growth, women's wages and working conditions, and gender equality. Those who hold a more optimistic view of the connections between the two have argued that gender inequality has been reduced in terms of wage differentials, access to jobs, and educational achievement (Dollar and Gatti 1999). On the other hand, those who take a less optimistic view argue that, for example in the case of the Asian tigers, economic growth was correlated to wage gender gaps, that is, growth was fed by gender inequality. Taking the second position, Seguino (2000) has shown that the Asian economies that grew the most rapidly had the widest wage gaps. Similarly, Hsiung (1995) illustrates how Taiwan's high level of flexibility and market adaptability has been solidly based on low wages and poor working conditions of women as home-based workers.

## The Ambiguities of Market Effects

The historical trends associated with globalization have changed women's connection to the market, influencing gender roles and gender relations, and altering the meanings of gender across countries and cultures. The extension and deepening of markets at the global level raises many relevant questions about their impact, both on women and men. What effect does being integrated in market activities have on individual behavior? More specifically, how are women affected as the relative weight of their paid labor time increases and that of unpaid work diminishes? Does it imply that women are increasingly adopting the norms of economic rationality à la the economic man? Are women becoming more individualistic, selfish, and less nurturing? Is market behavior undermining "women's ways of seeing and doing"? Are gender identities being reconstituted? The answer to these questions is far from being clear-cut. A nonessentialist view of gender differences implies that economic and social change are likely to influence gender (re)constructions and gender roles. As women become direct participants in the market, their motives and aspirations will be shaped by the ways in which they respond to it, probably adopting patterns of behavior traditionally observed more frequently among men. From casual observation, many of us think that this is already happening. However, there are areas of ambiguity, tensions, and contradictions in the answer to these questions.

To begin with, the market can have positive effects for women and men, such as the breaking up of patriarchal traditions like arranged marriages that limit individual autonomy and the liberation from divisions of labor associate with disproportional burdens for women. In this sense, the market can accelerate the diffusion of "liberating" practices. But we have pointed out that it can also introduce or intensify sexist or gender-based discriminatory and exploitative practices and it can introduce tensions regarding individual freedom and collective security.[13] Differences between countries can also be important as a result of historical circumstances and cultural factors. To illustrate, this is clearly reflected in the following quote from a World Bank report referring to societies of the former Soviet Union:

> Transition affects women much differently in some ways than it does men. In considering whether transition has increased welfare for women, the real test is whether it has left them freer than before, or more constrained. So far, at least, the answer in many transition countries appears to be the latter. (The World Bank 1996: 72)

Several authors have pointed out how gender ideology is changing in these countries, emphasizing that the transition has exacerbated "latent and manifest patriarchal attitudes," increasing women's vulnerability both culturally and economically (Moghadam 1993). Bridger, Kay, and Pinnick (1996) have written that "[T]he initial rounds of democratic elections in Russia have virtually wiped women off the political map and their re-emergence is now painfully slow and fraught with difficulty" (p. 2). In some of the Central Asian republics, new restrictions on women's lives were imposed during the post–1989 transition, such as the prohibition of appearing in public without a male or an elder woman, and restrictions on wearing pants and driving cars (Tohidi 1996). However, a key question is the extent to which market forces transform these norms and how the modernity spread through the market might break patriarchal forms and new regulations.

Ambiguity with regards to women's links to market society can be found in feminist discourses. For example, feminists have emphasized gender equality as a key goal, including the importance for women to have access to the public sphere and paid work in the same way and under similar conditions as men. In this sense, it is assumed that women can behave as men do—the emphasis here being on gender *equality*. On the other hand, feminist research and action has emphasized women's *difference*. Carol Gilligan (1982), for example, documented the "different modes of thinking about relationships and the association of these modes with male and female voices." These different modes arise, she argued, "in a social context where factors of social status and power combine with reproductive biology to shape the experience of males and females and the relationship between the sexes" (p. 2).

Although Gilligan's work has been criticized for its essentialist overtones, it illustrates the notion that a key issue for feminism is how to combine an emphasis on difference with the pursuit of equality, and how to preserve gender traits that contribute to individual, family, and human welfare without generating or perpetuating gender inequalities based on unequal power relations.[14] One danger, for example, is to perceive difference in essentialist ways, a problem that has often surfaced from oppositional views of gender differences, such as with the idealization of women's goodness and female superiority related to the construction of men as the opposite.[15] A different problem is to view gender differences and divisions in a rigid way, thereby making difficult the convergence of gender roles— for example in the case of men's need to share domestic work and child care with women. Related to this, ambiguity manifests itself around what we understand for women's ways of knowing and doing and the extent to which it is important to maintain, and even foster, them among women and men. In this sense, there is a tension between the equality vs. difference approaches that can only be worked out through social dynamics and women's agency. The example that follows illustrates the variety of ways through which this tension can manifest itself.

In an article in the *New York Times* (9/17/96) about the gender gap in the 1996 election in the United States, author Carol Tavris discussed the nature of women's and men's motivations and the reasons why more women than men tended to support President Clinton, the Democratic party candidate, than the more conservative Republican candidate, Senator Dole. Conservative explanations, she wrote, argue that women tend to be more sentimental, more risk-averse and less competitive than men; as a result, they are less inclined to be appreciative of free-market economics, claiming that the Democratic Party itself has become "feminized"—"just about the nastiest charge you can make." A Democratic explanation of the gender gap, she added, argued that women vote for that party "not because they are emotional and muddleheaded but because they are more compassionate and less aggressive than men, and thus attracted to the party that will help the weakest members of society."

What is interesting about the article is that the author wanted to demonstrate that women are neither sentimental nor irrational: they vote Democratic because "it's in their interest" the article emphasized. That is, Tavris wanted to emphasize that women behave like men—as equal agents in a market system based also on "rational economic woman"—thereby equating self-interest with a more "rational" form of behavior. Thus, while the Republican/conservative explanation of the women's vote was based on an emphasis on difference—viewed, in the case of women, as a backward trait rooted in pre-market relations—the Democratic version emphasized equality in market-oriented behavior. For the conservatives as well as for Tavris, the economic rationality associated with the market was superior to nonmarket perceptions of human welfare.

An alternative explanation is that women's vote was indeed based on a different mode of evaluating society's needs, human welfare, and politics—including a sense of solidarity with "the weakest members of society." Far from seeing this mode as "backward" or "irrational," it can be perceived as a source of inspiration for thinking about alternative ways of organizing society. The section that follows elaborates further these questions.

## Beyond Self-Interest?

*I don't need money, I want the river's color back*

—Silas Natkime, son of the Waa Valley Chief, Irian Jaya, Indonesia[16]

This moving quote, a clear affirmation of the value placed on a clean river over that of money, in many ways symbolizes one of the dilemmas of development, expressing an individual's choice to give priority to ecological over economic outcomes. It could also be interpreted as a reaction against the water-polluting effects of "development" or of the specific development model that has taken away the river's color. To return to Polanyi, his criticism of market society was that it is based on self-interest—leading to "disruptive strains" and "varied symptoms of disequilibrium" such as unemployment, class inequalities, "pressure on exchanges," and "imperialist rivalries." Environmental degradation can be added to his list of disruptive strains. Ultimately, Polanyi saw fascism as the outcome of these market-related strains, resulting from "the impasse reached by liberal capitalism." A different outcome was represented by a socialist transformation, defined by Polanyi as the tendency inherent in an industrial civilization to transcend the self-regulating market by consciously subordinating it to a democratic society. (p. 234)

For Polanyi, this tendency toward disequilibrium, or tensions generated by uncontrolled markets, led to the need for planning, or forms of market intervention that would counteract not only disruptive strains but also the domination of economic self-interest over all aspects of political and social life. This is more than history. We have seen that these strains have reappeared with the unfolding of global markets under neoliberal policies. To be sure, the global market has displayed its dynamism and ability to supply unprecedented amounts of goods and services and to generate new forms of wealth. But, as argued in chapter 1, it has also generated new imbalances and economic and social crises. Evidence linking globalization with increasing inequalities and maldistribution of resources within and between countries has been growing (ECLAC 1995; Freeman 1996; UNDP 1996, 1998, and 1999; World Bank 2000/2001). Social tensions—from increasing crime rates and urban insecurity to pressures to solve AIDs-related problems—have been on the increase as well.

Policymakers have been reluctant to incorporate in their agendas the notion that high unemployment or underemployment in many areas disrupts the social fabric of communities and countries. Here is where the economistic bias discussed in chapter 1 is often present, fostered by the heavy presence of orthodox economists in the higher circles of economic policy. Using a sample of countries from different regions and social structures, Rodrik (1997) has shown that those with a higher degree of social protection, such as the Scandinavian countries, are most prepared to face the consequences of economic openness. Given that globalization undermines social cohesiveness, he argues that this requires compensatory poli cies and the design of social insurance systems that most countries don't have. In some Latin American circles, the tendencies of the past two decades has led some authors to refer to the neoliberal model of development as "socially unsustainable" in the long run. In the same way, the Asian financial crisis raised new questions about the dangerous instability of financial markets that led to a new debate on global reforms and the need to establish national controls over capital flows. Current tensions in global capitalism have brought a turning point in the triumphalism of Davos Man, and an increasing number of people are decrying his excesses. Fifty years after Polanyi wrote *The Great Transformation*, his call for subordinating the market to the priorities set by democratic societies resonates as an urgent need, even though the channels toward achieving this goal have to accommodate to the realities of an increasingly globalized world.

This poses challenging questions for feminism, which, in its varied forms, can in fact be viewed as one of Polanyi's countermovements—linked to the search for gender equality but also to wider social issues. Some key questions are: Can women make a contribution to the quest for new directions toward human development? Can the alternative models discussed by feminists be used as guidelines for how to construct alternative societies? Can women provide different voices as they become more integrated in the market and public life? Can "difference," at least to the extent that it has unfolded historically and might be maintained, be a source of inspiration for progressive social change?

This means, for example, questioning rational economic man's objectives as the desired norm. For Polanyi, moving beyond economic man does not necessarily imply a rejection of markets as a way to organize production and distribution of goods and services. As he stated, "the end of market society means in no way the absence of markets" (p. 252). However, his view calls for subordinating markets to the objectives of truly democratic communities and countries. The goal is to place economic activity at the service of human or people-centered development and not the other way around—to reach an era in which productivity and efficiency are achieved not for their own sake but as a way to increase collective wellbeing. Hence, in the same way that it is possible to think of Christianity without hell, it is also possible to design ways to reduce the social costs of bankruptcy.

All of this implies placing issues of distribution, inequality, ethics, the environment, and other social goals—as well as the nature of individual happiness, collective wellbeing, and social change—at the center of our agendas. It follows that an urgent task for economists and social scientists is to translate these more general objectives into relevant theoretical, empirical, and practical work. For economists, the task of building a socially relevant economic theory should be a priority. What if, for example, production models assumed that the firm does not have to maximize profits and, instead, viewed profits as a leftover after key social objectives were met?[17] The range of possibilities is wide. Among the various objectives of the Zapatista movement in Mexico, one of the most emphasized issues is the need to provide individual and collective dignity. The dictionary defines dignity as "bearing conduct or speech indicative of self-respect," "worthiness," and "degree of excellence," definitions that take us back to the notion of human development: the "intuitive idea of a life that is worthy of the dignity of the human being ... for each and every person." To be sure, the concept of dignity might seem ambiguous to economists but the same can be said for the concept of utility around which a good part of economic theory is built. The notion of dignity for everyone suggests wellbeing associated with social equality, self-esteem, and respect/recognition across social groups. It raises questions about who contributes and to what extent to social welfare as well as questions of distribution, clearly topics worthy of scrutiny by economists. Many interesting questions surface along these lines. What if, instead of maximizing utility, economic models toyed with the notion of maximizing dignity? In what sense might this objective have different implications for gender-aware economic analysis? What implications might it have for distributive justice between capital and labor and for non-discriminatory, non-exploitative wage distribution and individual income?

People-centered development calls for transforming knowledge so as to rethink conventional approaches to theory and decisionmaking. As Elizabeth Minnich has put it:

> Behind any particular body of accepted knowledge are the definitions, the boundaries, established by those who have held power. To disagree with those boundaries and definitions, it has been necessary to recognize them; to refuse them is to be shut out even from debate; to transgress them is to mark oneself as mad, heretical, dangerous. (p. 151)

Definitions, boundaries, and power have a historical specificity. Polanyi dared to say that "[T]he passing of market-economy can become the beginning of an era of unprecedented freedom . . . generated by the leisure and security that industrial society offers to all" (p. 256). Written in the 1940s, at a time when it was difficult to predict the problems that state interventions would create in centrally planned economies, reality did not live up to his optimism. Yet, since the break in the Washington Consensus, the notion that "there is no alternative" to the neoliberal model seems increasingly less acceptable. Questions of global governance that would introduce checks and balances to uncontrolled markets are subject to debate. The present danger is that proposals for global governance might be introduced in a top-down fashion and without worldwide negotiations based on democratic forms of decisionmaking. The growing concentration of power in the hands of large global corporations and high-income country governments should be a source of concern to all those looking for alternatives. Feminism has been vital in the struggle for solutions at the decentralized, local, and institutional level; it has fought discrimination and inequalities at many levels; it has changed institutions and decisionmaking processes; it has incorporated new agendas in the politics of daily life; it has affected national policies; it has made an impact on international agendas; and it has been influential in first bringing human welfare to the center of debates on economic and social policy. It now has to meet the challenges posed by globalization.

Polanyi wrote that the endeavor of thinking of people first "cannot be successful unless it is disciplined by a total view of man and society very different from that which we inherited from market economy." The main message of this chapter is that this effort must be transformative and based on a "total view of wo/man and society." Rather than diminishing this view as "soft," "idealistic," and "female," we must dare to take up this theoretical and practical challenge and follow the concrete, bottom-up ways in which feminism has been a tremendous source of social change.

## CHAPTER 4

# Global/Local Connections: Employment Patterns, Gender, and Informalization

*Many still question claims that the patterns of working life are changing. But in the United Sates the anecdotal signs are increasing: more frequent job changes, more freelancing, more working at home, more opportunity but also more uncertainty. The old social contract between employers and workers is being shredded. It is still unclear what will replace it.*
—The Economist, 1/29/2000

This chapter shifts from the general questions regarding globalization and gender examined in chapter 3, to the more concrete analysis of labor market trends associated with it. It focuses on the nature of labor markets transformations that have resulted from economic restructuring, neoliberal policies, and reorganization of production both in high- and low-income countries during the past three decades. With an emphasis on understanding the tendencies toward labor market informalization and increasing inequalities, it analyzes the gender dimensions of these processes, pointing out some contradictory tendencies at work.

During the 1970s and early 1980s, relocation of production from high- to low-income countries gave rise to a large body of literature focusing on the threats of de-industrialization and massive loss of jobs in high income countries (Fröebel et al. 1980; Bluestone and Harrison 1982). Since then, many industrial processes have indeed been shifted in that direction, but many of the fears expressed in some of these studies did not materialize; the enormous growth of the service sector and the development of high tech industries and growth of the financial sector have maintained and even accentuated, the predominance of the richest countries in the world economy. This did not, however, prevent the deterioration of working conditions for specific labor sectors, even in high-income countries and even in periods of relative prosperity, such as during the 1990s in the United States. In both high- and low-income areas, labor market deregulation and increasing flexibilization of the work process generated new problems and challenges, particularly as globalization and increased market competition induced a search for lower production costs (Piore and Sabel 1984; Harrison and Bluestone 1988). Other factors such as trade liberalization and the formation of regional trading blocks have reinforced the competitive pressures of global markets. Taken together, these developments have resulted in profound processes of reorganization of production, technological innovation, and changes in the structures of firms and in employment conditions.

Since the 1980s, there has also been a growing body of literature focusing on the ways economic restructuring has led to decentralization of production, both geographically and vertically within firms (Dicken 1998). Institutional changes at the micro level have been deep—from downsizing and outsourcing to changes in work organization, skill requirements, and transformations in the composition of the workforce. Trade liberalization has had significant effects on changing skill requirements and on the dynamics of employment and relative wages within and across countries, particularly in terms of shifting labor-intensive processes of production to low-wage areas (Wood 1994). Needless to say, many of these transformations are gendered, with differential impacts on men and women that can vary according to a variety of factors. As analyzed in chapter 3, at the same time, we have witnessed the continuing process of feminization of the labor force at the domestic and international level—with the concept of feminization being used to refer to a) an increase in women's labor force participation, b) a relative decline in male employment, and c) the deterioration of working conditions in previously male jobs (Anker 1998; Standing 1999).

These changes have profoundly affected productive processes; they have transformed the structure of firms, as well as their functions and modes of operation, their employment patterns, wage hierarchies, distributive channels, and capital/labor relations. As a result, labor market structures have been destabilized and reorganized in multiple directions—from downsizing and shifting skill requirements to changes in the composition of the workforce according to gender, level of education, and other characteristics. Most importantly, the changing landscape of production at the micro level has led to profound changes in job creation and the generation of new forms of employment. For this reason, it is important to understand these transformations at the micro level of the firm and in terms of how they affect the labor market. As the quote heading this chapter indicates, the old social contract between employers and workers has indeed been shredded in many cases. The "Organization Man" of the post–World War II period, based on stable employment and attachment to a specific firm, is being replaced by a much less stable workforce, with profound consequences for lifetime work experiences (Capelli 1999; *The Economist*, 3/27/00) and with important distributive consequences. Speaking from a business perspective, Capelli has claimed that "the old employment system of secure, life-time jobs with predictable advancement and stable pay is dead" (p. 17). The result has been the declining employment security and other types of worker protection, and the increasing risks that employees and labor, in general, must bear. At the same time, a decline in labor union membership has taken place in many countries, contributing to the relative loss of power among labor and rising income inequality (Katz 2000).

This chapter focuses on the effects of economic restructuring on employment dynamics and on the nature of jobs and their characteristics, both in high- and low-income countries, and on their significance for labor and for gender divisions. What are the main trends leading to labor market informalization? Can we generalize across countries? What are the implications of the increasing informalization of employment and jobs? What emerging trends in informal activities do we observe both in high- and low-income countries? What are the gender dimensions of these processes and how women have been affected? I summarize the changes taking place at the micro level of the firm in order to contextualize their repercussions on employment dynamics and job formation/distribution, followed by a case study of the effects of a firm relocation from the United States to Mexico and an analysis of the ways in which gender differences appear in the process. I then focus on the growth of informalized and precarious jobs in developing countries, emphasizing the vicious circle that links these jobs to persistent poverty. The next section refers more specifically to women's participation in informal activities and the different forms it takes, followed by an analysis of the contradictory results and tendencies for women's employment. Taken together, these trends call for new policies and actions, some of which are discussed in the concluding remarks.

## The Micro Foundations

Since the 1980s, market penetration into the internal employment dynamics of firms has become increasingly common, often dismantling former internal labor market structures, with a growing direct influence of the market on the ways in which business is conducted. External labor market conditions have increasingly and directly influenced capital labor contracts, working conditions, the organization of production, employee training, and wage structures. At the same time, the internal structure of the firm and the new forms of capital/labor relations, in turn, have had repercussions on the dynamics of the external labor market. The following trends summarize the major changes along these lines.

- First, profound changes have taken place in terms of what many authors have referred to as *the new employment contract.* The old contract was linked to stable working conditions, long-term contracts, collective bargaining, and higher wages in large firms. Employment was assumed to provide health care and other fringe benefits, while internal labor markets setting wages and working conditions tended to significantly differentiate firms, with pay differentials normally following distinct patterns from firm to firm. The new contract has reversed many of these conditions, leading to more individualized and less stable contracts, with many workers holding often unrelated jobs and expected to shift regularly from job to job (Stone 2001). At the same time, individual workers are expected to constantly adjust to the more flexible and constantly changing labor market conditions.

- Second, here has been a *shift of employment from "core" to "periphery" activities* located in smaller firms and independent contractors (Harrison 1994; Hsiung 1996; Ybarra 2000). This has resulted in the reduction in the size of large firms, with downsizing being parallel to outsourcing and subcontracting. In the United States, the drive toward leaner production and shrinking workforce became particularly prevalent during the 1980s and 1990s, affecting not only low-skill workers but reaching management ranks as well. Global competition has created continuous pressures to lowering production costs. As Capelli (1999) has pointed out, downsizing refers to the dismissal of workers for reasons that are not related to their performance. These reasons have to do with the pressures on firms to "perform" and compete at the global level. Strategically, globalization has facilitated the reduction of core firm size by paving the way for the geographic expansion of the "periphery" to new outsourcing sites in other countries.

- Third, there has been a *reduction in hierarchical levels within core firms themselves*, resulting from several tendencies: a) the dismantling of internal labor markets based on merit, seniority, and other promotional factors; b) the elimination of middle management and the formation of "worker teams" and different forms of job rotation; and c) the concentration of high-skill jobs in core firms and the shifting of low-skill activities to locations outside the core (Harrison 1994; Batt 1996; Osterman 1999; Cappelli 1999). Highly

skilled, educated professionals increasingly concentrate in technologically based jobs at the core, including management, research,
and specialized work such as that provided by financial and legal
experts. At the same time, this professional and technical labor has
benefited from an expanded market at the global level and from
the opportunities provided by what has been referred to as a
"global driver's license" due to their high degree of employability
across countries. However, at least in the United States, the most
pronounced divide has evolved between top executives and other
employees due to the power of top executives and their highly
remunerative compensation schemes, which have been well documented during the past two decades (Capelli 1999).

• Fourth, except for the core of highly privileged professional and
technical labor, the changing employment contract shows a clear
tendency toward unstable employment. At the bottom of the
(wage) income scale, we find low-skill labor associated with *informalized work or temporary and part-time employment. It has
become the fastest growing part of the labor force in many countries,*
due to increasing reliance of firms on contingent work and decentralized production systems (Leigh 1995; Recio 2000). In the
United States, for example, the distribution of employment is such
that regular, full-time employees represented about 68.8 percent of
the total in the mid-1990s (Upjohn Institute 1997); it has been estimated that the fastest growing part of the economy in the state of
California is the temp business.[1] In the euro area, a study by Mor-
gan Stanley Dean Witter found that most of the net jobs created
between 1994 and 1998 were either part-time or temporary (*The
Economist,* 6/10/00). Although the ways this informalization
process takes place varies considerably by country and region, it
occurs in both high- and low-income countries and it is part of the
increasing economic insecurity registered even in countries experiencing sustained economic growth, such as the United States
during the 1990s. In developing countries, this trend has contributed to the high growth of the informal sector (see below).

• Fifth, the processes of informalization and decentralization affecting current labor market trends have produced a *sharp increase in
employment instability and in the number of workers experiencing the
stressful consequences of unemployment.* Job and labor market insecurity has a pronounced effect on workers at the lower end of educational and labor market hierarchies (Leigh 1995; Katz 2000).
However, an important feature of current insecurity is that it is felt
throughout the wide range of the occupational spectrum (ILO

1999; Standing 2002). In the United States, job tenure for men aged thirty-five and over has decreased since 1983, and the average thirty-two-year old has already worked for nine different firms.[2] For the working population, the chronically high unemployment rates registered in many countries represent a constant threat of losing access to income. This threat, of course, has been felt in countries with relatively high unemployment rates, such as many European countries, but also in those with relatively low levels of unemployment, such as the United States during the decade of the 1990s; despite almost a decade of uninterrupted economic growth, layoffs became increasingly widespread. Thus, the threat of dismissal has been on the increase. There is also evidence that persistent worker insecurity is intensified by capital mobility (Brofenbrenner 2000). However, the problem is particularly acute in developing countries with chronically high rates of unemployment and underemployment. Standing (1999) has estimated that the "effects of GDP growth on employment (and unemployment) suggest that to make a substantial difference there would have to be a long and sustainable period of high rates of economic growth" (p. 153). Instead, many developing countries have registered low or fragile economic growth and continue to do so.

• Sixth, many production processes that were illegal and viewed as part of the underground economy two or three decades ago are now considered to be legal or part of the regular economy, even if functioning under similar conditions. In addition, subcontracting and outsourcing have shifted many processes to this informalized production. In this way, labor conditions that would not have been acceptable as legal in the past have become normalized and much more adjusted to the needs of firms than to the norms and regulations that in the past were part of the modern economy. As Ybarra (2000) has pointed out for the case of Spain, there has been a loss of collective rights that have been replaced by individual rights in the search for survival. In this sense, he argues, the old "irregularities" have been accepted and socialized.

• Seventh, these tendencies have resulted in *growing income polarization in most countries,* resulting, on the one hand, in increasing job opportunities for skilled labor and, on the other, in a parallel reduction of opportunities for low-skilled workers. In 1979, the average college graduate in the United Sates earned 38 percent more than the average high school graduate; the current gap is 71 percent (*The Economist,* 1/29/00). In high-income countries, the outsourcing of production to low-wage areas, particularly in labor-intensive industries, has led to a gradual deterioration of the earnings for the those displaced. Studies show that when displaced workers find new jobs, the large majority tend to move to more precarious and lower-paid positions (see below) Likewise, trade liberalization has been shown to have a negative effect on unskilled workers (Wood 1994 and 1995; Rodrik 1997). The dismantling of internal labor markets produces pay structures closely linked to the external labor market; and rapidly changing technologies tend to remunerate young new hires rather than experienced workers, producing inequities that have negative repercussions on the morale of older workers (Capelli 1999). Statistics on income distribution are unambiguous on these growing inequalities, leading to the pessimistic views about the social consequences of globalization, technological change, and "the new economy" (UNDP 1999). For the 1980s and 1990s, this has been the case for OECD countries as well as for developing countries and Eastern Europe. In Latin America, despite the recovery of many economies during the 1990s and variations across countries, the concentration of income has remained the same or worse, with the continuous huge gap between the top and bottom 20 percent in the income scale (UNDP 1999), threatening to undermine the progress made through democratization.

• Eighth, *workers attitudes toward firms and the culture of work have been changing*. The "happy worker" model of the past, with stable employment and strong loyalty to the firm, has become less relevant for a large proportion of the working population. In turn, more unstable work contracts have had a negative influence on workers' commitment to the employer, absenteeism, and discipline. Survey data show that labor turnover rates have increased significantly, and that highly skilled professionals are the least committed to their employers because they are aware of their better chances to find jobs elsewhere (Capelli 1999). Younger and older workers often seem to differ in their commitment to the firm's objectives, as well as desired working conditions such as the length of the working day and other factors affecting the organization of work.[3]

• Finally, these tendencies have been registered in both high- and low-income countries, but *we observe conflicting forces at work*. A firm such as General Motors is offering lifetime employment at the same time that it envisions downsizing. As a result, young workers with new technical skills are hired while older workers are fired, many firms are firing and hiring at the same time ( *The Economist,* 9/12/99; 3/13/00; Ozler 2001). Some countries in the European Union suffer from labor shortages for specific segments of low- skill labor despite a high overall unemployment rate; a few of them also experience labor shortages at higher occupational levels.[4] The diminishing importance of internal labor markets has brought many advantages to some firms, such as the ability to respond quickly to market changes, lower long-term liabilities, flexibility in production, and reduced costs, at least in the short run. However, it has also created problems for them, particularly their inability to retain the best workers when the market is tight. At least in the United States, this has been illustrated by the prevalence of "poaching" or the "stealing" of high-level executives and professionals from competitors (Schell-hardt 1997). Finally, while many authors praise the possibilities offered by the "high road" to development—such as, high productivity and high wages—short-term strategic objectives on the part of private sector firms and "market failures" often lead to the "low road" that fails the test of human development objectives (Appelbaum and Batt 1994; Benería and Santiago 2001).

These trends have been observed, in different forms and intensity, in high- and low-income countries. The rest of this chapter discusses some of the specific forms which economic restructuring and subsequent labor market effects can take. The next section focuses on a case study of a firm relocation from the United States to Mexico.

## Industrial Relocation and Displaced Workers: Lessons from a Case Study[5]

How is globalization lived at the local level and what are the global and local connections? The answer to this question depends of course on the nature of each specific case and the conditions under which change takes place. The effects of trade liberalization, for example, will depend on whether the area in question is an importing or an exporting center—or both. Similarly, relocation of production creates unemployment in the locality that experiences layoffs but it generates jobs in the receiving area. This section explores a case study showing the impact that a large firm's relocation can have on the community that suffers layoffs. The study provides a detailed illustration of how the effects of relocation, in this case linked to trade liberalization, are felt at the local level. It refers to the case of Smith-Corona Corporation, the typewriter manufacturer that on July 21, 1992, announced its decision to transfer its manufacturing operations from Cortland, New York, to Tijuana, Mexico.

The announcement was the last of a series of moves over the preceding decade that reduced the firm's workforce in the community from its peak of 5,000 in the 1960s to 4,000 in 1981 and around 1,000 at the time of the announcement. Despite its large size and strong presence in the area, the firm was not unionized. The decision to relocate seems to have been related to a variety of factors, including the firm's relatively poor competitive position, a long period of litigation over dumping practices with Brother Industries (the Japanese firm that had been Smith-Corona's strongest competitor) and the possibilities offered by the implementation of NAFTA. Although, at that point, the firm was profitable, relocation aimed at taking advantage of the much lower labor and other costs in Mexico. According to a Smith-Corona executive, the firm was not technologically prepared to compete with the leading U.S. firms in the industry. However, the decisive factor seems to have been the expectation of savings from labor costs, esti mated at $15 million annually (Papaglia 1995) and the assumption that NAFTA would provide easy access to the Canadian and U.S. markets.[6]

During the three years that followed the announcement to close all Cortland manufacturing operations, 850 workers were gradually laid off as operations were transferred to Mexico. Cortland retained a group of about 150 to 200 employees working on marketing and sales operations. In many ways this was a typical case of a small town within a predominantly rural county losing its largest longstanding employer. After the Smith-Corona relocation of manufacturing operations, Cortland's economy showed signs of stagnation and deterioration. In 1998, Rubbermaid, one of the largest remaining manufacturing firms, also closed down, laying off almost 500 workers.[7] Even though Cortland's real per capita income increased from $15,930 in 1992 to $16,256 in 1995, average real wages and salaries decreased from $20,487 in 1992 to $18,584 in 1995. Other firms have closed down since then and all indications suggest that the downward trend for real income continues.

The research for this study took place over a three-year period, which allowed time to follow the labor market trajectories of the workers interviewed.[8] An examination of demographic characteristics of the workers interviewed indicated that approximately two thirds among them were women.[9] To give an indication of their educational levels, over 40 percent of the works had a high school degree, 43 percent had two or four years college education, and 10 percent had primary school only. The typical Smith-Corona worker was Caucasian, married or living with a partner, and female. The average age of respondents was forty-seven, with many years of experience (an average of twenty-two) working at Smith-Corona.[10]

Following the requirements of the 1988 Worker Adjustment and Retraining Notification Act (WARN), workers being laid off were given a sixty-day notice. Most of them also received unemployment compensation in addition to severance pay. The large majority of workers benefited from the provisions of the 1974 Trade Adjustment Assistance (TAA) Act which provided Trade Readjustment Allowance (TRA) funds for training for eligible workers. Thus, about two-thirds of all workers interviewed were able to further their education, attending local technical schools or colleges and obtaining a variety of degrees. In a few cases, these funds allowed them to enroll in graduate school and a small proportion (13 percent) enrolled in two different training programs. This stands in sharp contrast to the educational opportunities available to displaced workers not eligible for TRA funds; only 38 percent of men and 43 percent of women dislocated by the Rubbermaid closure sought retraining, by example.

Various local agencies provided assistance to displaced workers. A Smith-Corona Transition Center—established with a New York State grant—was set up to deal with the tensions created by the announcement of relocation and layoffs and to facilitate the subsequent labor market transitions. Local and state educational institutions provided the initial contacts and location for most recipients selected for their first training since layoff. Search counseling was also provided to nearly half of all workers interviewed and a smaller number also received job placement assistance.

The picture emerging from this information was that of a community that mobilized itself to deal with the shock and pain caused by the massive layoffs. Interviewed workers pointed out their longstanding contracts with the firm and Cortland's many concessions—for example, in the form of tax exemptions. With the collaboration of Smith-Corona and other local players, a concerted effort was launched to take action, even if limited by the constraints of the available federal, state, and local resources. The results were mixed. The findings tell a story of a difficult and often painful labor market transition for many workers. Although there were exceptions, the majority had to face significant short and long-term economic and noneconomic costs of relocation.

*Income Losses.* The magnitude of economic dislocation due to the layoffs becomes apparent when individual income before layoff is compared to income at the time workers in the sample were interviewed for a second time.[11] As illustrated by figure 4.1, there was a dramatic increase in the proportion of workers in lower income brackets ($0–$19,999). The mean income bracket moved to the left, due mostly to a large shift of workers from middle-income ($20,000–$39,999). Figure 4.1 also shows decreases in the number of workers in all but one of the upper income brackets (there was a 2 percent increase in the $40,000 to $49,999 group). Thus, instead of observing a return to individual income levels reported before the Smith-Corona layoffs, divergence from the original income distribution became increasingly marked during this three-year time period, reflecting the typical polarization of income observed throughout the U.S. economy.

Gender differences were important with respect to individual income and relocation effects. First, on average, men's pre-layoff individual income was higher than the comparable figure for women. Second, when individual income data is disaggregated according to gender, significant differences in income distribution were observed. Individual income at Smith-Corona before layoff assumed a bell-shaped distribution for women (see figure 4.2); the median individual income for women was estimated in the $20,000 to $25,000 bracket. At the time of the second interview, an overall shift to lower income brackets had taken place, with 78 percent of all women reporting individual incomes of $0 to $19,999. The shift of the curve to the left was therefore quite dramatic—indicating the extent of income loss for women.

For men, the income distribution before layoff shows two peaks: a large peak in the $30,000 to $39,999 range, and a smaller peak on the $20,000 to $24,999 range (see figure 4.3). By the time of the second interview, the income distribution curve for men indicates a pattern of increasing inequality. Furthermore, the majority of men reported a lower individual income, with approximately 28 percent of all men falling in the $0 to $19,999 category, compared to 78 percent of all women. Thus, post-layoff wages reflect

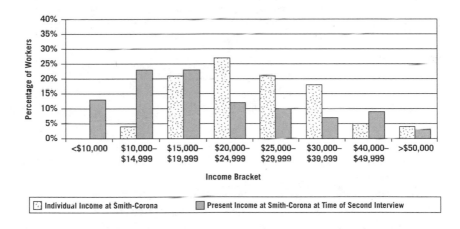

**Figure 4.1** Individual Income Before and After Layoff for Workers Employed at Time of Second Interview

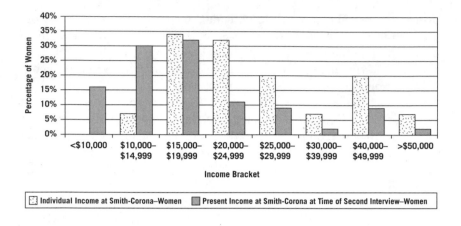

**Figure 4.2** Individual Income Before and After Layoff for Women Employed at Time of Second Interview

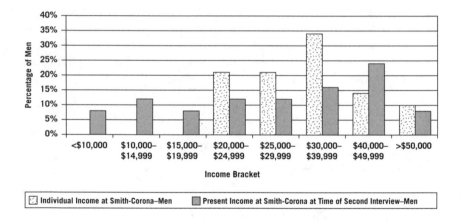

**Figure 4.3** Individual Income Before and After Layoff for Men Employed at Time of Second Interview

not only greater inequality among men but also a wider wage gap between men and women.

An estimate of earnings losses for Smith-Corona workers is provided in table 4.1. The approximate annual loss of earnings per worker was $8,147. If gender differences are considered, our estimates indicate that men lost an average of $8,917 per year, while women lost $7,727.[12] However, even though men experienced a greater income loss in absolute terms, women lost a larger proportion of their former income (26 percent and 35 percent,

**Table 4.1** Estimate of Annual Earnings Losses for Smith-Corona Workers[a]

| (A) INCOME BRACKET | (B) AVERAGE INCOME | (C) NET FLOW OF WORKERS | (D) INCOME GAIN (LOSS) | (E) NET FLOW OF MEN | (F) INCOME GAIN (LOSS) | (G) NET FLOW OF WOMEN | (H) INCOME GAIN (LOSS) |
|---|---|---|---|---|---|---|---|
| <10,000 | 5,000 | 22% | 95,000 | 13% | 20,000 | 27% | 75,000 |
| 10,000–14,999 | 12,500 | 20% | 212,500 | 20% | 75,000 | 20% | 137,500 |
| 15,000–19,999 | 17,500 | –1% | (17,500) | 7% | 35,000 | –5% | (52,500) |
| 20,000–24,999 | 22,500 | –18% | (337,500) | –3% | (22,500) | –25% | (315,000) |
| 25,000–29,999 | 27,500 | –12% | (275,000) | –13% | (110,000) | –11% | (165,000) |
| 30,000–39,999 | 35,000 | –12% | (350,000) | –23% | (245,000) | –5% | (105,000) |
| 40,000–49,999 | 45,000 | 2% | 90,000 | 7% | 90,000 | 0% | — |
| >50,000 | 55,000 | –2% | (110,000) | –7% | (110,000) | 0% | — |
| **Total Income Gain (Loss)** | | | (692,500) | | (267,500) | | (425,000) |
| **Average Gain (Loss) Per Worker** | | | (8,147) | | (8,917) | | (7,727) |

Total Sample 85
Men 30
Women 55

[a] All figures in U.S. dollars.

respectively). These findings make a contribution to the few studies that have focused on gender differences in plant closings and dislocation. Although we can not generalize from a case study, the findings indicate that layoffs could slow down the closing of the gender wage gap, which has been observed as a general trend in the United States. In the case of Rubbermaid, women's income was also significantly less than men's income both pre-and post-layoff. Although the wage gender gap closed slightly in jobs obtained after the plant's closure (with both men and women losing ground), women faced significant new costs in time and money while their median commuting distance increased to nearly three times that of men.

The results show a downward direction in the skill scale for a significant proportion of workers as they found new jobs. Half of the workers indicated that the skill level required for the first and second jobs accepted after layoff was lower than at Smith-Corona. Thus, the data points to a problem of "skidding" or downward job mobility—an indication of either an insufficient demand to absorb existing skills or of a mismatch between the skills supplied and demanded in the area. All this is consistent with the findings reflecting a polarization in the skills required in the new jobs. On the other hand, about 22 percent of the workers indicated that the skill level needed for the new placement was higher than at Smith-Corona. That is, for almost a quarter of the workers relocation implied an upgrading of their skills. However, for the large majority of the workers, the main problem was the mismatch between their skills supply and the insufficient demand for them in the local market.

Thus, the significant earnings losses experienced by Smith-Corona workers reinforce the findings from similar studies (Leigh 1995). The average Smith-Corona laid-off worker was a rural, female, blue-collar manufacturing worker with twenty-two years of experience. Each of these factors has been associated in the existing literature with an increase in the magnitude of earnings losses for displaced workers. The case study illustrates a trend toward a declining proportion of workers in middle and upper brackets, accompanied by their shift to lower brackets. Instead of observing a return to pre-layoff income, divergence from the original income distribution during the three-year period became increasingly clear, hence the tendency toward greater income inequality among the workers interviewed. This trend was echoed in the otherwise very different case study of the Rubbermaid closure.

*Length of Unemployment and Job Offers.*   Our study showed that the length of time from layoff to the first job offer was, on average, more than ten weeks. However, the time period was longer for women (11.8 weeks) than for men (9.5 weeks), with a greater standard deviation for men. This is consistent with data from the Bureau of Labor Statistics' *1995 Displaced Workers Survey,* which shows that women are less likely to be reemployed after dislocation (Spalter-Roth 1997). The first job after layoff tended to be of short duration for most of the workers interviewed; for 43 percent and 26 percent of those interviewed, its duration was eight and seven months, respectively. This reflected the "panic effect" of unemployment or rush to take the first offer followed by further search for a better job. In terms of employment by sector, figure 4.4 shows that more than half of the relocated workers were employed in the service sector at the time of the second interview, with manufacturing absorbing only 28 percent and retail trade accounting for 8 percent. This clearly shows, following the general pattern of post-industrial society, a shift from manufacturing to services and other sectors as sources of employment.

*Post-Layoff Training.* A significant proportion of the workers interviewed pursued some form of training using the post-layoff assistance received during one or two years. Funding sources for training and other expenses included transitional TRA funds, unemployment compensation, and combinations of both. Only a very small group (5 percent) did not receive unemployment benefits. Women had a higher degree of participation in training than men did (70 percent of the women versus 42 percent of the men). Thus, the social protection provided by TRA funds in the case of Smith-Corona was especially valuable to women. But these funds were unavailable to workers displaced by the Rubbermaid closure, and they reported far less access to education and training (43 percent of the Rubbermaid women in contrast with 70 percent in the case of Smith-Corona women; the corresponding figures for men were 38 percent and

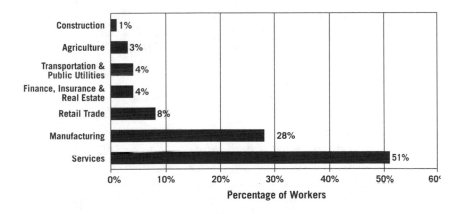

**Figure 4.4** Present Employment of Laid-off Workers by Major Industrial Division (Second Interview)

42 percent, respectively). Comments by Smith-Corona workers at the time of interviews suggested that the reasons for women's greater participation in educational programs ranged from a perception that, without training, women might have difficulty getting jobs, to a greater willingness among them to recognize the need for acquiring new skills. However, the training received was gendered in various ways. For example, the types of courses taken were not the same for men and women. To a great extent, the pattern followed gender stereotypes channeling women toward care work, such as courses on human services and childcare, and men toward other types of activities normally viewed as more appropriate for them, such as sales and computer programming. However, the list of courses taken by women had a wider range than the those taken by men, probably reflecting an effort on the women's part to not limit themselves to traditionally female activities.

*Health and Family Problems.* In addition to the loss of income experienced as a result of relocation, workers reported various health and family problems since layoff. These are important to take into consideration in estimating the costs of these transitional processes. The negative effects of unemployment are cumulative; they have an individual as well as a social impact, undermining and subverting personal and community life. Health concerns since layoff, such as emotional distress, depression, and anxiety, were reported by nearly half of all workers interviewed. Family problems since layoff were reported by 40 percent of respondents, with the most commonly identified being tension and stress, money-related issues, fighting and arguments, and children's behavior problems. Women were the most likely to report these types of distress at the household level.

Likewise, Rubbermaid workers reported postponing medical appointments and home repairs, falling into debt, selling their homes, needing to rely on food banks and sources of public assistance. At least 10 percent of the dislocated workers and their families left the community in search of better job prospects elsewhere (for the most part in the Southern part of the United States). These moves were often accompanied by experiences of stress and loss.

To summarize, these findings allow us to point out several implications: a) a variety of ad hoc measures taken at the local level, with some help from state and federal funds, were mobilized and were very helpful to smooth the painful transitions facing laid-off workers. However, the community had no systematic and comprehensive ways to compensate for the losses generated by relocation except for the use of federal TRA funds, which were very important for training purposes; b) layoffs and worker relocation contributed to increasing wage inequalities, which were parallel to the overall trends toward income inequality observed in the overall economy; c) increased labor market flexibility and plant closings affect women disproportionately and in various ways, including income losses and stress from related individual and household problems; and d) unemployment and a mismatch between supply and demand appear to have resulted from demand rather than from supply side insufficiencies. Several conclusions follow from this (which seem equally applicable to the Rubbermaid case).

First, the type of economic restructuring typified by Smith-Corona's relocation has as its main purpose the lowering of costs and increasing profits for the firms involved. This might be translated into lower prices for consumers buying the firm's products. However, at the community level where the layoffs take place, local communities rarely have systematic and comprehensive ways to estimate and compensate for the different layers of losses resulting from the firm's relocation. Thus, the theoretical principle, often mentioned in international trade theory, that winners should compensate losers still remains, as the twenty-first century unfolds, a golden rule waiting for more comprehensive policies and direct implementation. As market deregulation, trade liberalization, and globalization proceed, the costs associated with layoffs are disproportionately borne by the dislocated workers and their households and communities. If we can justify these processes on the basis of their benefits for the winners (particularly the employers) we should find ways to fully compensate those who lose out.

Second, the findings illustrate the extent of income losses for the dislocated workers and document the increasing wage inequalities associated with current labor market dynamics. Although a high proportion of the Smith-Corona workers found new jobs, relocation was associated with a significant polarization of income. While about one fourth among them were able to find jobs that required higher skills and paid higher wages, the large majority experienced a dramatic deterioration in their labor market position and income level. Women in particular suffered disproportionate losses despite their effort at acquiring new skills through training. This should be viewed as having a more general validity beyond our case study since it reinforces the conclusions from other studies (Howland 1998; Spalter-Roth 1997; Milkman 1997). Again, this points to the need to take gender into consideration in the design and implementation of compensatory policies.

Third, increased labor market flexibility and plant closings also can affect women disproportionately, as individual workers and as household members with a special responsibility for family well-being. This implies that policies addressing the problems associated with these transitions should incorporate measures dealing with women's specific roles and needs. Addressing the issue of gender inequality can have positive short-term effects, such as facilitating their transition to new jobs; in addition, special education, health programs, and other programs for women can improve their bargaining power and enhance their ability to deal with household and market work. Finally, these policies have to take into

were viewed mostly as separate and independent of each other, despite studies documenting their linkages and pointing out the shortcomings of dualistic divisions. For example, analyses of subcontracting processes showed the extent to which the two sectors were highly interconnected, particularly, but not solely, in the industrial sector through subcontracting and other links. They pointed out that, far from absorbing informal activities, the formal/modern sector often relied and fed on the former as a way to increase its competitiveness and profits (Bromley and Gerry 1979; Benería and Roldán 1987; Portes and Castells 1989). In this sense, the two sectors were not separate or independent of each other but highly linked and instrumental for the formal sector. The implication was that the conceptual separation between the two sectors was in many ways artificial, even if analytically useful to discuss different forms of employment.

If anything, the past two decades saw these tendencies intensified. We have witnessed an increasing reliance of firms and households on precarious forms of employment and a deterioration of labor market conditions for a large proportion of the workforce. To be sure, we need to distinguish between two types of informalized activities: those linked directly or indirectly to industrial and service work in more formal settings and those representing survival activities organized at the household and community level. The former are linked to profit-oriented operations and can include self-employment and wage work tied directly or indirectly to more formal production processes. This sector includes micro-enterprises and subcontracting arrangements, both in high- and low-income countries. The analysis in this section refers mostly to this type of informal work. Survival activities, on the other hand, tend to represent the most precarious forms of self-employment with weak or no links to the more formal processes and without possibilities for capital accumulation. These are, in fact, the most visible activities in the urban landscapes of Third World cities.

Another type of differentiation between these sectors results from the legal/illegal divide. The informalization of labor processes observed in high-income countries in recent times has mostly taken place within the context of legality, with important exceptions located in the underground economy. The many temp agencies that deal with contingent work operate within the confines of legality, even if they might not offer the protections of full time employment. This is much less the case in developing countries where, despite its growing importance, the informal sector lacks legal status and work takes place under the usual precarious conditions that have traditionally been associated with the sector. As a result, social protection and access to social benefits are rarely found among workers engaged in informal activities. Neither are they covered by national labor legislation. Hernando De Soto (2000) has argued that these are the activities that are "filling the vacuum left by the legal economy" (p. 49). Contrary to initial expectations, the proportion of the population engaged in them has not decreased. Table 4.2 shows, that, between 1980 and 1999, the relative importance of informal sector employment increased significantly in all regions. Charmes' estimates, reported in the table, reflect the growing importance of this sector for non-agricultural employment. The estimates seem very high, apparently resulting from the definition of the sector adopted by the fifteenth International Conference of Labor Statisticians in 1993, which included all nonagricultural "unincorporated enterprises owned by households." They include micro-enterprises as well as professional, domestic workers, and home-based workers; the figures also include family labor and "employees on an occasional basis."

Far from being absorbed by the formal sector, then, informal activities have been on the increase during the past two decades. In Latin America, for example, where labor markets have been deeply transformed since the 1980s, most observers agree in the diminishing centrality of formal employment. As Pérez-Sáinz (2000) has pointed out, there are a variety of reasons for the diminishing relative importance of formal employment in the region, from the effects of structural adjustment and market deregulation to the weakening of public employment due to budget cuts and privatization programs. Thus, although Latin America traditionally had high levels of informal employment, the past two decades have registered further growth; in urban areas, it represented 47.9 percent of total urban employment in 1998, up from 44.4 percent in 1990 (ILO 1999). A recent Inter-American Development Bank (IDB) study indicated that, in the mid-1990s, the micro-enterprise sector employed more than 50 percent of the labor force in most

**Table 4.2**   Trends in Informal Sector Employment, 1980–1999

| REGIONS | INFORMAL SECTOR AS PERCENT OF NONAGRICULTURAL EMPLOYMENT | | PERCENT OF WOMEN IN THE INFORMAL SECTOR | PERCENT OF SELF-EMPLOYMENT IN THE INFORMAL SECTOR |
|---|---|---|---|---|
| | 1980–1989 | 1990–1999 | | |
| North Africa | 38.8 | 43.4 | — | 51.5 |
| Sub-Saharan Africa | 68.1 | 74.8 | 52.3 | 90.0 |
| Latin America | 52.3 | 56.9 | 45.9 | 50.4 |
| Asia | 53.0 | 63.0 | 39.9 | 63.0 |

*Source:* Charmes 2000 (estimates based on national sources).

Latin American countries and that, between 1990 and 1995, an average of 84 out of 100 new jobs in the region were generated by micro-enterprises.

Women comprise a significant proportion of workers engaged in informal activities although this varies from region to region (see table 4.2). Hampered either by low marketable skills to their credit or by other obstacles such as lack of mobility and the need to combine work with child care and domestic activities, many women from poor households go into informal activities to generate whatever income they possibly can. Even when participating in micro-enterprises, their work in this sector serves as a means of subsistence rather than as a form of entrepreneurial or income producing activity.

These trends have led to the growing reliance on precarious forms of survival across countries, particularly for the poorest households but also affecting other sectors (González de la Rocha 2000; Oliveira 2000). Household survival strategies include very unstable links with the labor market, combining, often within short time periods, wage labor and self-employment as well as temporary migration (domestic and international). This instability led Bolivian sociologist Garcia-Linera (1999) to talk very appropriately about the phenomenon of "nomad labor," referring to survival strategies based on moving from one job to another or from a location to another. International migration, for example in the case of Bolivian workers working temporarily in Argentina and Brazil, had become an important part in these often precarious strategies up until the crisis in Argentina. In international development circles, the literature has used the notion of "labor exclusion" to refer to the vicious circle of poverty resulting from persistent levels of unemployment, underemployment, and marginality from regular sources of income. For example, weighted averages for Latin America show a 9 percent rate of open urban unemployment for 1999, "a figure above the 8.3 percent for 1985, at the height of the debt crisis" (Pérez-Sáinz 2000).[14] Even so, open urban unemployment rates mask a large number of persons in unstable, marginal, and precarious jobs. Thus, these rates do not capture the many people who subsist through multiple forms of poor labor strategies rather than through employment reflected in labor statistics.

Thus, marginality and precarious jobs have become an integral part of the labor market experience of a large proportion of workers in the South, leading to questions about the "erosion of work" and the disappearance of traditional forms of wage labor (McMichael 1999). As a study of current production processes in the outskirts of Cochabamba, Bolivia, has recently shown, some of the participants in this precarious employment are not even viewed as "workers" (Kruse 2000).[15] However, it must be emphasized that the informal sector tends to be very dynamic rather than backward and static as often assumed in (particularly) the earlier literature; it responds quickly to changes in the economic and institutional environment and adapts to evolving patterns of work organization in the more formal sector, taking up the gaps that it leaves behind.

Along these lines, we may ask what are the differences between current processes of informalization and the earlier stages in which the informal sector became a subject of study in developing countries? How can we compare current conditions with the 1970s in this respect? At least five observations can be made:

- First, since the 1980s, the macroeconomic context has changed in significant ways due to the introduction and predominance of neoliberal policies, and to the effects of globalization and economic restructuring. The expansion and deepening of markets has extended the links between formal and informal activities. At the same time, as Pérez-Sáinz argues for the case of Latin America, the distinction between the formal and informal has become increasingly vague. Market deregulation has blurred one of the basic distinctions that were used to differentiate between the two, for example, the association of different forms of regulation with the formal sector, and its correspondent legal/illegal breakdown. Over time, it has become increasingly problematic to define where the formal market ends and the informal begins. The pressures of global competition, combined with market deregulation, have led to the low road to development associated with precarious types of employment. Likewise, large firms in the formal sector have increased their involvement with informalized production through outsourcing and subcontracting. As activists and consumer campaigns against exploitative labor practices of large international retail chains have shown, the links between large and medium multinational corporations (MNCs) and the precarious working conditions in sweatshops, in both the North and the South, are well known and in continuous process of transformation.

- Second, the informal sector is no longer seen as the anomaly that will eventually be absorbed by the "modern" sector. On the contrary, the trend has been the opposite, as increasing global competition leads to lower production costs. Thus, the process is often justified in terms of low consumption prices. In fact, the "modern" sector is no longer exclusively identified with more formal and prestigious activities. In many countries, the public sector has become an increasingly less attractive source of employment due to budget cuts and retrenchment, leading to a continuous erosion in wages and benefits (Tripp 1987; Pérez-Sáinz 2000). Thus, the decline in the relative importance of formal employment in many countries has enhanced the attractiveness of informal activities, particularly as a source of livelihood for many workers and households. As suggested in ILO documents, we can now refer to the informal *economy* rather than the informal *sector*.

• Third, although the traditional association of informal employment with low skills and low productivity still holds, the past two decades have introduced changes. With the increase in outsourcing and subcontracting, many informal labor processes, such as those resulting from subcontracting chains with core firms, have their center of gravity in the formal sector. In this way, the core firms take up a principal role in the generation of informality and poor working conditions; they should be held accountable for these conditions, including the distributive mechanisms shaping wages and benefits. In fact, if technology transfers take place through outsourcing and subcontracting involving the use of modern equipment, the production tied to these processes is no longer likely to be associated with marginality or with low productivity.

• Fourth, the expansion of informal activities and the deterioration of labor market conditions in developing countries during the past two decades has taken place in an international climate that has been emphasizing political rights, individual agency, and empowerment. This has created obvious tensions between official discourses that emphasize these rights at the global and national level and the way in which a large proportion of the world's population live their lives. The contradictions between discourses that promote citizenship and rights, on the one hand, and disastrous labor market trends, on the other, are at as the root of social tensions and discontents. In this sense, globalization, growing inequalities, and concentration of economic power threaten the construction of democratic societies. I have mentioned in chapter 3 that in high income countries, the dismantling of the welfare state since the late 1970s, together with market deregulation and globalization, has resulted in the erosion of workers rights and labor unions (Tilly 1995; Standing 1999). Focusing mostly on Western Europe, Tilly has argued that while the rise of Western democracies led to the gradual and incremental establishment of workers' rights through the enforcement of contracts, intense labor struggle, and the creation of citizenship and democratic institutions, with globalization "great inequalities of economic power threaten democracy" (p. 22).

In developing countries where the welfare state has always been weaker or hardly existent, globalization has generated contradictory forces. To be sure, transnational investment thrives on the existing lack of workers' rights in many countries, as exemplified by the restrictions of rights in many export-processing zones scattered around the globe.[16] However, industrialization and individualization of decisionmaking associated with markets can contribute to the recognition of individual rights, even without a formal broadening of democratic institutions. For example, rural women's migration to urban areas for industrial and other forms of employment may foster their individual rights and increase their autonomy, releasing them from patriarchal practices *even though,* at the same time, they may be subject to discrimination and exploitative working conditions. Likewise, global links can generate pressure toward the recognition of workers' rights and labor standards, as illustrated by some of the recent debates on this issue in international forums (see below), but these links often exclude the large proportion of the labor force working within the boundaries of informality. Thus, the contradictions between public discourses and action on rights on the one hand and the realities of the labor market on the other are more intense than in the earlier stages of informalization.

• Finally, precarious jobs and economic insecurity translate into precarious lives and poor living conditions that appear to be a permanent feature of a large proportion of the population in developing countries. This is, of course, not a new phenomenon but, with labor market deregulation, increased flexibility in production, and global competition, it has taken new dimensions. In particular, the inability of many economies to generate jobs that provide at least minimum wages is key to understanding the persistence of poverty and increasing economic insecurity.[17] The following quote from Kruse's study of urban employment in Cochabamba is very explicit in reporting how men and women working in semi-informal[18] workshops and under very poor working conditions live their daily lives:

> [They] live a growing and powerful daily insecurity, with unpredictability in their *unilateral* labor contracts and mechanisms of retention, promotion, remuneration, and working time. In the face of such mechanisms, often the only *option* for defense, claim or resistance is to quit. To a great extent, these options explain their labor trajectories, marked by a notorious instability and horizontal mobility. . . . This limits the possibility to settle in any labor community and therefore the possibility to establish a social and political presence. (Kruse 2000)

Thus, the vicious circle of poverty and powerlessness is perpetuated—for men and for women, and for entire households and communities. As Kruse argues, such conditions are hardly appropriate for building stable communities and democratic participation in civic life. Needless to say, this is not the way to generate conditions conducive to human development. Instead, these conditions are part of a model that does not work for a large proportion of the world's population.

## Informalization and Women

At least since the 1970s, women have been highly involved in informal activities but given the labor market transformations of the past two decades, we can ask whether there have been changes in the extent and nature of this involvement. At least four observations can be made in this regard.

First, the feminization of the labor force during the past three decades has intensified the reliance of many women on informalized employment. Table 4.2 shows that the proportion of women in the sector varies according to region, with Sub-Saharan Africa leading with a proportion of 52.3 percent in 1999. Given that self-employment reflects this trend, the proportion of self-employed in the female nonagricultural labor force increased in all regions, including the "developed regions" (see also table 4.3). More specifically, table 4.4 illustrates the weight of informal sector employment and of women's contribution to GDP generated by this sector in various countries, showing that in some African countries like Benin, Chad, Mali, and Kenya this contribution reached levels above 50 percent for the years reported. Although statistical information regarding the scope of informal activities where women concentrate is deficient, studies have shown that they range from subcontracting processes linked to export-oriented industrialization—including home-based work—to street vending and other trade and service activities that evolve around survival strategies.

Subcontracting and home-based work illustrate many of the problems associated with women's informal employment. A recent study of subcontracted work in five Asian countries (The Philippines, Thailand, India, Pakistan, and Sri Lanka) shows that earnings lower than in the formal sector prevail, with no consistency in work contracts, difficult working conditions, and long hours of work (Balakrishnan and Huang 2000). The study points out the difficulty of organizing workers for the purpose of increasing their bargaining power, and it illustrates that "subcontracting makes it very difficult to hold one employer responsible for protecting workers' rights" due to "the many layers of chains" (p. 14). Several studies mention that married women with children are often preferred by subcontracting firms (Dangler 1994; Boris and Prugl 1996). Due to their limited mobility and narrower range of options in the labor market, married women in particular offer greater labor force security for firms (Hsiung 1995). Although they can not have direct control over work done at home and, hence, they can not directly monitor workers, firms can take advantage of the discipline imposed on women by their need to both remain at home to care for children and other domestic activities, and to earn whatever income they can.

Another study differentiates between two types of home-based workers —"independent own-account producers" and "dependent subcontract workers"—pointing out that the term "homeworkers" refers to the second category (Carr, Chen, and Tate 2000). Table 4.5 shows that women represent the large majority of home-based workers in many areas, reaching beyond the 80 percent level in some countries. Although the variations between countries are large, the table shows that in some cases women

**Table 4.3**   Self-Employment in the Female Nonagricultural Labor Force

| | PERCENT OF SELF-EMPLOYED IN FEMALE NONAGRICULTURAL LABOR FORCE | | |
| --- | --- | --- | --- |
| | 1970 | 1980 | 1990 |
| Developed regions | 10.4 | 9.7 | 11.1 |
| Africa | 38.1 | 59.3 | 62.8 |
| Latin America | 28.6 | 29.2 | 32.1 |
| Asia | 27.9 | 26.7 | 28.7 |
| World | 24.0 | 28.4 | 27.6 |

*Source:* Charmes 2000 (estimations based on national sources).

**Table 4.4**   Employment and Contribution of Women in Informal Activities, Various Countries and Years

| | PERCENT OF WOMEN'S CONTRIBUTION IN | |
| --- | --- | --- |
| | INFORMAL SECTOR EMPLOYMENT | INFORMAL SECTOR GDP |
| Benin (1992) | 59.7 | 51.1 |
| Burkina Faso (1992) | 41.9 | 61.4 |
| Chad (1993) | 53.4 | 62.3 |
| Mali (1989) | 71.9 | 68.2 |
| Kenya (1998) | 60.3 | 46.2 |
| Tunisia (1994–1996) | 18.1 | 15.7 |
| India (1993) | 22.7 | 22.1 |
| Indonesia (1998) | 43.1 | 39.5 |
| Philippines (1995) | 46.3 | 44.2 |

*Source:* Charmes 2000; author's estimations based on official labor force statistics and national accounts.

**Table 4.5**  Home-Based Workers, Various Countries and Years

|  | NUMBER OF HOME-BASED WORKERS | PERCENT OF NONAGRICULTURAL LABOR FORCE | PERCENT OF WOMEN |
|---|---|---|---|
| Tunisia (1994) | 86,267 | 4.8 | 71.3 |
| Kenya (1999) | 777,100 | 15.0 | 34.9 |
| Benin (1992) | 595,544 | 65.8 | 74.1 |
| Thailand (1999) | 311,790 | 2.0 | 80.0 |
| Philippines (1993–1995) | 2,025,017 | 13.7 | 78.8 |
| Chile (1997) | 79,740 | 1.8 | 82.3 |
| Peru (1993) | 128,700 | 5.2 | 35.3 |
| Brazil (1991) | 2,141,972 | 5.0 | 57.1 |
| Brazil (1995) | 2,700,000 | 5.2 | 78.5 |

*Source:* Charmes 2000 (estimations based on national sources).

represent a significant proportion of the nonagricultural labor force. Home-based work in the service sector has also been expanding in high-income countries such as France, the United Kingdom, and the United States where much of this work is of clerical nature, including typing, word processing, editing, and telemarketing (Carr, Chen, and Tate 2000).

Second, in the North as well as the South, at least three aspects of economic restructuring have implications for the informalization of work, with a variety of gender dimensions:

- At the micro level, industrial restructuring has profoundly transformed the linkages between core firms and the different levels at which production has been decentralized. Production through subcontracting provide examples across countries and industries. A study of the shoe industry in Spain's Mediterranean region, for example, has illustrated the ways in which the larger firms have reduced their size through the formation of smaller firms and through decentralized production based on more informal labor contracts many of which have gone underground. Ybarra (2000) has estimated that total employment has been halved since the 1980s, despite the increase in the number of firms. Women have concentrated at the lower levels of production, particularly in home-based work in which labor norms are "rarely implemented" (p. 213). The underground work carried out by women has been estimated to comprise between 35 and 40 percent of the work generated by the sector.

- Layoffs and relocation of production do not necessarily affect men and women workers in the same way. As the above case study of the Smith-Corona relocation shows, transitions after layoffs can result in gender-related differences in income loss, length of unemployment, transitional strategies adopted, and in the impacts from layoffs and unemployment experienced at the household and community levels.

• The literature on "commodity chains" and peripheral urban growth has also contributed examples of the ways in which labor market informalization can affect women. Gereffi and others have analyzed the connections between globalization and the formation of commodity chains through which large buyers tend to control the links between inputs and outputs. (Gereffi and Korzeniewicz 1994). Along the same lines, Carr et al. (2000) have pointed out that technological change has facilitated "lean retailing" that demands the "quick and timely supply of goods associated with the just in time inventory system" (p. 126). According to these authors, this system has resulted in an increase in homework in the garment sector, particularly in countries close to the main markets of Europe and North America. Thus, the traditional precarious conditions in the informal sector have been reinforced by the dynamics of globalization in these new productive processes.

Third, women's primary involvement in domestic work and child care responsibilities continues to be a source of economic vulnerability for them, not only because this is unpaid work but also because it diminishes women's mobility and autonomy to design their labor market strategies. The effort of the past two decades (described in chapter 5) to account for and analyze unpaid work and its consequences for women's participation in paid production has not been sufficiently translated into practical action and policies. In developing countries, middle- and upper-class households can rely on poor women to take up the responsibilities of domestic work and child care and to facilitate professional women's incorporation in market work. Domestic service still represents a very large proportion of women's informal employment in many low- and middle-income countries.[19] In the North, the crisis of care is particularly met with the hiring of immigrant women from the South, thus creating another care crisis for the families left behind (Ehrenreich and Hochschild 2002).

In any case, involvement in unpaid work and child care responsibilities often ties women to informal employment and continues to have an impact on their choices and ability to participate in paid production on an equal basis with men—even if differences exist according to class and social background. We have seen that the implementation of austerity policies tends to increase women's work and multiple responsibilities. However, these policies have not included appropriate provisions addressing the different problems faced by men and women as a result of adjustment, nor have they taken into consideration existing legislation. A typical example of the latter is provided by the existence of ILO Convention 103 on maternity protection which has been ratified only by thirty-seven countries. This low rate of ratification points to the low priority given to this issue in most countries, let alone the fact that "maternity protection," in contrast to "parental protection," represents an intrinsic bias in the assignment of child care to mothers without equal share with fathers. With the increasing informalization of jobs, the implementation of ILO standards seem even more remote. In fact, within the framework of deteriorating labor conditions created by globalization, the ILO standards have been disregarded and subject to new scrutiny (ILO 1997).

Fourth, one of the differences between the earlier periods of informalized labor and the present time is the degree to which women have been able to take up actions at the national and international level. Structural adjustment and economic crises have led women to organize around labor issues as well as around tensions related to unpaid work and household survival strategies. An interesting example has been women's key role in getting the ILO Convention on Home Work approved in June of 1996. Elizabeth Prugl (1999) has argued that its approval was a feminist victory, with some international networks such as HomeNet and the Self-Employed Women's Association (SEWA), providing extensive information and using the special relationship that its members had built with unions in advance of the conference to get their arguments on the floor. Although the convention's rate of ratification at the country level is very low, it provides concrete goals and a regulatory tool around which to organize further action. Organizations focusing on women and informalized work such as SEWA have gained international recognition for its accomplishments on behalf of homeworkers, particularly in India. Its increasing international influence has been important in the formation of other groups such as South Africa's Self-Employed Women's Union (SEWU). Similarly, Women and Informal Employment Globalizing and Organizing (WIEGO) has organized a network of workers, activists, and academics focusing on the informal sector, including home-based workers and linking their interests and actions with research and work on improving statistical information on this sector at the global level.

## Contradictory Tendencies for Women

During the past three decades there have been positive changes for women that need to be taken into consideration in order to evaluate the complex and often contradictory tendencies affecting women's work. As argued in chapter 3, the effects of globalization and reorganization of the work process is highly uneven among women within and across countries. Thus, generalizations need to be qualified, particularly as the conditions affecting women's employment are very varied and often complex. There are several reasons behind this complexity.

First, gender gaps in education have been decreasing significantly across regions. For example, the Arab countries have experienced some of the most dramatic increases in women's educational indicators, with women's literacy rates doubling between 1970 and 1990. South East Asia and the Pacific countries also made very significant progress during the period. In many Latin American countries educational indicators for women have surpassed those of men (UNDP 1999). Figure 4.5, using 1997 figures for net enrolment ratio in secondary education, indicates that this was the case for five out of the thirty-four countries in Sub-Saharan Africa, six out of twenty-one in Asia and the Pacific, three out of eleven in Central and Western Asia, and eighteen out of twenty six in Latin American and the Caribbean. To be sure, many countries continue to have a very low female/male enrollment ratio, particularly in Sub-Sahara Africa and Asia and the Pacific. In addition, indicators might be misleading because they tell us nothing about the quality of education.

There is much agreement on the notion that the improvement in women's educational status is a crucial step toward gender equality, women's advancement, and social development as a whole. However, while a correlation exists between schooling and labor force participation, and while this correlation tends to be higher for women than for men, women's educational achievements do not necessarily translate into labor market gains. Obstacles to women's advancement such as those resulting from occupational segregation and gender-based discriminatory practices, reduce these possible gains. In addition, the progress made in women's education is far from complete. For example, gender differences in illiteracy rates and other indicators of educational achievement are still substantial in many countries. Illiteracy rates are extremely high in some African and Asia countries while female primary and secondary school enrollment has not achieved parity with men in many areas.[20] To the extent that a high concentration of women in informalized production can be partially a result of their lower educational status, educational policies are crucial to deal with women's economic vulnerability and other aspects of women's lives. At a bare minimum, the elimination of illiteracy is an urgent objective for educational policies in the countries affected.

Second, there are clear indications that women's higher educational levels and rising labor market participation have contributed to a gradual increase in women's participation in managerial and professional occupations. The improved working conditions and social mobility of women in higher education stands in contrast with the precariousness and low-income levels received by the majority. This polarization seems to be at the root of growing income inequalities among women. Although more studies are needed to

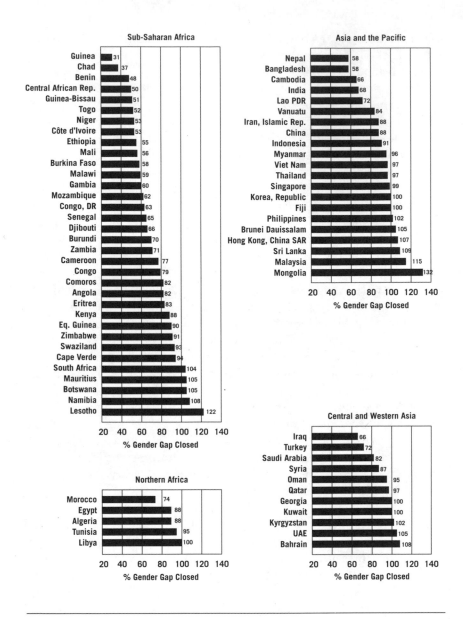

**Sub-Saharan Africa**

| Country | % Gender Gap Closed |
|---|---|
| Guinea | 31 |
| Chad | 37 |
| Benin | 48 |
| Central African Rep. | 50 |
| Guinea-Bissau | 51 |
| Togo | 52 |
| Niger | 53 |
| Côte d'Ivoire | 53 |
| Ethiopia | 55 |
| Mali | 56 |
| Burkina Faso | 58 |
| Malawi | 59 |
| Gambia | 60 |
| Mozambique | 62 |
| Congo, DR | 63 |
| Senegal | 65 |
| Djibouti | 66 |
| Burundi | 70 |
| Zambia | 71 |
| Cameroon | 77 |
| Congo | 79 |
| Comoros | 82 |
| Angola | 82 |
| Eritrea | 83 |
| Kenya | 88 |
| Eq. Guinea | 90 |
| Zimbabwe | 91 |
| Swaziland | 93 |
| Cape Verde | 94 |
| South Africa | 104 |
| Mauritius | 105 |
| Botswana | 105 |
| Namibia | 108 |
| Lesotho | 122 |

**Asia and the Pacific**

| Country | % Gender Gap Closed |
|---|---|
| Nepal | 58 |
| Bangladesh | 58 |
| Cambodia | 66 |
| India | 68 |
| Lao PDR | 72 |
| Vanuatu | 84 |
| Iran, Islamic Rep. | 88 |
| China | 88 |
| Indonesia | 91 |
| Myanmar | 96 |
| Viet Nam | 97 |
| Thailand | 97 |
| Singapore | 99 |
| Korea, Republic | 100 |
| Fiji | 100 |
| Philippines | 102 |
| Brunei Dauissalam | 105 |
| Hong Kong, China SAR | 107 |
| Sri Lanka | 109 |
| Malaysia | 115 |
| Mongolia | 132 |

**Northern Africa**

| Country | % Gender Gap Closed |
|---|---|
| Morocco | 74 |
| Egypt | 88 |
| Algeria | 88 |
| Tunisia | 95 |
| Libya | 100 |

**Central and Western Asia**

| Country | % Gender Gap Closed |
|---|---|
| Iraq | 66 |
| Turkey | 72 |
| Saudi Arabia | 82 |
| Syria | 87 |
| Oman | 95 |
| Qatar | 97 |
| Georgia | 100 |
| Kuwait | 100 |
| Kyrgyzstan | 102 |
| UAE | 105 |
| Bahrain | 108 |

**Figure 4.5** Secondary Net Enrollment Ratio, Female/Male 1997
*Source:* Progress of the World's Women 2000, New York: UNIFEM.

## Latin America and the Caribbean

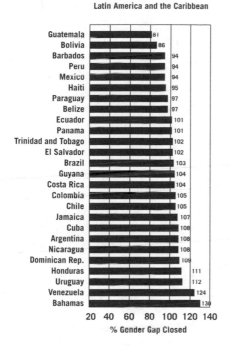

| Country | % Gender Gap Closed |
|---|---|
| Guatemala | 81 |
| Bolivia | 86 |
| Barbados | 94 |
| Peru | 94 |
| Mexico | 94 |
| Haiti | 95 |
| Paraguay | 97 |
| Belize | 97 |
| Ecuador | 101 |
| Panama | 101 |
| Trinidad and Tobago | 102 |
| El Salvador | 102 |
| Brazil | 103 |
| Guyana | 104 |
| Costa Rica | 104 |
| Colombia | 105 |
| Chile | 105 |
| Jamaica | 107 |
| Cuba | 108 |
| Argentina | 108 |
| Nicaragua | 108 |
| Dominican Rep. | 109 |
| Honduras | 111 |
| Uruguay | 112 |
| Venezuela | 124 |
| Bahamas | 130 |

% Gender Gap Closed

## Western Europe and Other Developed Countries

| Country | % Gender Gap Closed |
|---|---|
| Switzerland | 92 |
| Malta | 96 |
| Germany | 99 |
| Austria | 99 |
| Japan | 100 |
| United States | 100 |
| Australia | 100 |
| Sweden | 100 |
| Netherlands | 100 |
| Ireland | 100 |
| France | 100 |
| Belgium | 100 |
| Norway | 101 |
| Iceland | 101 |
| Denmark | 101 |
| New Zealand | 102 |
| Spain | 102 |
| Italy | 102 |
| Finland | 102 |
| United Kingdom | 103 |
| Portugal | 103 |
| Greece | 104 |
| Canada | 108 |

% Gender Gap Closed

## Eastern Europe

| Country | % Gender Gap Closed |
|---|---|
| Bulgaria | 95 |
| Latvia | 100 |
| Czech Rep. | 100 |
| Romania | 101 |
| Croatia | 102 |
| Hungary | 103 |
| Estonia | 103 |
| Poland | 105 |
| Russian Fed. | 107 |

% Gender Gap Closed

**Figure 4.5** (*continued*)

document this tendency for different countries, available evidence for Brazil and the United States points in the direction of what McCrate has called a "growing class divide among women" (Lavinas 1996; McCrate 1999). The more favorable real earnings for women and the decline in the pay gender gap in the United States have resulted in significant differences among them. As with men, the less educated are gradually falling behind as wage and earnings disparities by education have grown (Bertola et al. 2001: 267).

Third, despite the persistence of gender discrimination and obstacles to women's advancement, women's relative wages have improved in relation to male wage across countries. As figure 4.6 indicates for 1980 to 1997, in industry and services this improvement took place in twenty-two out of twenty-nine countries, and the list includes both high- and low-income countries. Similarly, in manufacturing and for the same period, gender wage disparities decreased for twenty out of twenty-two countries. For the transition economies of Eastern Europe, Figure 4.6 also shows an improvement in women's relative wages for four out of seven countries. To be sure, this narrowing of the wage gender gap might be due to the fact that the relative wage for male workers has deteriorated. In any case, no country has achieved wage equality; the female/male wage ratios for 1997 range between a low 45 percent for South Korea to 95 percent for El Salvador, followed by Australia, Sri Lanka, and Sweden (90 percent). A related issue is that a higher level of formal education does not assure that women will be able to upgrade their skills with the speed required by technological change and shifting labor markets.

To add complexity to this issue, a UN (1999) report on the role of women in development pointed out that there is mixed evidence on whether the gender wage gap has increased or decreased. The report argues that in some countries, like the United States, the gap indeed seems to have narrowed, while in others, such as Japan, it appears to have widened. Similarly, the survey reports that trends vary among developing countries, with a narrowing of the gap in countries like El Salvador and Sri Lanka and a widening in some Asian countries like Hong Kong, Singapore, and Taiwan.

Fourth, I have argued that much has changed since Ester Boserup (1970) emphasized the need to "integrate women in development." As she saw it, women had lost out in the process of development for a variety of reasons. One of them had to do with the ways in which industrialization, particularly under import substitution policies, had resulted in the marginalization of women due to the replacement of craft production with modern industry employing predominantly male labor. During the past three decades, we have seen that the new preference for women workers, particularly in the manufacturing and service sectors, has contributed to the feminization of the labor force, thus reversing the trend mentioned by Boserup. Although the new processes of industrialization have provided many illustrations of

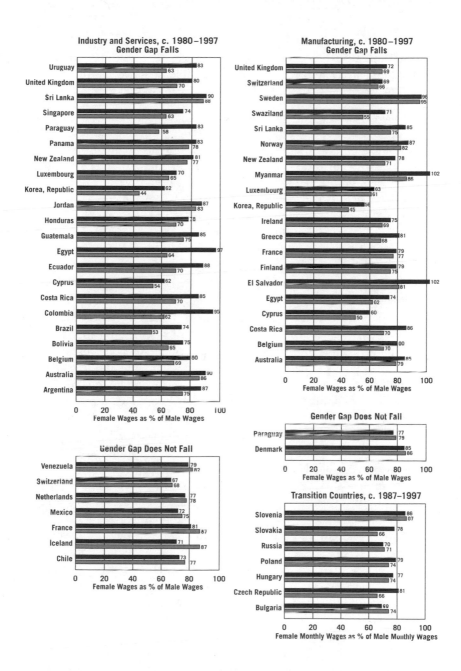

**Figure 4.6** Change in Female Wages as Percent of Male Wages
*Source:* Progress of the World's Women 2000, New York: UNIFEM.

the precariousness of women's employment, they have also contributed to raising women's income and autonomy, therefore generating contradictory results. Along these lines, we can distinguish at least between three different outcomes associated with the feminization of the labor force.

1. Cases that have generated gains for women. Under rapid growth and absorption of labor into labor-intensive export manufacturing, women have experienced wage increases as their share of industry employment has expanded. I have pointed out that, contrary to the initial literature on the subject in the South East Asian region, Lim (1983) argued, with respect to the South East Asian countries, that rapid export-led growth benefited women by providing them with formal, well-paid employment. In particular, she argued that multinational firms paid higher wages than national capital. Subsequent research has focused on the mass economic implications of this wage inequality, namely that rapid growth in South East Asia was partly based on a high degree of gender and wage inequality. This is the case with Seguino's argument that low female wages served as an incentive for investment and exports, "by lowering unit labor costs, [and] providing the foreign exchange to purchase capital and intermediate goods which raise productivity and growth rates" (Seguino 2000: 29). Thus, the improvement in women's employment conditions in the South East Asian region must be seen within the wider framework of gender and wage inequalities.

   Wage gains can not be the only factor to evaluate the benefits of change for women. As Seguino has pointed out, women's socialization in Asia has led them to "accept their economic and social status, reassuring investors that labor strife will be unlikely," adding that "Women's lower wages and, in some cases, dismissal from employment upon marriage, have maintained their lower bargaining power not only relative to employers but also to men" (p. 51). Hence, an evaluation of the effects of employment for women need to take into consideration what happens at the level of gender socialization and power relations. Studies focusing on socio-cultural aspects of women's involvement in paid work have analyzed the different and often contradictory aspects of women's participation in the new processes of industrialization (Ong 1987; Feldman 1992). Their analyses of women's agency, of changing gender identities, and of women's capacity to contest oppressive practices—at work or in their lives in general—have added important dimensions for an evaluation of women's employment.

2. Cases where growth in female share of industry employment has been held in check and women's wage gains are limited. An example

is provided by Fussell's study, mentioned, in chapter 3, on the maquiladora industries along the U.S.–Mexico border. Using a Labor Trajectory Survey for Tijuana, Fussell (2000) argues that maquiladora wages did not improve over the years as employment expanded in the area. This contradicts Lim's assertion that export-oriented employment raises wages for workers and improve women's labor market position. As already suggested, the difference between the two cases can be attributed to the conditions prevailing in Mexico in comparison with those in South East Asia. While the maquiladora area continued to attract an almost unlimited labor supply, the rapid growth in South East Asia resulted in tight labor markets and high productivity increases, both of which contributed to raising real wages. Three more factors have contributed to this situation in the maquiladora industry: a) economic restructuring and the introduction of high tech production systems have bene-fited male labor, thus decreasing the proportion of women workers from its peak in 1985; b) due to high levels of unemployment and migration from rural areas in Mexico, young male workers in par-ticular have replaced women, particularly because they have been willing to take up previously female jobs (Cravey 1998); and c) reports about the effects of China's recent membership in the WTO indicate that countries like Mexico are suffering from the erosion of their relative comparative advantage as the much lower labor cost in the giant Chinese economy threaten to shift production away.

An interesting study of the effects of export-led growth on gen-der wage inequality in Taiwan provides another example (Berik 2000). Using industry-level panel data, the study shows that eco-nomic restructuring and technological change since the 1980s, together with greater export orientation, shifted employment opportunities in manufacturing from wage to salaried employ-ment. This was accompanied by a disproportionate loss of employment opportunities for women and an increase in gender wage inequality. Technological change brought higher real wages for men and lower real wages for women. Thus, in industries that underwent faster techological change women wage workers expe-rienced both absolute losses and losses relative to men. This rever-sal of feminization due to the introduction of new technologies in the maquiladora industries, in Taiwan, and other cases occurs for a variety of gender-biased reasons; they include men's greater opportunities to upgrade their skills and to benefit from the intro-duction of high technology—for example, through after-work training programs that are less accessible to women due to their domestic responsibilities. Likewise, women's difficulties in adjusting to schedules of flexible production are due to these responsibilities. Hsiung (1995) provides a similar evaluation of the Taiwanese experience from an ethonographic perspective.

3. There are also cases of mixed results with increases in female share of industrial employment but under highly volatile employment conditions or contingent on continuation of favorable circumstances for international capital. A study of gender differences in employment in Turkey's export-led industrialization provides an interesting example (Ozler 2001). Based on a large plant-level data set of Turkish manufacturing, Ozler argues that trade liberalization has led to the feminization of the labor force, with job creation for women significantly higher than for their male counterparts. However, the volatility of women's jobs is also significantly higher. Thus this case reflects a preference for women workers but for jobs that are insecure. Mixed results are represented also by the process of de-feminization described for the cases of Taiwan and the maquiladora industry, and similar changes have also been observed elsewhere.[21]

Finally, the pressures of global competition can create ambivalent situations with respect to women's employment. For example, Kabeer (2001) has argued strongly that the imposition of international labor standards can be detrimental for women workers in Bangladesh on the grounds that implementation of higher standards might drive investment away from the country. Hence, the ability for women to benefit from international investment might be limited by the threat of adopting even minimum core standards. Again, referring to Bangladesh, the contradictory results of women's employment have been emphasized by authors looking at the multidimensional aspects of gender constructions, arguing that its effects must be seen as resulting from the different dimensions of power relations at the workplace and elsewhere. These include women's agency and resistance to exploitative conditions as well as the dynamics of evolving traditions (Feldman 2001).

Taken together, these cases imply that the initial 1970s literature emphasizing the adverse effects of industrialization on women's employment by global capital was simplistic at best. Global capital was, and continues to be, exploitative and causes disruptions and adverse effects in many cases, but its specific effects need to be examined case by case so as to take into consideration the range of variations in labor market conditions as well as the ways in which gender inequality affects the outcomes.

These examples also show that much has changed in terms of the profound transformations in gender roles in the workplace and outside of it, both for women and men. More specifically, Richard Anker's 1996 study of gender segregation across countries illustrates how, over a period of about three decades, men have been losing their labor market advantage— in the sense of having their "own" occupations protected against female competition. There are, however, some exceptions, and results differ between industries, countries, and regions. Anker's analysis for the OECD countries illustrates the extent to which the increase in women's labor force participation has taken place in female-dominated occupations, particularly in the 1970s, as well as in male-dominated occupations in the 1980s. We have come to view gender and gender differences in a dynamic way, reflecting its changing meanings over time. As illustrated by Matthew Gutmann in his ethnografic study of changing relations is Mexico City, "Gender identities, roles and relations do not remain frozen in place, either for individuals or for groups" (Guttman 1996: 27).This implies discarding stereotypes about the gender division of labor, employment conditions, and other factors affecting gender relations and gender differences. It also implies that a focus on women only is incomplete and often inaccurate for any type of gender analysis since it leaves out the changing nature of gender roles and locations, and their implications for power relations.

## Concluding Remarks

This chapter argues that economic restructuring and the enormous increase in precarious employment and informalized production that has resulted from globalization and the implementation of neoliberal policies need to be understood within the context of the changes taking place, first, at the micro-level of the firm and, second, in terms of their repercussion on the labor market and the labor force. These changes have represented a massive redistribution of resources away from labor and an increase in social inequalities across countries. They are part of the low road to development pursued as a result of global competition, particularly for labor-intensive industries. The deterioration of conditions and relative power for labor is at the root of the stubborn persistence, and even increase, in poverty and economic insecurity among millions of workers and their families across countries, including high income countries. Chapter 1 points out that, aware of the increasing problems of poverty, during the past few years international organizations and development agencies have paid growing attention to programs of poverty alleviation. An implication of the analysis in this chapter is that poverty eradication programs will continue to be ineffective unless they emphasize the urgency of generating decent jobs, the need to design social protection policies, and to rethink the structures that regulate distributive and redistributive channels.

Action is needed at different levels, from the adoption of new forms of social protection to international agreements on core labor standards, social policies, and minimum wages. Given the extent to which resources have shifted from public to private hands during the past decades, the time has come to put pressure on the private sector for its responsibility in the creation of precarious jobs and living conditions. In the same way that the environmental movement has succeeded in increasing the responsibility of private firms for environmental degradation during the past three decades, it is time for a similar effort addressing, at the global and national level, the problems of precarious employment.

The case of subcontracting and outsourcing is a good example: large firms constitute the center of gravity in the creation of subcontracting chains, yet they have been an avenue through which previously acquired labor gains in terms of wages, working conditions, and other benefits have been reduced or eliminated. This raises the question of whether and how this trend can be reversed or changed, and in what ways subcontractors and workers in the periphery could participate in some of the benefits provided by core firms. The responsibility of the private sector in responding to these questions and dealing with the roots of poverty and inequality can not be underestimated.[22] The voluntary adoption of codes of conduct on the part of large MNCs is an encouraging step in this direction. However, voluntary codes rely on self-monitoring and, in addition, they only represent a small proportion of the huge task ahead. Much more needs to be done toward the adoption of regulatory measures providing global standards.

Regarding women's work, this chapter provides an illustration of how economic restructuring and labor market developments have generated change with gender dimensions in the North and the South. A basic argument is that it is difficult to generalize about the effects of economic restructuring on women's employment, given that there are contradictory forces at work. On the positive side, the improvement in women's educational levels across countries and the preference for women's labor in low-wage employment must be noted. Yet improvements in education do not always result in corresponding gains in labor market conditions for women. At the same time, the observed "preference" for female labor in export-led employment is often accompanied with greater insecurity of women's jobs in comparison with men's, even though all jobs, in general, are becoming less secure. This calls for policies to solidify and upgrade women's educational gains, particularly in view of rapidly changing technological requirements. Most of all, given the connection between precarious jobs and poverty, women and their families will benefit from policies addressing the problems of labor market insecurity, low pay, and gender inequalities in informal employment.

## CHAPTER 5

# Paid and Unpaid Labor: Meanings and Debates

*One of the defining movements of the 20th century has been the relentless struggle for gender equality. When this struggle finally succeeds—as it must—it will mark a great milestone in human progress. And along the way it will change most of today's premises for social, economic and political life*
—UNDP, Human Development Report, 1995: 1

This chapter shifts our attention from the wider issues of development, globalization, and labor markets to the debates around paid and unpaid labor. It is centered around what I have called the "accounting for women's work project." Its central theme is the analysis of how conceptual and theoretical conventions are at the root of statistical biases leading to the underestimation of women's work in labor force and national accounting statistics across countries. Initially viewed as a way of making women's work more visible, the project has gradually evolved to include all unpaid work, mostly performed by women but also by men, although to a smaller extent. In addition, this project presents an illustration of how the questions raised by feminists have a relevance that transcends feminism and challenges basic tenets in conventional economic thinking. Finally it is also a project with domestic and global dimensions.

For me, this challenge first surfaced when I witnessed what I have come to call "the paradox of Cheshaouen," named after the picturesque town in Northern Morocco, which I visited in 1978 while working at the ILO. Preparing for the trip, I had looked at statistics showing that the labor force participation rate for men and women in Morocco differed widely—over 75 percent for men and less than 10 percent for women. However, what I saw in the streets of Cheshaouen the morning after my arrival told me a very different story from that reflected in these statistics. I saw many women moving about the busy streets, some carrying dough on their heads to bake bread in public ovens, others carrying wood on their backs or clothes to be washed in the brook bordering the town; still other women were carrying baskets or bags on their way to shopping, often with children at their side. The men were less busy; many of them were sitting outside their shops, idle and chatting, perhaps waiting for the tourist season to increase the demand for the beautiful crafts sold in many stores. I immediately thought that there was something wrong in the statistics I had seen. It was the first time I had paid attention to this type of discrepancy, but I soon learned how prevalent it was across countries and regions.

Others had been concerned about this issue as well. Ester Boserup had pointed out that "the subsistence activities usually omitted in the statistics of production and income are largely women's work" (p. 163). Boserup was a pioneer in emphasizing the time-consuming character of these activities, which, in rural economies, included physically demanding tasks such as fetching wood and carrying water as well as food production and the "crude processing of basic foods"—with great variations across countries in the time taken. Earlier in the United States, Margaret Reid, in her book *Economics of Household Production,* published in 1934, had been concerned about the exclusion of domestic production in national income accounts and had designed a method to estimate the value of housework.

Since the late 1960s, the international women's movement and the debates among feminists had prepared the ground for a new look at this topic. Many in the movement saw this issue as symbolic of society's undervaluation of women and of their contribution to social well-being. The various UN World Decade of Women Conferences were instrumental in including the issue in their agendas and in subsequent plans of action. Individual authors, research institutions, and governments also contributed to the effort. Marylin Waring's book *If Women Counted,* published in 1988, made a significant contribution by making the analysis of this issue and of its implication for action more readily accessible to a larger audience. Finally, during the past two decades, an increasing number of governments and individual researchers and activist groups took up this project and prioritized it in their agendas.

This process unfolded gradually, despite initial skepticism and even hostile reactions to the overall project. Its objective was officially sanctioned and summarized in the Platform of Action adopted in 1995 at the Fourth World Conference on Women in Beijing which called for the design and implementation of suitable statistical means to recognize and make visible the full extent of the work of women and all their contributions to the national economy including their contribution in the unremunerated and domestic sectors, and to examine the relationship of women's unremunerated work to the incidence of vulnerability to poverty. (UN 2001: 93)

In the past and over the years, an important body of literature not necessarily imbued with feminist goals has developed, addressing time allocation data that includes unpaid work. In fact, the first systematic collection of this data goes back to 1924 and is from the USSR, with the objective of obtaining information about variables such as leisure time and community-oriented work (Juster and Stafford 1991). Since the 1960s, national and comparative studies of time use have been carried out for a variety of purposes, such as the expansion of national accounting statistics and the analysis of household behavior. This work has taken place both in industrialized and developing countries.[1] However, although useful and often with parallel objectives to those of the "accounting project," these studies do not contain a specific feminist concern regarding their implications for women and for gender equality. This chapter presents a summary of some of the theoretical and practical issues involved in this project as they have evolved during the past two decades.

## The Accounting Project

The underestimation of unpaid work in national and international statistics is reflected in labor force as well as GNP and national income data. Labor force statistics and national income accounts were designed primarily to gather information about the level of economic activity and changes over time, and to provide a basis for economic policy and planning. Given that, in capitalist economies, the market has been considered the core of economic activity, participation in the labor market was historically defined as engagement in work "for pay or profit" (as defined by the International Conference of Labor Force Statisticians in 1954). Likewise, the inclusion of production in national income accounts was defined by its connection to the market. The typical story about the decrease in GNP when a man marries his housekeeper is well known by readers of introductory economics textbooks even if, as a wife, her household activities might not have changed or might, in fact, have increased. This is because the wife, unlike the housekeeper, is not paid a wage and her work is not part of the market, therefore her work is not considered economically significant.

Thus, the problem of undercounting springs from the way "work" has been defined, in theory and in conventional statistics, as a paid economic activity linked to the market. Until World War II, statistics on the economically active population were gathered through population censuses, but the unemployment problems derived from the Great Depression generated a growing interest in the collection of reliable labor statistics. In 1938 the Committee of Statistical Experts of the League of Nations recommended a definition of the concepts "gainfully occupied" and "unemployed," and drew up proposals to standardize census data with the purpose of facilitating international comparisons. As a result, many countries expanded the collection of what, from then on, would be called "the labor force" (League of Nations 1938; ILO 1976). In 1966, the UN Statistical Commission updated the earlier definitions for the purpose of providing not only a measure of the unemployed but of labor availability. The adopted definition of "economically active population" referred *to all persons of either sex who furnish the supply of labor for the production of economic goods and services.* The objective of this definition was to facilitate not only estimates of employment and unemployment but of underemployment as well.[2]

Another aspect of this definition was the link assumed between the labor force and the national product—active labor being defined as that which contributes to the national product plus the unemployed. This definition leads to questionable measurements of work. Family members working part time can be classified as employed or underemployed when working in unremunerated agricultural activities but not when engaged in household production. A large proportion of unpaid work was therefore excluded from national product and income accounting as well as from labor force statistics under this definition. However, the problem of underestimation of unpaid work and the reasons behind it differ for each of the four sectors in which it predominates—namely, subsistence production, the household economy, the informal sector, and volunteer work.

*The Subsistence Sector*

Despite considerable efforts made since 1938 to improve labor force and national accounting statistics, the basic concepts remained essentially untouched until the past two decades. One important exception was the effort to include estimates of subsistence production in GNP accounts. As early as 1947, Kuznets had warned about the need to improve the then-still young system of national income accounts and argued for the inclusion of subsistence production in the accounts. Methods to estimate the value of this type of production and the proportion of the population engaged in it were recommended in the UN system of national accounts during the 1950s, particularly for countries in which this sector had a relatively important weight. Thus, countries such as Nepal, Papua New Guinea, Tanzania, and others developed methods of estimating the contributions of this sector to GNP. By 1960 a working party of African statisticians recommended that estimates of rural household activities, such as the cultivation of back-yard vegetables, could and should be added to those of subsistence produc-tion in agriculture, forestry, and fishing (Waring 1988). However, the recommendation was not accompanied with an implementation effort.

This process was consolidated with the 1966 definition of labor force recommended by the International Conference of Labor Statisticians, which referred to *all persons of either sex who furnish the supply of economic goods and services* (ILO 1976). Whether this supply was furnished through the market was irrelevant in this case. Thus, although what constituted "economic goods and services" was not clear, the new definition introduced an exception to the market criterion—justified by the notion that subsis-tence production represents "marketable goods." As a result, it seemed logi-cal to view the labor engaged in the sector as part of the labor force, including "family labor." Thus, despite the practical difficulties in estimat-ing the market value of subsistence production, it became an accepted practice without important theoretical or conceptual objections. The objective was to arrive at more accurate estimates of GNP and of economic growth. To quote Ester Boserup,

> [T]he present system of under reporting subsistence activities not only makes the underdeveloped countries seem poorer than they really are in comparison with the more developed countries, but it also makes their rate of economic growth appear in a more favor-able light than the facts warrant, since economic development entails a gradual replacement of the omitted subsistence activities by the creation of income in the non-subsistence sector which is recorded more correctly. (Boserup 1970: 163)

In practice, however, the participation of women in subsistence production was not fully accounted for, given that the boundaries between agricultural and domestic work can be difficult to trace, particularly for women. To the extent that women's unpaid agricultural labor is highly integrated with domestic activities—such as with food cultivation, the fetching of wood, care of animals, and many others—the line between the conventional classi-fications of family labor (in agriculture) and domestic work becomes thin and difficult to draw unless some clear-cut convention is established. The result has been a tendency to underestimate women's work in subsistence production, particularly whenever it is classified as domestic work.

The same problem appeared when censuses classified workers according to their "main occupation." In such cases, the tendency to underreport women family workers in agriculture or any other type of nondomestic production has been prevalent. Historically, such underreporting has been observed across countries and it was already pointed out by the ILO in 1977, referring in particular to North Africa and Southwest Asia where "... the female unpaid family workers were, to a large extent, not recorded" (ILO 1977, vol. VI: 11). Since then, there have been efforts to include this category of workers in many countries' labor force statistics. Even so, there are still reasons to believe that underreporting continues to be a problem; they range from the relative irregularity of women's work in agriculture— for example in cases when it is mostly seasonal or marginal—to the deeply ingrained view, subject to multiple cultural and historical variations, that women's place is in the household. The result of these problems has been the nonexistence or the unreliability of national statistics regarding women's work and the difficulties in making meaningful comparisons across countries.[3]

### The Informal Sector

A different type of problem is represented by the sparse statistical information on the informal sector at least until recently. This sector comprises a wide array of activities ranging from underground production of goods and services, to street vendors, to officially sanctioned micro-enterprises in all sorts of industries, including construction, garment, toys, and even shoes. In this case, the measurement problem is not one of conceptualization, given that it represents largely paid activities and therefore it falls within conventional definitions of work; the problem has to do with the difficulties of obtaining reliable statistics.

The absence of appropriate and systematic data collection on the informal sector becomes a significant problem given the large (and growing) proportion of its workforce in many countries.[4] For women, the informal sector often provides a primary, even if precarious, source of income. Informal activities range from homework (industrial piecework) to preparing and selling street foods, to self-employment and work in micro-enterprises. As analyzed in chapter 4, rather than being gradually replaced by formal sector activities as the earlier literature had expected, the tendency in many countries has been the opposite—the size of the informal sector has been growing, and it has absorbed the largest numbers of people who have remained marginal to the "modern economy" or expelled from it when unemployment has increased. To be sure, many case studies and efforts of data collection of informal activities have been undertaken, but the difficulties of gathering systematic, sectoral information are enormous; they derive from the invisible and even underground character of significant parts of this sector—illegal activities or at the borderline of illegality— and from its unstable, precarious, and unregulated nature.

Periodic and systematic country surveys, however, can realistically be elaborated to provide estimates of the sector's weight in the labor force and GNP estimates—as it has already been done in many cases. In the early 1990s, several branches within the UN prepared conceptual and methodological guidelines for the measurement of women's work in this sector—including industry, trade, and services—and carried out useful pilot studies, such as in Burkina Faso, Congo, the Gambia, and Zambia (UN Statistical Office/ECA/INSTRAW 1991a and 1991b; INSTRAW 1991). In each case, microeconomic survey data—for example for individuals and households—was combined with macroeconomic information, depending on data availability for each country. Similar efforts have been undertaken by other organizations, governments, and individual authors (Charmes 2000; De Soto 2001). This information-gathering effort is key to facilitate policy design and actions to improve the working conditions of those who participate in the sector.

## Domestic Work

In the case of domestic production and related activities, the problem is not so much one of underestimation as of total exclusion because it has been conceptualized as falling outside of the conventional definition of work. Historically, even authors who have been open to the possibility of defining domestic work as "production," did not give much priority to the project. As stated by Blades (1975), "the production boundary should encompass non-monetary activities *which are likely to be replaced by monetary activities as an economy becomes more specialized.*" But he concluded that "Because of the practical difficulties of measurement *the case for including housewives' general services is considerably weaker*" (emphasis mine).

As mentioned earlier, with few exceptions such as Margaret Reid's, this exclusion of domestic work from labor force statistics was not much questioned until the late 1970s. Boserup argued strongly for the inclusion in national accounts "of food items obtained by collecting and hunting, of output of home crafts such as clothing, footwear, sleeping and sitting mats, baskets, clay pots, calabashes, fuel collected by women, funeral services, hair cuts, entertainment, and traditional administrative and medical services," together with "pounding, husking and grinding of foodstuffs and the slaughtering of animals" (pp. 162–63). However, she saw these activities as subsistence production—"marketable goods," not as domestic work. Although Boserup mentioned the omission of "domestic services of housewives" from national accounts, she was less vociferous about it than in the case of subsistence production. Yet, she did emphasize the need to include production for own consumption, which she pointed out was larger in the economically less-developed and agricultural countries than in the more industrialized ones.

To some degree, a reversal in the historical trend for domestic work to shift from the household to the market as countries develop has been observed. As labor costs have increased in the high-income countries, self-help activities such as home construction, carpentry, and repairs, often performed by men, have also increased significantly. This has been added to the bulk of unpaid work at the household level, a trend reinforced by the decreasing tendency in the hiring of domestic workers as countries develop (Langfeldt 1987; Chadeau 1989; UNDP 1995).[5] In the United States, for example, some authors have estimated that the time allocated to unpaid work by men and women converged between the 1960s and 1980s (Bittman and Pixley 1997). The same tendency has been observed in other industrialized countries.[6] However, this convergence thesis ignores the extent to which multiple tasks are performed simultaneously. As Floro (1995) has argued, there is growing evidence that the performance of overlapping activities over prolonged periods especially by women is not an isolated phenomenon. Her conclusion is that, as women's participation in market work has increased, work intensification resulting from overlapping activities requires a revision of the convergence thesis.

To sum, production tends to shift out of the household at some stages in the development process while at least part of it might return at later stages, regardless of whether it is performed by women or men. If household production is not accounted for, growth rates are likely to be overestimated when this production shifts to the market; on the contrary, they are likely to be underestimated when paid activities are taken up by (unpaid) household members. Given the predominant division of labor and women's role in the domestic sphere, the exclusion affects mostly—but not exclusively—women's work. This takes into consideration the fact that some tasks are often carried out simultaneously—such as when a housewife is cooking, doing the wash, and caring for the children at the same time.

*Volunteer Work*

Like in the case of domestic work, the wide range of tasks in the volunteer sector creates both conceptual and methodological problems for measurement because it is not directly linked to the market. Conceptually, volunteer work refers to work whose beneficiaries must not be members of the immediate family. In addition, there cannot be any direct payment—it's unpaid work by definition, and the work must be part of an organized program. That is, volunteer work is clearly different from domestic work even though there are close connections between the two—as when volunteer work takes place in one's neighborhood or community—which can make the boundaries difficult to draw in some cases. In addition, while some volunteer tasks can easily be defined as production, such as in the case of job training and home-building organizations, others are more difficult to classify, such as some of the activities associated with charitable or church-related work. Yet even in the later case, some accounting of these tasks seems important if they provide free substitutes for what otherwise would be paid market work. To illustrate, in the United States, reliable data on volunteer work has existed since 1987. Estimates for 1995 indicate that 93 million Americans volunteered an average of 4.2 hours per week per person, with a total of 15.7 billion hours of formal volunteering and 4.6 billion hours of informal volunteering.[7] The 15.7 billion hours of formal volunteer time were estimated to represent the equivalent of 9.2 million full-time, private-sector employees. At a wage of $12.84 (the average hourly wage of a nonagricultural worker in 1995), the monetary equivalent for volunteer work is $201.5 billion. This work is often of a professional nature, as in the case of the relatively high number of volunteers in the health sector (Gora and Nemerowicz 1991).

Many factors influence the extent to which people engage in volunteer work—gender being one them since gender asymmetries in this type of work are abundant. Thus, in the U.S., women are more likely than men to engage in volunteer activities, particularly women who are married and relatively well educated with children under eighteen.[8] These gendered disparities have many dimensions. For example, in 1984 New Zealand women mobilized around the notion that, while monetary contributions (often male) to charity are tax-deductible, time contributions (often female) are not. The result of this mobilization was the inclusion of a question about time dedicated to volunteer work in the 1986 Census of Population, a pioneer effort to New Zealand's credit (Waring 1988).

Similarly, volunteer work varies according to social characteristics. In the United States, a survey conducted in 1996 showed that volunteering correlated with income: the highest proportion (62 percent) of volunteering was among people with income above $75,000 and the lowest among those with income below $20,000 (AARP 1997). However, these differences might be misleading since much remains to be done to document volunteer work worldwide. Among the poor, volunteering can represent very significant individual and collective actions in times of crises. A well-known example was provided by the collective soup kitchens in the Andean countries during the 1980s and 1990s. Organized and run mostly by women, soup kitchens functioned as survival strategies to deal with the drastic deterioration of living standards that resulted from structural adjustment policies and increasing urban poverty. It has been estimated that in Lima, Peru, 40,000 low-income women formally organized a federation of self-managed communal kitchens, located in 2,000 sites in Lima's poor neighborhoods, and pooled their resources to feed about 200,000 people as often as five times a week (Barrig 1996; Lind 1997). Managing such an impressive endeavor requires a wide range of skills—from contacting food providers to handling money and dealing with charitable institutions and other funding sources—some of which were acquired by women as they engaged in survival work for their families and neighbors.

Collective food kitchens, in fact, raise questions about the conventional definition of volunteer work, since the beneficiaries often include both the immediate family *and* the community/neighborhood. Hence, these workers perform both domestic and volunteer work. Food kitchen volunteering also raises questions about the extent to which participation in volunteer work results from choice or lack of it; participation springs from the urgent needs of survival and from the inability of individual households to meet their needs on their own. Collective soup kitchens are clearly not exclusive to the Andean region. They take different forms and can also be found in high-income countries. For example, in the United States, soup kitchens that serve the poor, unemployed, and homeless are often run by women,[9] again pointing to the importance of documenting and analyzing the significance of this type of unpaid work.

To sum, the project of accounting for women's work was twofold from its beginning. First, it required the refinement of categories and improvement of data collection in the areas of paid work that were, in theory at least, included in conventional statistics. Second, it resulted from the need to rethink and redefine the concept of work and to develop ways to measure unpaid activities involving mostly domestic and volunteer work. In what follows, I will concentrate largely on domestic work.

## The Contributions of Two Decades

Although questions and objections about the extent to which unpaid work should be measured still remain, much progress on the practical issues involved has been made since the 1980s. This progress has proceeded mainly on three fronts: conceptual, theoretical, and methodological. On the *conceptual* front and as a result of the initial Nairobi conference recommendation, the International Research and Training Institute for the Advancement of Women (INSTRAW) and the Statistical Office of the UN Secretariat took the lead to review and promote the revision of national accounts and other statistical information on women's work, with several meetings held for this purpose since 1986. A significant consensus has been built on the need to measure unpaid domestic work on the basis that it makes an important contribution to welfare. Most recommendations have opted for the development of separate or supplementary accounts that would permit the generation of "augmented" estimates of GNP (UN Office of Vienna 1989).

The purpose of such "satellite accounts" is to measure unpaid production of goods and services by households and to provide indicators of their contribution to welfare. This can be done by using time as a form of measurement—as done in time-use surveys—or by imputing a monetary value to time inputs or to the goods and services produced. Given the numerous and varied tasks being performed in the home, the question of which tasks to include or exclude has been an important focus of the discussion. The most accepted operational criterion is still Margaret Reid's *third-person principle,* according to which domestic production should refer to unpaid activities that can also be performed by a third person in a paid form. While tasks such as shopping, cleaning, food preparation, and child care are included under this criterion, watching television and getting dressed are not. This still leaves some ambiguities (the very rich or the ill might have a paid person to help them dress) but as a whole it represents an important step in setting a standard of definition that can allow, for example, comparisons between countries.

The third-party principle has been criticized for assuming the market as the model of economic activity and therefore precluding "the existence of economic activity unique to the household, since anything that does not, or does not yet, have a commodity equivalent cannot be considered economic" (Wood 1997: 50). However, although the principle does assume market production as the point of reference, it does not follow that a domestic activity without a market equivalent cannot be included; it can, as long as a third person can perform it. Wood goes further in criticizing the principle for its exclusion of personal activities such as "emotional care-taking, sex and childbirth from definitions of economic activity" (Wood 1997: 52). This argument, however, takes up the discussion of what should be considered as "work" to a level of ambiguity that makes it difficult to define. In any case, what needs to be emphasize here is that, overall, a significant shift has taken place in the conceptualization of economic activity toward the inclusion of tasks that contribute to social reproduction and the maintenance of the labor force and which are not directly connected with the market.

At the *theoretical* front, significant changes preceded or were parallel to the conceptual and practical work of the last two decades, particularly in terms of a greater understanding of the nature of domestic production. Since the 1950s and even more so since the 1960s, economic analysis focused increasingly on the household—within the framework of different theoretical paradigms and with different objectives. As pointed out in chapter 2, the neoclassical literature, particularly the New Household Economics, analyzed household production as a way to understand the gender division of labor and the participation of men and women in the paid labor force. Feminist versions of this analysis have pointed out some of its shortcomings and have placed greater emphasis on the social construction of gender roles and the extent to which it results in gender discrimination (Blau and Ferber 1986). On the other hand, within the Marxian paradigm, the domestic labor debate of the 1970s emphasized the importance of domestic work for the daily maintenance and reproduction of the labor force. The emphasis was on understanding the nature of domestic work, its links to the market, and the economic and social power relations established between paid and unpaid domestic work and between men and women (Gardiner 1985; Molyneux 1979; Deere 1990). As mentioned earlier, questions about the application of the notion of exploitation to domestic work were also raised (Folbre 1982).

From a feminist perspective, neither of these two approaches placed enough attention to gender and power relations within the household. However, they were useful to enhance our understanding of the economic significance of domestic work and the need to develop methods to evaluate its contribution to production and welfare. In addition, the more strictly feminist analyses further contributed to elaborate the theoretical dimensions of domestic work as well as its political implications (Hartmann 1976a; Folbre 1994; Bergmann 1995).[10]

A different debate has centered around one of the main obstacles to measuring household production and volunteer work, namely, the difficulty of comparing them with market production: can this comparison be made given that they take place under very different conditions and norms of behavior? In particular, domestic work is not subject to the competitive pressures of the market and therefore productivity levels might be very different in the two sectors. Likewise, the quality of outputs can differ substantially, according to whether these are performed at home or in the market, such as in the case of childcare, meals, nurturing services, and many other activities. Similar arguments can be applied to volunteer work. Could we then be comparing apples and oranges? We will return to this issue below in more detail, but we should keep in mind that *there are several purposes to the project of measuring and documenting unpaid work.*

First, an important objective has been to make household work more visible and socially appreciated. Second, it facilitates the establishment of indicators to evaluate its contribution to social well-being and the reproduction of human resources, and it provides the basis for revising GNP and labor force statistics. Third, its measurement is crucial to analyzing the extent to which total work (paid and unpaid) is shared equally at the household and society level. Fourth, both at the micro and macro levels, measurement can provide information on how time is allocated between work (paid/unpaid) and leisure. Fifth, it is a crucial input for the project of "engendering budgets" in order to make explicit that they are not neutral tools of resource allocation (Bakker and Elson 1998). Sixth, measurement of unpaid domestic work has other practical uses such as in litigation and in estimating monetary compensation in divorce cases (Cassels 1993; Collins 1993). Seventh, even if productivity levels are not comparable, time-use indicators can be used to analyze tendencies and trends in the share of paid/unpaid work overtime. Finally, this information can help governments and other entities to design policy and action more effectively.

At the *methodological* level, substantial progress has been made on two fronts. One is the revisions of data-gathering methods to capture with greater accuracy the contributions to GNP made by the various types of unpaid work. The other is the progress in dealing with the complex task of designing different methods to measure its value. Here, I will refer mostly to domestic work, differentiating between input and output-related methods and showing the difficulties and advantages of each. Time budget studies and surveys carried out in many countries have provided the empirical base for such a task, often with large samples. In addition, empirical studies have been useful in analyzing the actual content and complexities of domestic work and household dynamics. Two main approaches to measuring the value of domestic work have been introduced: one based on the imputation of value to labor time (i.e., an *input-related method*) and another based on the imputation of market prices to goods and services produced in the domestic sphere (i.e., an *output-related method*).

For each approach, different estimation methods have been used. For the input-related method, a key problem is which value to impute to labor time. Three main methods have been identified:[11]

- The *global substitute* method uses the cost of a hired domestic worker, assumed to be paid to carry out all types of household tasks.

- The *specialized substitute* method uses the average wage of a specialist with skills for each specific household task.

- The *opportunity cost* method is based on the wage that the person performing domestic work could receive in the market.[12]

Each method has some advantages and disadvantages. The global substitute method tends to yield very low estimates given that domestic workers are at the lower end of the wage hierarchy. Also, a domestic worker is not likely to perform all of the work of the household. Therefore, unless the full contribution of all household members is estimated and added up, this approach will further reinforce the tendency toward low estimates. On the contrary, the specialized substitute method tends to generate high estimates, even though it is more indicative of the market value of household production. One practical problem associated with this method is the need to desegregate each task, with the corresponding problems, mentioned earlier, of comparing unpaid and paid work.

The opportunity cost method yields the widest range of estimates, depending on the skills and opportunity wage of the individual involved. This can result in rather absurd estimates since, for example, a meal produced by a doctor will be imputed a higher value than an identical meal prepared by an unskilled worker, even if the latter is a better cook. Another problem in this case has been pointed out repeatedly: the tautology suggested by the fact that, if the cook is a full-time housewife, her opportunity costs (i.e., the income she would get in the paid labor force) are, in turn, correlated to her condition as a full-time housewife. To quote Ferber and Birbaum (1980), "a person who has been out of the labor market, especially when it has been a long time, will not have reliable information about how much s/he could earn . . ." (p. 389).

As for output-related estimates, they require methods of imputing value to domestic production and deducting the cost of inputs from it. The problem again is to determine which market goods and services are equivalent to those produced at home, and what price to impute to inputs such as labor and raw materials not purchased in the market (for example, wood gathered by family members or home-made utensils). A different problem, again, is the disparities in the quality of goods and services produced, which in the case of nonmarket work can not be captured by an imputed price. At the empirical level, it is a tedious method requiring time-budgets data, hourly wages, and a relatively high number of input and output prices. While a proportion of such data can be obtained from existing censuses, most have to be generated through surveys. This is precisely the type of information that satellite accounts could provide periodically. How often they should be elaborated depends on available resources and projected needs. They could be obtained every few years instead of annually.

Input vs. output methods raise other issues with respect to their usefulness. For example, if the time needed to fetch water increases, input-related accounting will show an increase in time input while there is no increase in output. This suggests that, in terms of welfare, an output-related method is superior since it shows more accurately changes in welfare. Yet, from the perspective of documenting the time needed for domestic work, the input-related method is more explicit. In addition, the institutional and social dimensions of time complicate this issue. As Floro (1997) has argued, the notion of time and its uses is different across countries and cultures, and, in some cases, activities that Westerners might see as recreational—such as traditional festivities and gift exchange—can, in fact, represent unpaid work in other societies.

Although real, these difficulties are not insurmountable. The practical progress made so far and the guidelines provided by international organizations have laid a foundation from which to proceed. At the practical level, the efforts to measure unpaid work have been on the increase. Although they can be costly, in the last resort it is a question of priorities and political will. Table 5.1 presents an illustration of some of the attempts carried out at the country-level during the past two decades. It shows that the large majority of measurements are based on time-use data although input-output methods have been used in some countries. As can be observed, the proportion of childcare time provided by women across the countries included in the table ranges from 64 percent (Denmark) to 88 percent (Japan).

At the international level, special mention should be made of the pioneer effort that UNDP undertook in preparing its annual *Human Development Report* in view of the 1995 UN Conference in Beijing. The report included estimates of the share of paid and unpaid work across a variety of countries. Based on time-use data for different years, it showed that, for both developing and industrial countries, on average women work more hours than men—their work representing 53 percent of total time in developing countries and 51 percent in industrial countries. In both groups of countries, only 34 percent of women's work was included in national income accounts; the corresponding figure for men was 76 percent for developing countries and 66 percent for industrial countries.

However, as tables 5.2 and 5.3 illustrate, country data vary widely and the rural-urban differences within countries are significant. Among selected developing countries, the urban difference between women's work burden and that of men's (table 5.2) ranges from 3 percent (Kenya) to 12 percent (Colombia); in the rural context, the range is between 10 percent (Bangladesh) and 35 percent (Kenya). Among selected industrial countries, table 5.3 shows that the corresponding figures for the country as a whole range between −2.0 percent (Denmark) and 21.1 percent (Italy). Although a good proportion of the data used for the report relied on the "third-person criterion" for its estimates, these figures were based on studies that varied in data collection methods—raising methodological questions about comparability.[13] Recognizing this problem, the report points out that, in the absence of better data, these estimates provide "a valuable glimpse of the general pattern of time use by women and men" across countries.

**Table 5.1**  Measuring Unpaid Work

| COUNTRY | SCOPE OF MEASUREMENT (AND AGENCY RESPONSIBLE) | YEARS SURVEY UNDERTAKEN | MEASUREMENT METHODS USED | SOME HIGHLIGHTS AND PERCENTAGE OF CHILD CARE TIME PROVIDED BY WOMEN[a] |
|---|---|---|---|---|
| Australia | National (every 5 years) (Australian Bureau of Statistics) | 1987 (pilot), 1992, 1997 | time-use | 78% |
| Austria | National (Vienna, Austrian Central Statistical Office) | 1981, 1992 | time-use | 76% |
| Bangladesh | National | 1989, 1992 | time-use | Average hours per week of housework: Women = 31, Men = 5[a] |
| Bulgaria | Multinational Comparative (Bulgarian Academy of Science—1965) National (Sofia, Central Statistical Office—1988) | 1965, 1988 | time-use | 81% |
| Canada | National (Ottawa, Statistics Canada) | 1961, 1971, 1981, 1986, 1992 | –time-use –input/output also for 1981, 1986[c] | 71% |
| Denmark | National (Copenhagen, Danish National Institute of Social Research) | 1987 | time-use | 64% |
| European Union | EUROSTAT (European Union, Statistical Office) | 1996 (pilot), 1997 | time-use | A harmonized time use survey for countries in the EU is proposed for 1997 with the pilot in 1996[b] |

| Country | Source | Year(s) | Type | Percentage |
|---|---|---|---|---|
| Finland | National (Helsinki, Central Statistical Office of Finland) | 1979, 1987, 1990 | –time-use –input/output also for 1990[c] | 75% |
| Former USSR | Multinational Comparative (1965—Academy of Sciences of the USSR) Join US-USSR Project (1985—Russian Academy of Sciences) | 1965, 1986 | time-use | 75% |
| Germany, Federal Republic | National (Germany, Staticher Bundesamt) | 1965, 1991, 1992 | time-use | 71% |
| Hungary | National Way of Life Survey (Budapest, Central Statistics Office) | 1976, 1986 | time-use | 64% |
| India | National | 1989, 1992 | time-use | Average hours per week of housework: Women=34, Men=10[a] |
| Israel | National Time-Budget Survey (Israel, Central Bureau of Statistics) | 1991, 1992 | time-use | 75% |
| Italy | National (Rome, National Statistical Institute of Italy) | 1988, 1989 | time-use | 75% |
| Japan | National (5 yearly) (Tokyo, Bureau of Statistics) | 1976, 1981, 1986, 1991 | time-use | –88% –Women work 9 times the amount of unpaid times as men do[a] |
| Korea, Republic of | National (Seoul, Korean Broadcasting System) | 1987, 1990 | time-use | 80% |
| Latvia | National (Riga, Institute of Economics) | 1972, 1987 | time-use | 69% |
| Lithuania | National (Helsinki, Central Statistical Office of Finland) | 1974, 1988 | time-use | 75% |

**Table 5.1** Measuring Unpaid Work (*continued*)

| COUNTRY | SCOPE OF MEASUREMENT (AND AGENCY RESPONSIBLE) | YEARS SURVEY UNDERTAKEN | MEASUREMENT METHODS USED | SOME HIGHLIGHTS AND PERCENTAGE OF CHILD CARE TIME PROVIDED BY WOMEN[a] |
|---|---|---|---|---|
| Nepal | National | 1989, 1992 | time-use | Average hours per week of housework: Women = 42, Men = 15[a] |
| Norway | National (Oslo, Norweigian Central Bureau of Statistics) | 1980, 1981, 1990 | time-use | 71% |
| Poland | Time Budget Survey of Working People (Warsaw, Cent. Stat. Office) | 1984 | time-use | 69% |
| Spain | –National (Madrid, Instituto de Economia y Geografia) –Catalonia, Institute Catalá de la Dona | 1991 2001 | time-use time-use | 86% % increase in GNP contributed by domestic production 66%[d] |
| Sweden | National (Stockholm, Statistics Sweden) | 1990, 1991 | time-use | 72% |
| United Kingdom | Daily Life Survey | 1984 | time-use | 76% |
| United States | National (Univ. of Michigan—1996) (Univ. of Maryland—1986) | 1965, 1986 | time-use | 72% |

*Sources:* [a] United Nations: The World's Women 1995: Trends and Statistics; [b] Luisella Goldschmidt-Clermont and Elisabetta Pagnossin-Aligisakis (1995), "Measures of Unrecorded Economic Activities in Fourteen Countries," Human Development Report Occasional Papers; [c] Duncan Ironmonger, "Counting outputs, capital inputs and caring labor: estimating gross household product"; [d] Comajuncosa et al. (2001).

**Table 5.2**  Burden of Work by Gender, Selected Developing Countries

| COUNTRY | YEAR | WORK TIME (MINUTES A DAY) | | | WOMEN'S WORK BURDEN COMPARED WITH MEN'S (% DIFFERENCE) |
|---|---|---|---|---|---|
| | | AVERAGE | WOMEN | MEN | |
| *Urban* | | | | | |
| Colombia | 1983 | 378 | 399 | 356 | 12 |
| Indonesia | 1992 | 382 | 398 | 366 | 9 |
| Kenya | 1986 | 581 | 590 | 572 | 3 |
| Nepal | 1978 | 567 | 579 | 554 | 5 |
| Venezuela | 1983 | 428 | 440 | 416 | 6 |
| Average | | 471 | 481 | 453 | 6 |
| Percentage share | | | 51 | 49 | |
| *Rural* | | | | | |
| Bangladesh | 1990 | 521 | 545 | 496 | 10 |
| Guatemala | 1977 | 629 | 678 | 579 | 17 |
| Kenya | 1988 | 588 | 676 | 500 | 35 |
| Nepal: | 1978 | 594 | 641 | 547 | 17 |
| –Highlands | 1978 | 639 | 692 | 586 | 18 |
| –Mountains | 1978 | 592 | 649 | 534 | 22 |
| –Rural hills | 1978 | 552 | 583 | 520 | 12 |
| Philippines | 1975–77 | 499 | 546 | 452 | 21 |
| Average | | 566 | 617 | 515 | 20 |
| Percentage share | | | 55 | 45 | |
| *National* | | | | | |
| Korea, Republic of | 1990 | 479 | 488 | 480 | 2 |
| Average for sample countries | | 514 | 544 | 483 | 13 |
| Percentage share | | | 53 | 47 | |

*Source:* UNDP, *Human Development Report*, 1995, Table 4.1.

Indeed, although these are rough estimates, they provide an indication upon which it is possible to construct more accurate measures.

Overall, these figures illustrate several basic facts. First, unpaid domestic work is important in relation to total work time. Second, women bear a larger burden of total work time. Third, a disproportionate amount of women's work is not included in national income accounts. There is much, however, that these figures cannot capture, given that they are based on averages. For example, working time for men and women vary across social class. Likewise, there are areas of activity, such as shopping and driving the children to

**Table 5.3**  Burden of Work by Gender, Selected Industrial Countries

| COUNTRY | YEAR | WORK TIME (MINUTES A DAY) | | | WOMEN'S WORK BURDEN COMPARED WITH MEN'S (% DIFFERENCE) |
|---|---|---|---|---|---|
| | | AVERAGE | WOMEN | MEN | |
| Australia | 1992 | 443 | 443 | 443 | 0 |
| Austria | 1992 | 416 | 438 | 393 | 11.5 |
| Canada | 1992 | 430 | 429 | 430 | −0.2 |
| Denmark | 1987 | 454 | 449 | 458 | −2 |
| Finland | 1987/88 | 420 | 430 | 410 | 4.9 |
| France | 1985/86 | 409 | 429 | 388 | 10.6 |
| Germany | 1991/92 | 441 | 440 | 441 | −0.2 |
| Israel | 1991/92 | 376 | 375 | 377 | −0.5 |
| Italy | 1988/89 | 419 | 470 | 367 | 28.1 |
| Netherlands | 1987 | 361 | 377 | 345 | 9.3 |
| Norway | 1990/91 | 429 | 445 | 412 | 8 |
| United Kingdom | 1985 | 412 | 413 | 411 | 0.5 |
| USA | 1985 | 441 | 453 | 428 | 5.8 |
| Average for sample countries | | 419 | 430 | 408 | 5.8 |
| Percentage share | | | 51 | 49 | |

Source: UNDP, *Human Development Report*, 1995, Table 4.3.

school—consumption and reproduction tasks—that could be considered "work" but conventionally are not. We will return to these issues below.

## The Emergence of New Issues

The accounting project continues to be important as current labor market trends have raised new questions about the links between paid and unpaid work and about their distribution and boundaries. We are witnessing a significant transition in the ways this distribution is affecting individuals, households, and communities across countries. Several developments are contributing to these trends.

First, the increasing participation of women in the paid labor force has reinforced the importance of how paid and unpaid work are shared among family members. Together with changing constructions of gender roles and of women's positioning in society, it is likely to decrease women's tolerance for gender inequality in the distribution of working time and to increase their autonomy and bargaining power. Hence the "crisis of care" already being felt in many countries is intensified by the fact that, as Mary Daly (2001) has argued, "care work tends to be squeezed to the margins of many people's lives" (p. 6). Estimates of the extent and requirements of unpaid work will be necessary whether the solution to the crisis of care is worked out through the market, the provision of public services, or through more equal sharing of those activities between men and women.

Second, in high-income countries those who are unemployed and marginalized from mainstream economic life have to negotiate survival strategies involving a shifting reliance on unpaid work, including forms of labor exchange that are not captured in conventional statistics.[14] The same can be said for developing countries undergoing structural adjustment or the consequences of financial policies leading to the intensification of unpaid work in the household and in communities; as argued in previous chapters, they tend to increase the number of activities that are not included in conventional statistics.

Third, high incidence of underemployment and of part-time work results in cyclical or fluid combinations of paid and unpaid activities related to changes in the economy and affecting women and men in different ways. As will be argued below, measuring the extent of these changes is important in assessing variations in living standards and contributions to social well-being. Similarly, discussions about the thirty-five-hour week that have taken place, particularly in Western Europe, have many gender implications regarding the distribution of paid/unpaid work. These discussions are carried out under the assumption that a reduction in working time will be helpful in dealing with unemployment. But as Figart and Mutari (1998) have argued, the underlying assumption is that "full time, year-round employment is a social norm constructed around gendered assumptions," such as that "a full-time worker, presumably male, faces limited demands from unpaid work and family life" (p. 2). A different assumption, they argue, is that the concentration of women in part-time work will continue, regardless of their choice. This suggests that statistics documenting who performs unpaid work can be useful to understanding the distribution of working time. In the same way, households with multiple earners need to address this question if they are concerned about gender equality and about the fair distribution of caring work among household members.

Finally, given that unpaid work represents roughly 25 percent to 50 percent of economic activity, depending on the country and methods of estimation, its exclusion from national accounts is difficult to justify. In terms of domestic work, there is some evidence showing that unpaid labor is increasing more rapidly than market production. Australian data, for example, indicate that between 1974 and 1992 household work grew at a

rate of 2.4 percent per year, while the corresponding rate for market production was 1.2 percent (Ironmonger 1996). The increase in domestic work
can be attributed to a variety of reasons: rapid rise in the number of small
size households—resulting in a loss in economies of scale—to the aging of
the population and the changing preferences of more affluent societies.
Ironmonger notes that this increase in unpaid labor has happened despite
raising women's labor force participation rates and despite the diffusion of
new household technologies that are labor-saving.

All of these factors explain why there has been an increasing awareness
of the extent to which paid and unpaid work are unequally distributed
among men and women. The quote from the *Human Development Report*
that heads this chapter underlines this point clearly. Likewise, the 1996
report of the Independent Commission on Population and the Duality of
Life, *Caring for the Future*, includes a call for the redefinition of work and
for equality in the distribution of its output:

> The Commission proposes . . . to redefine work in a broad sense that
> encompasses both employment and unpaid activities benefiting
> society as a whole, families as well as individuals, and ensuring an
> equitable distribution of the wealth generated. (p. 147)

To sum, the project of redefining and measuring unpaid work has gained
much support in recent decades. However, and as expected given that we are
dealing with a complex issue, there is also opposition to it. The following
section discusses the various arguments casting doubts on the project.

## The Continuing Debate

At least three types of objections to the accounting for unpaid work project
have emerged. Two of them actually derive from feminist circles, while the
third springs out from the core of orthodox economics.

### Useless Effort

We may call this objection "the waste-of-time argument." It results from the
fear that the effort and use of resources necessary to generate statistics on
unpaid work will not make any difference to those engaged in it, particularly women. To what extent, for example, can the information be used to
decrease the burden of poor women who toil many hours a day or to
empower the urban housewife with no income of her own? Could it be
used to increase their bargaining power at some level? Can it *really* make a
difference to those individuals engaged in unpaid activities? On the contrary, this argument goes, greater social recognition of the importance of
domestic work might, in fact, reinforce a division of labor that relegates

women to activities providing no financial autonomy and little control over the resources they need. This would therefore not contribute to gender equality; it would instead perpetuate women's dependency on men.

I call this type of argument "the post-Nairobi blues," reflecting the doubts some of us felt after the 1985 UN Conference on Women, which took place in Nairobi, Kenya. For the first time, the official report of the conference, *Forward-Looking Strategies for the Advancement of Women*, strongly recommended appropriate efforts to measure the contribution of women's paid and unpaid work "to all aspects and sectors of development." The report significantly moved the action forward and, in doing so, it also raised questions and doubts about whether setting this agenda would make any difference to women.

A similar version of this argument has been offered by Barbara Bergmann who, although not objecting to the effort itself, thinks too much energy is spent on it. Feminists, she argues, should emphasize the need for women to engage in paid work in order to reduce their dependency on men and increase their bargaining power in and outside of the home. Thus, she believes that feminists should first place their efforts on the design and implementation of policies that facilitate the incorporation of women into the paid labor force, such as child care provision and maternity leave. Likewise, they should work on policy and action leading to the enforcement of gender equality in the labor market such as pay equity, affirmative action, and comparable worth. Bergmann is skeptical about the possibility that better information on unpaid work "can help a single woman," in the same way that "the inclusion in the GNP of food produced in the subsistence sector does not make any difference to farmers."[15] She also fears that statistics on housework are likely to be used by those who want "to glorify the housewife," as in the case of some right-wing groups in the United States, which "can argue that housework is irreplaceable because it performs crucial services to society." Hence, she concludes that "there is an anti-feminist implication in valorizing housework."

This type of objection ignores the fact that action, policy design, and implementation of projects affecting those engaged in unpaid work requires as much systematic information as possible in order to make optimal estimates. We should remember the problems created by lack of information. In the words of Indian feminist Devaki Jain, "One of the greatest difficulties in assisting women has been the absence of any reliable data regarding their number, problems and achievements" (Jain 1975). This applies not only to obvious problems requiring urgent solutions such as violence against women or wage discrimination; the weight and distribution of unpaid work can be important in many ways. For example, high estimates of time spent in fetching water by women in any country might prevent authorities from giving low priority to the installation of running water on the grounds that fetching water does not take much of women's time. Likewise, time-use information about time spent on traveling with children can be an important input for transportation policies.

To elaborate with another example, it is important to know the extent to which an economic slowdown that increases unemployment and reduces household income results in unpaid labor picking up the slack, for example through the intensification of domestic work or subsistence production. We do know that the financial crises and adjustment policies of the past two decades led to coping strategies that required the intensification of unpaid work, with a disproportionate burden for women. In such cases, a decrease in real income may or may not result in a corresponding decline in family welfare—depending on the extent to which unpaid work makes up for the reduced income. An evaluation of these shifts cannot be done without systematic statistical information on unpaid work. As Floro (1996) has argued, a more precise information on people's daily activities helps us to assess the quality of their lives more accurately and develop indicators of work intensity, performance of multiple tasks, stress, individual health, and even of child neglect. This is because varied dimensions of work—such as work intensity and the length of the working day—have been shown to be related to stress and health of workers and their families (Floro 1996).

Thus, the accounting project must be viewed, on the one hand, not as an end in itself but as a means to understand who contributes to human welfare and human development—and to what extent. The symbolic value of estimations of unpaid work should not be underestimated. As a male economist who participated in the first attempt to calculate the value of domestic activities in Catalonia, Spain, stated in his presentation of the report, it was not so much the specific figures arrived at but what he had learned about the significance of this work that changed his views about it (Comajuncosa et al. 2001). On the other hand, these estimates can provide information for the design of policies to distribute the pains and pleasures of *work* in a more egalitarian fashion. The fear that some political groups might use the information for their own purpose must be weighted with the fact that it can also be used for a variety of positive outcomes, including the more accurate design of social policies as in the case of social security payments, pensions, and other forms of social insurance.

### The Importance of "Difference"

A second objection, concerning mostly domestic and unpaid caring work, is perhaps more difficult to deal with since it springs from the notion that this type of activity includes personal and relational aspects that make it qualitatively very different from market work. Sue Himmelweit

(1995) has argued that, although recognizing unpaid labor as "work" is an important way to make it visible and to validate women's contributions in the home, something is lost in the process. She questions "whether the best way for women's contribution to be appreciated [is] to force it into a pre-existing category of 'work,' borrowed from an economics which inherently failed to value most of what made women's domestic contribution distinctive" (p. 2).

As an example, Himmelweit argues that "caring" is an ambiguous notion that can stretch from physical to emotional care; while the first "might to some extent be independent of the relation between the career and the person cared for," the second requires that "the person doing the caring is inseparable from the care given" (p. 8). She points out a second characteristic of caring work—namely, its self-fulfilling quality. Hence, Himmelweit is reluctant to view as conventional "work" the time spent on activities that provide emotional care and support, which, in addition, are also very difficult to quantify.

Himmelweit concludes that not everything needs to be seen as "work" or "nonwork," particularly since this may lead to the social undervaluation of activities that do not fit into the first category:

> By insisting that domestic activities gain recognition by conforming to an unchallenged category of work, the significance of caring and self-fulfilling activities remains unrecognized. (p. 14)

This argument, although interesting, seems problematic for different reasons. First, greater visibility and documentation of these unpaid activities is likely to increase the recognition of their significance for human welfare, particularly if their nature is well understood and emphasized. As we have seen, recent history demonstrates that this is exactly what the theoretical, methodological, and practical efforts of the last three decades have accomplished. The shift of a significant proportion of caring work from the unpaid reproductive sphere to the market has not always taken away some of its basic characteristics. For example, work motives associated with solidarity, altruism, and caring can be found in the market as well as in unpaid work. Second, many unpaid activities are not caring and self-fulfilling while some paid activities are. Hence, it is difficult to argue that there is no personal and relational aspects in some of the paid services offered through the market, even though the service is offered in exchange for a monetary reward.

To be sure, some market-oriented caring services are not likely to provide the same quality of care and emotional support that a loving family member can offer—whether or not the caring work might be based on motives such as love and affection, a sense of responsibility, respect, intrinsic enjoyment, altruism, or informal *quid pro quo* expectations. However, it is not difficult to find exceptions to these cases. To illustrate, there can be market-based care providing selfless emotional support beyond the exchange contract. On the other hand, there can be family care based on selfish expectations (an inheritance) or on some form of coercion (as in the topical case of a wife having to take care of her inlaws even when there might not exist much affection between them). As for Himmelweit's argument that something is lost in the process of evaluating unpaid caring work, it needs to be contrasted with the fact that something is also won.

Third, there is a dialectical relationship between market and nonmarket work, in such a way that, to some extent, the skills used in one sphere can be used in the other and vice versa.[16] Thus, a paid nanny or nurse might provide a high quality of personal care with skills learned at home; and managerial skills learned in the labor market might be used as a way to reduce unpaid working time in the household. This means that it is difficult to draw a clearly defined dividing line between the two.

Fourth, in addition to caring labor, unpaid work includes other types of activities that are only indirectly related to caring, such as gathering wood, taking care of domestic animals, cleaning the house, and participating in community activities. These tasks vary by country, cultural factors, and social background of participants. In this sense, Himmelweit's argument has a built-in bias—reflecting the activities of an urban nuclear family rather than those typical of rural settings.

Overall, this is not to dismiss Himmelweit's important arguments. They raise the question of the extent to which the self-less, caring work that is conventionally attributed to domestic labor can be projected on to other activities outside of the household, including market activity, a subject further discussed below.

### Theoretically Misguided

The third type of objection to the project of measuring unpaid work is related to theoretical and methodological questions that spring from more conventional value theory in economics. Despite criticisms emanating from these circles, very few have been expressed in writing.[17] The discussion that follows is based on a paper by economist Sujai Shivakumar (1996), which represents a pioneering effort and in many ways captures many of the unwritten criticisms. In what follows, I will focus exclusively on this paper.

One of Shivakumar's objectives is to show that the *monetary imputation* of unpaid work "is not consistent with present conceptions of the theory of value in economics" and that this imputation is merely a "rhetorical effort" without theoretical foundation or a "dubious game of statistical football" (p. 374). To elaborate this argument, he includes a historical account of the development of value theory in economics leading to three main criticisms. First, he claims that the accounting project is a socialist-feminist effort in terms of its rhetoric, forms of analysis, and policy prescriptions—using gender as the central "tool of analysis," presenting alternative visions of economic processes, and centering economics around the notion of "provisioning of human life." Second, he argues that the project is based on Ricardian-Marxian notions of value based on the labor theory of value instead of the "modern" orthodox value theory based on subjective preferences and expressed through market prices; as such, he views the project as theoretically unacceptable:

> Modern economic theory does not support time-use analysis as a basis for imputing the monetary value of work. . . . The labor theory of value on which this type of analysis is based has roots in Ricardian-Marxian theory of value that is no longer recognized in economics. (p. 333)

In this sense, Shivakumar states that the money value estimates, such as those included in UNDP's 1995 *Human Development Report*, are meaningless because they are based on time-use data.

Third, Shivakumar criticizes the methods used to estimate the value of unpaid work. In doing so, he repeats many of the methodological objections that have previously been recognized and addressed by different authors, including those involved in the project. However, rather than pointing out the ways in which methodologies might be improved, he does not see much redeeming value in the attempt to do so. Thus, comparing the accounting effort with that of the environmentalists who want to take environmental costs into consideration in national accounting statistics, he writes:

> With no theoretical guideline on how to choose among alternative ways of conducting the valuation, the selection among alternative ways of imputation in environmental accounting then comes to reflect on the relative strengths of competing political interests. . . . (p. 405)

Hence, Shivakumar views the value estimates such as those of the 1995 *Human Development Report* as "meaningless." Although the estimates present problems, as mentioned earlier, due to poor or insufficient data, a more constructive approach is to see them as a pioneering but nevertheless important effort in need of improvement. Shivakumar points out the problem of comparability between market and nonmarket time. However, he does not mention the fact that most advocates of including unpaid work in national income accounts recognize this problem (hence, the use of satellite accounts referred to earlier, to avoid the mixing of apples and oranges).

Shivakumar's critique is more fundamentalist in his insistence on the issue that any monetary evaluation "displays an ignorance of the concept of value *as something realized through the exchange process*" (p. 27, emphasis added). That is, he views the exchange process as the only source of value, despite the fact that the value of nonmarket goods in subsistence production has been estimated for many years, and that many economists make use of "shadow prices" in their work. As argued above, this practice has been supported by the notion that subsistence production represents "marketable goods." Yet, a good proportion of domestic work is marketable and, with economic growth, increasing portions of it are taken up by paid work, including, food production, cleaning services, and childcare.

Thus, there is a double standard in Shivakumar's critique since he does not make reference to these facts. Within neoclassical economics, the imputing of market prices to household production is a standard practice. Shivakumar does not make any reference to the fact that, in many ways, the New Household Economics pioneered the application of "modern" human capital theory to household production and decisionmaking and that other economists have also taken seriously the task of analyzing household production (Fraumeni 1998). It would be ironic to categorize the work of human capital theorists like Jacob Mincer, Gary Becker, and many other neoclassical economists as socialist-feminist and based on the labor theory of value.

In associating the effort to measure unpaid work to Ricardo and Marx, Shivakumar ignores the fact that orthodox Marxist theory would agree with his insistence on seeing value as originated only through the exchange process. In addition, it is far from clear that Marxian value theory is based on labor inputs without regard to the weight of demand to determine market value (Itoh and Yokokawa 1979; Elson 1979). Although he is right in affirming that gender as an analytical category and "the provisioning of human life" are central to feminist economics, this is not specific to any branch of feminism. Feminist economists of different persuasions would probably agree with his statement. He also ignores that the actual work toward measuring unpaid labor includes a large number of feminists and professional men and women with diverse theoretical approaches and practical politics.

Beyond these basic points, some of Shivakumar's criticisms are not well informed, as with his statement that feminists "have not spelled out any particular policy prescription other than to seek to better inform policy makers" (p. 394). Feminists *have* called for and suggested gender-aware policies in areas such as labor market policy, public services, structural adjustment packages, and agricultural policy (Sen and Grown 1987; Palmer 1991; Elson 1992 and 1995; UNDP 1995; Deere and León 2001). Many of these policies would benefit from more systematic statistical information and documentation regarding unpaid work. Shivakumar's attribution of self-interest to feminists recommending these changes—claiming that "the called-for increases in female participation in policy-making will differentially advantage those who call for such increases"—is far-fetched and even discriminatory, given that it would be difficult to hear a similar charge made to men suggesting changes in statistics and policy. What one reads in Shivakumar's paper is a strong irritation about the spoiling of a neatly-defined, presumably "objective" economic paradigm by what he sees as the "normative" prescriptions of feminism. Although, to his credit, he does present some recommendations "to satisfy the Beijing mandate," his alternatives fall short of the task to be accomplished and, as he points out, do not solve some of the problems analyzed. In any case, we are thankful for his effort to take this project seriously and to bring it to the heart of economic theory.

## Concluding Comments

The main argument of this chapter takes us back to the eternal question of what is *value* and what is *valuable* to society. Much has been written about this subject and a discussion of it falls outside of the scope of this chapter. Ultimately, we are left with the basic question of how to measure and evaluate human well-being and how to recognize those who contribute to it. The point repeatedly being made is that current GNP statistics include what is bad for our health—such as the production of food with carcinogenic chemicals—or for the environment—such as the output of polluting factories. Yet, there has been resistance to the measuring of work and production of goods and services that sustain and enhance life. In Nancy Folbre's terms, societies and individuals need to know, among other things, "who pays for the kids?" This requires an effort to evaluate time spent and costs involved.

We also want to know, for example, who contributes to the survival strategies of the poor so that we can design gender-aware and social class-aware policies to overcome poverty. Unpaid work is not unevenly distributed across class and social groups. While affluent households can employ (mostly) women for domestic work, they can also purchase goods and services that poorer households produce at home and without outside help. When lower-income women participate in the paid labor market, either their workload increases or the standards in home-produced goods and childcare need to be lowered (Giménez 1990). There is a significant difference in the total number of hours that women from different income levels and social backgrounds dedicate to domestic work. An empirical study carried out in Barcelona, Spain, showed that the absolute value of domestic work was higher for middle-income households, followed by the lower-income and higher-income categories. However, the value of domestic work in lower-income households represented a higher percentage of total household income, which included social income or the value of public services perceived (Carrasco 1992).

There is more to the challenge of measuring unpaid work since it calls for, in Elizabeth Minnich's terms, "transforming knowledge" or moving beyond the boundaries of conventional paradigms. This includes the rethinking of "mystified concepts," or "ideas, notions, categories, and the like that are so deeply familiar they are rarely questioned" and which result in "partial knowledge" (Minnich 1990). The challenge leads us to question the ways in which we measure well-being and to understand who contributes to it in our communities and in society as a whole. Further, it leads us to question the assumptions behind received knowledge—in this case, those that conceptually link "work" to paid labor time and the market.

Finally, we have seen that the discussion about the difference between paid and unpaid work leads to questions about the extent to which economic rationality assumed to inform market-related behavior is the norm and to what extent human behavior is based on other motives and norms most commonly linked to unpaid work, such as love, compassion, altruism, empathy, individual and collective responsibility, and solidarity. This chapter reinforces the arguments in chapter 3 about the need to construct alternative models other than those based on market-oriented motives of rational economic man.

## CHAPTER 6

# Development as if All People Mattered

*Por el agua, por la vida* (for water, for life)[1]

*Another world is possible*

—slogan from the alternative Global Justice movement

Most of this book was written before the tragic events of 9/11/01, which changed the world in a way that reinforces many of the arguments made throughout these pages. In 1987, I coauthored a book whose concluding chapter was titled "Development as if Women Mattered." I could repeat the title for this chapter. However, that would fall short of my objectives. Concerns about women do not exclude concerns about the whole society. Understanding gender divisions implies looking at both men and women from a feminist perspective and with a special emphasis on women's subordination and the pursuit of gender equality. If anything, globalization and increasing world tensions have created an enormous challenge for women to think globally and to search for solutions affecting not only women but humankind. Along these lines, the main general arguments in this book can be summarized as follows.

1. From the perspective of a large majority of people living in low- and even middle-income countries—and for all concerned with global justice—development as we know it has failed to meet expectations. Since the late 1970s, neoliberal policies introduced a shift in development models toward market-oriented, export-led, and more globalized economies. This generated unprecedented economic prosperity for many areas in the North and some sectors in the South, fostered by reorganization of production, global

competition, technological change, and financial accumulation. However, for many developing countries, foreign debt problems and financial crises have forced them to adopt structural adjustment policy packages designed under the umbrella of the Washington Consensus. The social costs generated by these policies include the persistence, and even rise, of poverty in many countries, social tensions, increasing economic and social insecurity, and a general pessimism about the prospects of development. These costs have affected the poor and the middle classes, as well, even though they often have been accompanied by improved macroeconomic indicators. The contrasts between the way different social groups have experienced the effects of these changes, together with the growing North-South disparities and the powerlessness and resentment felt by millions in the South, threaten world stability, while social inequalities have risen beyond any sense of social or global justice.

2. The crisis of development reflects the crisis of orthodox economics as a discipline—described as *autistic* by many to reflect its economistic biases toward market-based solutions without regard to social needs. Human development must be people-centered and it must respond to the needs of all social groups. It must incorporate multiple objectives, not just economic targets, although economic resources are important as a means to reach democratically chosen ends. One of the dilemmas facing the world today has to do with the contradictions between democratic principles, on the one hand, and the increasing concentration of wealth and power, on the other. That is, tensions between political and economic democracy are increasing. Unregulated markets are repeating history—they are fostering greed, corruption, exploitation, and insecurity in the midst of plenty. Mainstream economics does not deal openly with issues pertaining to the realm of political economy. The profession sees its functions mostly as technical and narrowly defined—though de facto it fosters market fundamentalism and economism. A world regulated by material pursuit leads to the neglect of the spirit and to the avoidance of epistemological questions linked to human wellbeing; it also fosters the identification of happiness and security with material accumulation.

3. Feminist economists have contributed to the critique of orthodox economics. They have questioned the androcentric biases in the profession and have introduced gender as a central category of analysis in theoretical and empirical work. In addition, they have engaged with policy and action, raising questions about alternatives and directions for economic and social policy—from anti-

discriminatory measures in the labor market to family policy and welfare reform. In the field of gender and development, they have contributed to a wide range of debates—from the nature of macroeconomics and the gender dimensions of structural adjustment to gender analysis of land reform, trade, and employment policy. Feminist economists also have emphasized that an excessive emphasis on the study of choice has led to the neglect of the study of provisioning, human welfare, and human development. For that purpose, they have pioneered the analysis of the meaning and importance of unpaid work and fostered its measurement. The gradual integration of gender in economics has made an impact on different fronts, including academic and policy circles. Overall, however, it is probably accurate to say that the profession has not paid *much* attention to these efforts, despite the fact that they address core questions in the discipline.

4. Globalization and the feminization of the labor force in most countries have changed the distribution and location of women's and men's work. At the international level, export-led development and global competition have resulted in employers' preference for women workers, especially in labor-intensive manufacturing, where they provide a cheap and flexible work force. Female labor has also been absorbed in the service sector across countries, including the global offices of the insurance, banking, airlines, and other industries. Globalization and the increasing mobility of women have facilitated the employment of migrant women from the South in specific areas of services in high-income countries, such as in care work. We are only beginning to evaluate the impacts of such phenomena on individuals and families, both in the South and the North. All of these changes have had significant impacts on gender roles and gender relations. Professional women have moved into privileged male jobs, contributing to decreasing gender wage gaps in some countries. On the other hand, most women remain at the bottom of labor market hierarchies, hence there is some evidence showing that these trends are generating increasing inequality among women.

5. The expansion of markets and the more intense commercialization of life have resulted from deep economic restructuring across countries. Responding to the pressures of domestic and global competition, cost cutting, and reorganization of production have generated relocation of production and the introduction of high technologies. These processes have benefited capital but also consumers who have gained from lower prices in a variety of products. However, they have also been at the root of downsizing and layoffs,

with an increased proportion of workers experiencing unemployment. Mergers and acquisitions, fed by and contributing to the accumulation of financial resources, have intensified the tendency of corporations to grow and concentrate resources and power. Labor market trends have benefited the professional, well-educated, and often global elites, but this has been accompanied with the loss of income and decreases in real wages for many workers, particularly those at the bottom of the educational and income scale and often including middle income workers. Hence, the resulting tendency toward increased inequalities and social polarization. The race to the bottom in cost-cutting strategies has led to the increasing informalization of jobs and rising economic and social insecurity, often tied to poverty. The new labor contract linked to insecure and precarious employment has had a profound impact on the ways workers approach their labor market strategies. Studies show that these processes have a variety of gender dimensions, symbolized by the loss of male collar jobs in high income countries and the growth of female, low paid jobs in manufacturing and services across countries.

6.  The effects of these changes for women are not easy to evaluate because they are often contradictory and rife with tensions. Paid employment tends to increase women's autonomy and bargaining power, and the market can break up old patriarchal forms. At the same time, during the past decades, an important expansion in education has resulted in higher female/male enrollment ratios is many countries. Wage gender gaps also have decreased in some countries. However, despite these important gains, the majority of women remain at the bottom of the social ladder, burdened by domestic and market responsibilities, and immersed in the daily struggles of poverty. Without much change in the share of domestic work and childcare between men and women, women's responsibilities in the reproductive sphere places them in a disadvantaged position in the labor market. The result is their high degree of participation in part-time, temporary, and precarious jobs and their concentration in highly female sectors such as home-based work. In developing countries, the increasing importance of the informal sector has absorbed a large proportion of women. Finally, and despite the progress made, much remains to be done on the educational front—for example, in terms of eradicating illiteracy, which still remains high among women in many countries.

7.  The greater visibility of women in public life has deeply transformed their ability to engage in active agency at all levels of social

and political life. The mobilization of women during the past few decades represents an unprecedented historical transformation, responding to profound changes in women's (and, to some extent, men's) consciousness and visions of social change. Women's agency has been manifested from the microcosm of the family, the household, and the community to the multiple layers of activity where women have been present. Symbolized by the various international UN conferences on women, from Mexico City in 1975 to Beijing in 1995, these transformations have been global, although with differences and specific characteristics across countries and cultures. This new visibility and activism has reflected the increase in women's participation across many fronts—from research and academic work, to urban and other social movements, to professional organizations, labor unions, indigenous struggles, and global networks. Responding to very different approaches to feminism, perhaps one of the most common underlying tendencies in the process has been not just the questioning of male biases at all levels but the search for solutions from the bottom up. In terms of development work, the progress made has also encountered many obstacles, some of which are underlined in the following section.

### Plus ça change . . . Global Governance and Development

Despite these positive transformations, it is difficult at this turn of century to feel optimistic about current global trends. At the more specific level of development work channeled through international organizations, there are many obstacles on the way toward the type of progressive social change argued for in this book. To illustrate, I will refer to the work that was organized in connection with the UN Conference on Financing for Development, which took place in Monterrey, Mexico, on March 2002. Originally convened in 1997, this global meeting—organized by the UN jointly (for the first time) with the World Bank, the IMF, and the WTO—had been prepared with many expectations about the possibility of adopting new paths for financing development. As in the case of other UN conferences, it included governments and NGOs (about 750 of them), even though the latter had been assigned a small number of seats in the official meetings. More than fifty heads of state attended and at least 200 ministers (of finance, foreign, development cooperation, and other government representatives) were present. This was not unlike other conferences of this kind. I am focusing on Monterrey as a way to illustrate the tensions involved.

The official document that was finalized before the conference, called the "Monterrey Consensus," went through several drafts since the summer of 2001. The initial draft included innovative ideas and initiatives on ways to finance development efforts, particularly for the poorer countries. It included new initiatives referring to the use and disposition of global public goods, the desirability and feasibility of global taxation—such as in the implementation of a currency transaction tax and carbon taxes—and a call for an international tax organization to develop a system of transfers from the richest to the poorest world regions in a coherent and efficient manner. A section with the title "Toward a Fully Inclusive Equitable Organization" called for the adoption of policies that would contribute to "reversing the increasing polarization between the haves and have-nots." The document included one section on global governance and proposed the strengthening of the UN and the General Assembly as "chief policy making." However, most of these proposals were dropped in subsequent drafts, including a section on reforming the international financial institutions. According to participants at the session to discuss the initial draft, the United States was opposed to considering any type of global redistributive measures. Instead, the U.S. position emphasized the importance of fostering markets to help the plight of poor countries and, more specifically, the role of foreign trade. In the face of the U.S. government opposition, the European Union and other high-income countries did not make an effort to keep the initial proposals, and the document was revised accordingly.

As a result of this process, financing for development was left to country offers of foreign aid, a funding model that depends on the political will of donor countries. Judging from the past, foreign aid does not have a shining record, either in terms of quantity provided nor in reaching the roots of development problems. The conference *did* lead to increases in the amounts of foreign aid promised.[2] This, however, fell short of developing more systemic, reliable, and less dependency-inducing ways of distributing the world's resources. Although much fanfare accompanied the announcements of the increases in foreign aid, the fact that they represented a small proportion of military expenditures in many countries was not lost on critical observers. The initial conference expectations had been crushed, and poor countries were left with the continuing powerlessness that has characterized their position during the past two decades and beyond. Symbolically enough, the conference ended with a lavish banquet for its distinguished participants, compliments of Mexico's president Vicente Fox, another illustration of the insensitivity of world leaders to the plight of the poor.

To be sure, more positive interpretations of the conference were made and should be mentioned. Some participants have pointed out that the Monterrey gathering represented a shift toward a more important leadership role on the part of the UN in development finance; as having moved the discussion on global public goods foward; and as having established a participatory process for the different players in international finance—including possible partnerships between the private and public sectors. The Monterrey document stressed the importance of international linkages; it emphasized the need for partnerships among countries and the importance of respecting the rights of developing countries to take their own initiatives regarding good governance and the mobilization of resources. Finally, although the proposals in the document seemed vague, participants pointed out that they could be used for concrete action and for future follow-up planning.

Gender-related issues were incorporated in the agenda particularly through the initiatives and work carried out by UNIFEM and DAW within the UN, and through the involvement of many NGOs. To be sure, official and nonofficial sessions focusing on gender were mostly attended by women and seemed typically marginal. Although some interesting sessions were held, for example, on the subjects of gender, finance, and trade, they represented the typical "add women and stir" approach. At a meeting organized jointly by NGOs and a UN unit, a high-ranking official who arrived at the end of the session spoke in a celebratory mood about the progress made, pointing out that "we are getting this debate turned around—and not just for the guys; we can't do anything without 50 percent of the world's human capital." He was, of course, referring to the world's women, but it was difficult to share his suggestion that that the debate had been turned around. In fact, it was painful to watch that his presence, so well received by the women crowding the room, seemed to be the highlight of the session, thus suggesting that paternalism was alive and well.

Monterrey illustrated the ways in which development agendas continue to be dominated by the interests of international elites and powerful countries. Although we must recognize the many efforts to the contrary, the results do not produce people-centered, much less women-centered, development. That it typifies other such meetings explains the frustrations of many involved in this difficult task.[3] Still trapped in economistic approaches and institutional limitations, these agendas are unable to deal appropriately with the real problems linked to "powerlessness, voicelessness, vulnerability and fear."

Along these lines, I turn to the following eight guidelines, suggested as starting points in an agenda for human development and the design of more concrete paths of action and policy measures:

1. Begin with the general notion of development as a process that is multidimensional and relational, collective rather than individual, leading to shifts in the balance of power toward those who hold very little of it. Development is much more than increases in GDP and the growth of markets; it's about the fulfillment of human

potential, in all its dimensions—for each and everyone. It's about economic as well as political democracy.

2. Link the cultural politics of recognition with the economic and social processes of distribution. In order to do so, we need to question theoretical models of production and distribution—who gets what and why—and to rethink existing channels of distribution and redistribution. These have to do, for instance, with wage and salary formation, profits and financial rewards, taxes and government subsidies, gender gaps in the distribution of resources, access to education, antidiscriminatory laws, welfare policies, pensions, health, and other forms of insurance.

3. Rethink current forms of ownership and control of resources, and press for measures leading toward economic democracy. Progressive social change cannot ignore the questions suggested by Fanny Puntaca, a shopkeeper and grandmother of six from Arequipa, Peru, who participated (for the first time) in a demonstration against the privatization of two state-owned electrical firms to be bought by a Belgian company: "I had to fight. The government was going to sell *our companies* and *enrich another country.*"[4]

4. Design policies that take into consideration the importance of unpaid work for gender equality and social well-being, and find ways to share work and leisure time by men and women on an equal basis. In order to do so, generate statistical information able to accurately reflect how the contributions to human welfare by paid and unpaid work are shared.

5. Design systems of social protection to deal with the negative effects of economic restructuring and globalization. These include unemployment benefits and other forms of compensation for the losses associated with plant relocation and trade liberalization, labor-saving technological change, and downsizing.

6. Take a global approach to the design of effective regulation of markets. In particular, work-related measures such as labor protection and labor standards will not be effective unless they are approached globally so as to avoid the current race to the bottom that results from countries competing through poor environmental and labor standards.

7. Emphasize the importance of education and training to deal with our highly competitive, globalized, and fast-moving world, keep-

ing in mind that equality in education is a necessary but insufficient condition to deal with gender-based and other forms of inequality due to discriminatory practices. Hence, there is a need to press for antidiscriminatory policies on different fronts.

8. Promote all forms of women's agency with the goal of reaching not only gender equality but the "intuitive idea of a life that is worthy of the dignity of the human being . . . for each and every person."

# Notes

## Introduction

1. A selection of the papers presented at the conference was published in Kate Young, Carol Wolkowitz, and Roslyn McCullagh, eds., *Of Marriage and the Market. Women's Subordination in International Perspective* (London: CSE Books, 1981).
2. Other estimates of income and wealth inequalities show variations over the same theme, such as those indicating that 7.2 million people control about one third of the world's wealth (*The Economist*, 6/16/01).
3. To illustrate with a few examples, General Motors' GDP sales surpassed the GDP figure for Malaysia and Norway; Ford Motor and Misui and Co. surpassed that of Saudi Arabia; Misubishi that of Poland, and Itochu that of South Africa (UNDP 1999).
4. *The Financial Times*, 7/2/02.
5. An illustration of this tendency is provided by a special report on "The new wealth of nations" published by *The Economist* (6/16/01). Arguing that the world is getting both wealthier and less equal, the report discusses the "problems associated with being, and particularly with becoming, exceptionally wealthy" (p. 13). The concern is not so much about inequality and what it means for the less privileged members of society; rather, it is about how to generate a better acceptance of social inequalities, including the question of whether the very rich "would get better approval ratings from a public that still generally frowns on wealth" (p. 15). *The Economist*'s solution is an increase in philanthropy among the wealthy. No questions are asked about the economic and institutional channels through which income and wealth are distributed—that is, about the economic and sociopolitical factors determining wages or the "the sociology of wage determination." The report assumes that distribution is meritocratic and just, particularly in high-income countries, with no questions raised about the right of all who work in joint production processes to a fair share of the wealth generated. It also argues that, since the rich have many ways to evade taxes, taxation can not be an important tool for redistribution. To quote from the report:

> Rather than trying to constrain the rich, as they have done for the past century, populists ought to look at the freedoms the rich enjoy and try to make them more generally available. (p. 18)

One does not have to have read much Marx or other critical non-Marxists authors to ponder at the naivete with which the subject is treated in this text, regardless of its consequences for issues beyond distribution. It is difficult to understand how an important publication such as *The Economist* can ignore the basic facts of distribution and trivialize social inequality and the importance of redistribution.

6. Quoted in *The New York Times*, 7/25/01, p. A6.
7. *The Economist*, 8/4/01, p. 43.
8. *The New York Times*, 7/21/01, p. A1.
9. *The Economist*, 8/4/01, p. 43.

# Chapter 1
## On Development, Gender, and Economics

1. The collection of papers presented can be found in Conseil d'Analyse Economique and World Bank, 2000.
2. For more detail, see Stiglitz 2002.
3. For example, the average fertility rate for OECD countries and for the 1995–2000 period was 1.7 per woman, but it ranged between 2.0 in the United States to 1.2 in Italy and Spain, the lowest rates in the world (UNDP 2001).
4. A different concern regarding the activities related to gender in international organizations is the risk of duplication of work among the different agencies and programs. Although there is a division of labor that contextualizes the work of international organizations, the extensive literature that has appeared during the past two decades provides numerous examples of duplication. To be sure, this might be inevitable and the problem is not exclusive to gender-related programs. However, it calls for an evaluation of possible overlaps and of ways to avoid them, particularly as a way of saving resources while providing the possibility to expand into other directions representing innovative and important projects.
5. Circulated through the listserv of the International Association of Feminist Economics, August 15, 2001.
6. See McCloskey 1996, p. 138. An elaboration of this position was made by McCloskey at her Cornell University lecture, July 17, 2001.
7. The illustrations are numerous. See, for example, Hart 1992; Folbre 1994; Sen 1996; Harriss-White 1998; and several of the articles in the special issue on Gender and Globalization, *Feminist Economics*, Vol. 6, No. 3 (November 2000).
8. A large body of literature has developed around this topic—a discussion of which is beyond the scope of this chapter. See, for example, Bardhan and Klasen 1999 and Dijstra and Hammer 2000, among others.
9. See, for example, Bardhan and Klasen 1999; Dijkstra and Hammer 2000; and Nussbaum 2001.

10. See, for example, Stiglitz 2002.
11. David Gonzalez, "Lima Street Vendors Caught Between Police and Poverty," *The New York Times*, January 6, 2002.
12. In the social sciences, this influence was constrained by the difficulty of reconciling postmodern analysis with some of the objectives of the respective disciplines. For example, deconstruction and destabilization of categories create methodological problems for social research requiring some stability in the categories used. Lee Badgett, a feminist economist who has written on sexuality and sexual orientation, put this succinctly when asking how can we "construct survey instruments or empirical research projects without defining and restabilizing theories?" (Badgett 1995).
13. For example, the domestic labor debate and the discussion about the nature of the working-class family that took up much energy among many feminist circles during the 1970s tended to generate this type of polarization. For a discussion of these earlier debates and the lessons learned, see Molyneux 1979.

## Chapter 2
### The Study of Women and Gender in Economics

1. *Economic Heresies: Some Old Fashioned Questions in Economic Theory* (New York: Macmillan, 1971).
2. For a complementary list to the sources mentioned throughout these chapters, see Albelda 1997.
3. See, for example, the "Dialogue" section in *Feminist Economics* 2 (1) Spring 1996: 67–120, and the debate "Gender, Market and Community on Femecon, IAFFE's listserve, in May and June 1994," printed in *Feminist Economics* 2 (2), Summer 1996: 1–39; see also Deirdre McCloskey, "Love and Money" in the same issue: 137–40.
4. See, for example, the special issue of *Feminist Economics* on Children and Family Policy 6(1), March 2000.
5. See, for example, the articles from the Symposium on Equal Opportunities and the Employment Change in Western Economies, edited by Irene Bruegel and Jane Humphries, *Feminist Economics*, 4(1), Spring 1998, and Ammott and Matthaei 1991; Power and Rosenberg 1995; Blau and Ferber 1998; Rubbery et al. 1998. This is far from an exhaustive list since the contributions to these topics are numerous.
6. Briefly, the emphasis in these packages has been on promoting the market as the main allocator of economic resources and on creating the conditions for the expansion and deepening of markets. Although some details might have varied from country to country, the basic characteristics can be summarized as falling under four major policy arenas: 1) adjustments in the area of foreign exchange, often including a devaluation of the national currency; 2) drastic cuts in government spending and privatization of government-run firms; 3) deep economic restructuring and deregulation of markets, including labor and capital markets; 4) trade liberalization and the easing of rules regulating foreign investment,

thereby increasing the degree of globalization of national economies and shifting production toward exports relative to domestic markets. For more detail about SAPs, see Benería 1999.

7. See, for example, Elson 1992; Benería and Feldman 1992; Blackden and Morris-Hughes 1993; Floro 1995; Floro and Shaffer 1998; Çagatay, Elson, and Grown 1996; Grown, Elson, and Çagatay 2000.

8. This was the case with the series of papers on adjustment and market liberalization in African countries carried by a group of researches associated with the Food and Nutrition Policy Program at Cornell University in the early 1990s. Using social accounting matrix (SAM) estimates to evaluate the effects of adjustment, their initial conclusion was that adjustment and liberalization had been beneficial for the poor and for women. Other studies that focused on the effects of adjustment at the micro level were much less optimistic (Geisler and Hansen 1994), hence highlighting a contradiction between the macro and micro evaluations. However, even in the case of the Cornell studies, there was an eventual recognition that there were some losers as a result of reform: "Of particular concern has been the plight of some of retrenched workers and women. While the evidence regarding both groups is mixed, the heterogeneity of the poor suggests the need not to neglect dimensions such as gender in the analysis." (Sahn, Dorosh, and Younger 1994).

9. Quoted in Taylor 1990, p. 1.

10. See, for example, the articles by Braunstein; Lim; Floro and Dymski; Arndt and Tarp; Warner and Campbell; and Evers and Walters in the special issues of *World Development* (July 2000), mentioned earlier.

## Chapter 3
## Markets, Globalization, and Gender

1. Quoted in Anderson and Cavanagh 2000, p. 92.

2. Gary Becker's analysis of altruism in the family is often pointed out as a notable exception, which, in fact, has been much criticized by feminist economists. (See, for example, Ferber and Nelson 1993; Folbre 1994; Bergmann 1995).

3. From a refrain attributed to Westerners in a *New York Times* article on the Asian financial crisis (WuDunn 1998). The article argues that, during the crisis, corporations in Asia failed in record numbers but without disappearing from the market (i.e., without "going to hell").

4. The opposition to structural adjustment policies, which, as argued below, were instrumental in introducing market deregulation programs in many developing countries, was very loud in many cases. In Latin America, for example, protests around economic and social conditions that followed these policies have been numerous throughout the past two decades and, in some countries, have continued to the present. This includes women's organizations that were instrumental in voicing their protests during the 1980s and early 1990s (Montecinos 2001). In Argentina, the continuous financial crises experienced for more than a decade and culminating in a practical default in late 2001 has brought thousands of people to the streets, contributing to political crisis and government changes. In high-income

countries, the fiscal pressures, unemployment, and the weakening of the welfare state associated with neoliberal policies and globalization also has generated strong contestations. For example, the political debates during the 1997 French election provided a clear illustration of how the public perceived the objectives of the European Union's Maastricht Treaty as contrary to the interests of a large proportion of the population. Similar protests emerged in the Asian countries affected by the 1997 economic crisis.

5. To be sure, economic interests are not the only driving forces behind such schemes. In the case of the European Community, for example, the political objectives of European unification were important, from its early stages, as a way to overcome historical tensions and divisions in the continent. However, trade liberalization and economic integration schemes have largely been promoted by the financial and industrial, including transnational corporations, financial capital, and specific economic sectors expecting to profit from expanding and less-regulated trade and foreign investment. For some specific examples, see Epstein et al. 1990.

6. For a more detailed analysis of this point, see World Bank 1996.

7. Despite continuous debates and even resistance to these changes, the evidence supporting this shift has been overwhelming. As an article in *The New York Times* put it, "[W]ith the growth of free markets generally accepted around the world, debates focus less on whether greed is good or bad than on specific checks on excess: on when or which superpayments may be deserved." (Hacker 1997) For a typical view of the pre-eminence of productivity as a social objective, see "The Future of the State. A Survey of the World Economy," *The Economist*, (9/20/97).

8. The reference is to the annual meeting in Davos, Switzerland, of "people who run the world." The Chatham House refers to the "elegant London home" of the Royal Institute of International Affairs where "diplomats have mulled the strange ways of abroad" for "nearly 80 years" ("In praise of the Davos man," *The Economist*, 2/1/97).

9. This could be observed even in academic circles. At a meeting to discuss development studies I attended in the mid-1990s, a representative of a business school announced proudly that in his school it was assumed that there was no need to teach foreign languages since the international business world could function perfectly in English. This was a few years before the U.S. government realized that, as a result of the 9/11/01 events, it didn't have enough people who understood Arabic.

10. Lim, for example, discusses how a figure of 800,000 for Thailand, estimated by ECPAT in 1993, has been seriously questioned by other sources that have found it exaggerated.

11. Some exceptions to the more general trends can be found in the economies of the former Soviet Union where the post–1989 period created contradictory tendencies. Women in these countries had registered very high labor force participation rates during the Soviet era, but they have suffered disproportionately from the social costs of the transition, including unemployment, gender discrimination, and reinforcement of patriarchal forms. In many cases, the transition to more privatized market economies reduced women's employment opportunities and relegated

women to temporary and low-pay jobs (Moghadam 1993; Bridger et al. 1996; World Bank 2000). At the same time, the new market forces have generated jobs for women as a source of cheap labor, particularly in labor-intensive production for global markets. Hence, contradictory tendencies have been observed.

12. In the Mexican case, the proportion of women in the maquiladora labor force, which originally reached levels above 60 percent, began to decrease since the mid-1980s. This was due to several reasons, including technological shifts in production toward more flexible production systems requiring new skills and increasing employment and availability of male labor (due to unemployment and migration, particularly of young males willing to work for low wages).

13. These tensions are specially relevant for specific groups such as indigenous women (and perhaps also for indigenous men) who might feel torn between the freedom that the logic of the market might provide for them and the logic of collectivity within which their identity and security has been shaped. Agarwal (1994) and Deere and León (2001) provide many illustrations.

14. At Cornell University, where I teach, three well established fields that served traditionally feminized service professions—nursing, social work, and teaching in childhood education—were discontinued in the mid-1990s, reflecting a loss of interest in these fields on the part of both students and the university. These were fields that had originally been set up as an extension of women's traditional domestic responsibilities. As female labor force participation increased over time, these activities were viewed as "feminine" and appropriate for women. They also offered lower wages than "masculine" jobs. However, as a result of the women's movement and as the intense criticisms of these divisions became increasingly more manifest during the past three decades, these professions have been associated with nineteenth and early twentieth-century gender stereotypes. Interestingly, however, some women students at Cornell questioned the cancellation of these fields at the university level. They argued, for example, that "[A]t a time when capable and enthusiastic teachers and nurses are in short supply, Cornell is discouraging some of the most intelligent and talented candidates from pursuing these careers" (Harris 1997). They also pointed out that "[A]lthough encouraging women to enter traditionally male occupations is a step forward for feminism, discouraging involvement in traditional 'women's work' is a step backwards." This discouragement was viewed as resulting from a type of feminist rhetoric, which disdains "feminine qualities" and particularly the "ability to care." I have chosen this example to illustrate the type of tensions and contradictions that I am emphasizing here.

15. An example is provided by some of the literature associated with ecofeminism. For a feminist critique of this approach, see Agarwal 1991.

16. "Goldrush in New Guinea," *Business Week*, 11/20/95.

17. This is not sheer wishful thinking. While finalizing the revisions to this book, I am reading an article in the *Financial Times* (7/12/02) about Vald Birn, a Danish cast metal parts maker with 1,300 employees, whose managing director, Christian

Pedersen, is quoted as saying that maximizing profits is not the company's main goal. He refers mostly to the firm's compliance with Denmark's strict environmental laws. Non-profit organizations also offer examples of the possibilities to organize economic activities whose goal is not primarily organized around gain (Rose-Ackerman 1996).

## Chapter 4
## Global/Local Connections

1. Estimates indicate that during the late 1990s the service industry in California, which has a large proportion of temporary workers, added as many jobs as the software and electronic equipment industries combined (*The Economist*, 1/29/00).

2. The decrease in job tenure for men fifty-five and over has been particularly sharp, with an acceleration of this trend since the early 1990s. For more detail, see "Career Evolution," *The Economist*, 1/29/00.

3. For example, young workers prefer longer working days in order to have longer weekends, whereas older workers opt for more traditional weekly schedules (*Wall Street Journal*, 3/13/00).

4. Hence, the reliance on immigration to fill job vacancies at the bottom of the labor hierarchy and, in cases such as Germany, the efforts to facilitate the immigration of computer technicians despite protests on the part of some groups.

5. This section relies on a paper coauthored with Luis Santiago and based on a study carried out in the mid-1990s. For more details, see Benería and Santiago 2001.

6. At the time relocation was announced, Smith-Corona's president, William Henderson, quoted an average of $18 per hour per worker at Cortland, including wages, insurance, and benefits. The corresponding average in Tijuana was expected to be just over $3 per hour.

7. All information about the Rubbermaid closure included in this chapter has been provided by Jennifer Tiffany's doctoral dissertation survey (work in progress).

8. The main data collection method used for this study consisted of two standardized questionnaires, which were administered either in person or (in some cases for the second questionnaire) over the telephone from 1993 to 1996. For more detail on the methodology used and results, see Benería and Santiago 2001.

9. This was a similar proportion to that of a larger sample of 679 workers from the Smith-Corona Dislocated Worker Survey released in November 1997, in which women represented 58 percent of the total (Papaglia 1994).

10. While the average number of persons per household remained almost the same during the period of the study, the number of people employed per household increased from 1.9 at the time of layoff to 2.8 when the second interview was conducted. This increase is likely to have resulted from the strategies followed by

households to compensate for employment instability and decreased individual (and household) income.

11.  For workers, economic losses were measured in terms of the reduction in wages upon re-employment. Data on individual income distribution was collected at two points in time: 1992, the year in which the Smith-Corona layoff was announced, and the time at which the second interview was conducted. The analysis that follows considers respondents who gave information about their individual income and were employed at these two points in time.

Even though individual income data was available for other time periods, the focus was restricted to the previous two points in time for two reasons. Since the first point refers to pre-layoff income, it only includes wage income. The second point minimizes income distortion because the income data was obtained at a time when unemployment and training funds were no longer available to workers.

12.  By way of comparison, in Howland's study of dislocated workers in metalworking machinery, electronic components, and motor vehicles industries, it was estimated that the financial loss for a white, male, blue-collar worker with a twelfth-grade education who was displaced in 1979 or 1981 and who had worked for a firm for twenty-five years was $52,000 in five years, or $10,000 annually (Howland 1988).

13.  The Clinton administration, for example, placed great emphasis on the need for Americans to further their education and adjust to the requirements of an increasingly more technological society. Although few would quarrel with this argument, it does not necessarily imply that there is a shortage of skilled workers (for more detail, see Mishel and Teixeira 1991; Gordon 1996). The problem can be seen as resulting from insufficient demand.

14.  For some countries, unemployment rates in 1999 reached much higher levels, such as in Argentina (14.5 percent), Colombia (19.8 percent), Panama (13 percent), and Venezuela (15.3 percent) (Pérez-Saínz 2000).

15.  Kruse reports the case of a worker in a blue jeans sweatshop who asked the owner's wife whether the workers would get a day off on May Day, to which she replied: "Do you suppose you are a worker?"

16.  The literature on this subject is abundant. See, for example, Bureau of International Labor Affairs, Workers Rights in Export Processing Zones, Washington, D.C. 1989–1990.

17.  Standing (2001) has disaggregated the different forms of labor market insecurity generated by these processes as follows:
   • *Labor market insecurity* has grown almost globally, with much higher unemployment, slower rates of employment growth, and higher "labor *slack*."
   • *Employment insecurity* is high and rising, with growing proportions of those in the labor force having insecure employment statuses and with more workers lacking employment protection.
   • *Work insecurity* has become greater, due to more people being in work statuses without coverage by protective institutions and regulations.

- *Job insecurity* has worsened, with more workers having to switch jobs and learn new tricks of working.
- *Skill reproduction insecurity* is considerable, in part because skills become obsolescent more quickly and because few workers are receiving career skills.
- *Income insecurity* is greater for those employed, due to flexible wages and so on, and for those outside formal employment, due to explicit and implicit disentitlement to benefits.
- *Representation insecurity* is growing due to de-unionization, erosion of "tripartite" institutions, and the changing character of collective bargaining.

18. That is, workshops that are difficult to classify because they include legal and illegal operations.
19. To illustrate with the case of Brazil, estimates of the proportion of employed women in domestic service range between 16 percent and 20 percent; one study found an average of 19 percent for the 1990s (Benería and Rosenberg 1999).
20. To illustrate, the 1997 female illiteracy rate was 97.1 percent in Ethiopia, 92.8 percent in Niger, and 79.3 percent in Nepal (UNDP 1999).
21. See, for example, an extensive study by Martha Roldán's of the gender effects of economic restructuring in the auto industry in Argentina, illustrating the multiple links and meanings of the process of defeminization (Roldán 1994 and 2000). My own (unfinished) research on the Catalan textile industry also indicates that, since the 1970s, a process of de-feminization took place in an industry that had been predominantly female.
22. At the time of this writing, a pending suit against Microsoft Corporation in the United States represents an interesting example illustrating the shifting boundaries between distributive channels benefiting different actors. The firm, in addition to regular employees, has utilized the services of independent contractors without access to the employment benefits of regular employees. Following a federal employment tax examination in 1990, the Internal Revenue Service questioned the status of these subcontractors and, as a result, Microsoft reclassified some of them as regular employees. However, most workers were only given the option to convert to temporary workers (temps) or lose their working ties with Microsoft. Other contractors were reclassified as temps without having an option. To date, a case is still pending regarding the right of some of the initial subcontractors to participate in Microsoft's tax-qualified Employee Stock Purchase Plan (ESPP). The case illustrates how the boundaries between jobs in the core and periphery of firms can be fluid and therefore questionable and subject to change with respect to the distribution of benefits to workers.

# Chapter 5
## Paid and Unpaid Labor

1. For a summary of the literature and relevant definitions, see Goldschmidt-Clermont 1982, and Juster and Stafford 1991.

2. UN Statistical Commission 1983. For a more detailed account, see Benería 1982.
3. For further detail, see Benería 1982.
4. See chapter 4 for more detail.
5. There are, of course, exceptions to this trend, such as the phenomenon referred to as the "nanny bubble" since the late 1990s in the United States, representing an increase in employment of immigrant domestic workers among the very rich. If anything, this trend has accelerated in high-income countries, as discussed in chapter 3, particularly as a result of the crisis of care work.
6. Based on data from Canada, Denmark, Holland, Japan, Norway, the United Kingdom and the United States, Juster and Stafford (1991) show that men's unpaid domestic work increased for most countries between the 1960s and the 1980s while women's decreased in larger proportions.
7. Data prepared for the Inaugural Meeting of the National Commission on Philanthropy and Civic Renewal, Washington, D.C., September 1996. Formal volunteering was defined as "specific commitments of time to organizations" and informal volunteering as "less structured arrangements like helping one's neighbors."
8. Ibid.
9. A soup kitchen that I visited in an East Los Angeles church in 1996 was run entirely by Spanish-speaking women and served daily dinner for about 100 men.
10. See chapter 2 for more detail.
11. For more detail, see, for example, Goldschmidt-Clermont 1982 and 1987; Benería 1992; Fraumeni 1998.
12. A variation of the opportunity cost method is the *lifetime income approach* (Fraumeni 1998).
13. The sample of countries used was selected "on the basis of availability and reliability of time-use data" but with variations in the methods of data collection.
14. These strategies may consist of types of paid work outside of the mainstream monetary system, as with some cases in which the creation of a local currency facilitates exchanges. One such case has been developed in Ithaca, New York, where "Ithaca money" is issued locally and used to exchange labor services as well as to purchase from the local stores that accept it. Even though these cases have little weight for the economy as a whole, they can be important at the local level and they provide interesting examples of work not recorded in conventional statistics.
15. Based on my conversation with Barbara Bergmann on this topic, March 14, 1998.
16. I wish to thank a participant in a seminar I gave at Radcliffe's Public Policy Institute on this topic for this point. She mentioned her own experience in using managerial skills learned at home for her market work, and vice versa, to argue that it is often difficult to neatly differentiate between paid and unpaid work in terms of Himmelweit's analysis.
17. For example, some World Bank economists have been critical of the UNDP's efforts to include estimates of unpaid work in its *1995 Human Development Report*. However, to my knowledge, the objections have mostly be voiced in discussions and meetings rather than in a written form.

*Chapter 6*
*Development as if All People Mattered*

1. Slogan used by the citizen coalition against the privatization of water in Cochabamba, Bolivia, Spring 2000. The coalition was set up after the Bolivian government rescinded the concession contract to water rights and system management to a subsidiary of Bechtel. The multinational, an engineering and construction firm with income almost twice that of Bolivia's GNP, has demanded $25 million in compensation from the Bolivian government through commercial arbitration at the World Bank.

2. The European Union announced that it would increase its annual aid by $7 billion, to be added to the then current amount of $25 billion. The United States, which represented the lowest donor in per capita aid, also announced gradual annual increases to be added to the $10 billion already in place at the time.

3. Just a few months later, the World's Food Summit that took place in Rome on June 2002 closed with the general impression that once again little had been accomplished in terms of the initial expectations. One of the main items on the agenda was the problem of hunger and the danger of starvation facing millions of people, particularly women and children. Agricultural ministers from all countries gathered for the meeting convened by the World Food Organization for the purpose of discussing how to feed the world in the years to come. Some observers pointed out that the agenda had no plans to discuss the world food system organized around the production of expensive feed for cattle that provide for meat diets at the expense of cheaper (and healthier) foods. Thus, a key problem for dealing with the world's food problems was set aside.

4. *The New York Times*, 7/19/02 (emphasis added).

# Bibliography

AARP (American Association of Retired Persons). 1997. *The AARP Survey of Civic Involvement.* Washington, D.C.

Adelman, Irma, and Sherman Robinson. 1989. "Income distribution and development." In H. Chenery and T. N. Srinivasan, eds. *Handbook of Development Economics,* Vol. II. Amsterdam: Elsevier Science Publishers B.V., 949–1003.

Agarwal, Bina. 1991. "Engendering the Environmental Debate: Lessons from the Indian Subcontinent." CASID Distinguished Speakers Series No. 8. Michigan State University.

———. 1992. "Gender relations and food security: coping with seasonality, drought, and famine in South Asia." In Lourdes Benería and Shelly Feldman, eds. *Unequal Burden, Economic Crises, Household Strategies and Women's Work.* Boulder, Colo.: Westview Press, 181–218.

———. 1994. *A Field of One's Own: Gender and Land Rights in South Asia.* Cambridge: Cambridge University Press.

———. 1997. "Bargaining and gender relations: within and beyond the household." *Feminist Economics* 3(1), Spring: 1–51.

Albelda, Randy. 1997. *Economics & Feminism: Disturbances in the Field.* New York: Twayne Publishers and Prentice Hall International.

———. 2001. "Welfare to work, farewell to families? U.S. welfare reform and work/family debates." *Feminist Economics* 7(1), March: 119–36.

Allen, Aileen, and Lourdes Benería. 2001. "Gender and trade issues within Mercosur." Report written for UNIFEM's Southern Cone Regional Office, April.

Ammott, Teresa L., and Julie Matthaei. 1991. *Race, Gender and Work: A Multicultural Economic History of Women in the United States.* Boston: South End Press.

Andrade, X., and Gioconda Herrera, eds. 2001. *Masculinidades en Ecuador.* Quito: FLACSO.

Anker, Richard. 1998. *Gender and Jobs: Sex Segregation of Occupations in the World.* Geneva: ILO.

Appelbaum, Ileen, and Rosemary Batt. 1994. *The New American Workplace: Transforming Work Systems in the United States.* Ithaca, N.Y.: Cornell University ILR Press.

Arbona, Juan. 2000. "The Political Economy of Micro-Enterprise Promotion Policies: Restructuring and Income-Generating Activities in El Alto, Bolivia." Ph.D. dissertation. Ithaca, N.Y.: Cornell University.

Aslanbeigui, Nahid, and Gale Summerfield. 2000. "The Asian crisis, gender and the international financial architecture." *Feminist Economics* 6(3), November: 81–103.

Badgett, M. V. Lee. 1995. "The last of the modernists?" *Feminist Economics* 1(2): 63–65.

Bakker, Isabella. 1994. *The Strategic Silence: Gender and Economic Policy.* London/ Atlantic Highlands, N.J.: Zed Books.

Bakker, Isabella, and Elson, Diane. 1998. "Towards engendering budgets." In *Alternative Federal Budget Papers.* Ottawa: Canadian Center for Policy Alternatives.

Balakrishnan, Radhika. 1994. "The social context of sex selection and the politics of sex selection in India." In G. Sen and R. Snow, eds. *Power and Decision: The Social Control of Reproduction.* Cambridge, Mass.: Harvard University Press.

Balakrishnan, Radhika, and M. Huang. 2000. "Flexible workers—hidden employers: gender and subcontracting in the global economy, report on a research project of the women's economic and legal rights program." Washington, D.C.: The Asia Foundation.

Bardhan, Kalpana, and Stephan Klasen. 1999. "UNDP's gender-related indices: a critical review." *World Development* 27(6): 985–1010.

Barker, Lucilla. 1995. "Economists, social reformers and prophets: a feminist critique of economic efficiency." *Feminist Economics* 1(3), Fall: 26–39.

Barrett, Michele. 1999. *Imagination in Theory: Culture, Writing, Words, and Things.* New York: University Press.

Barrig, Maruja. 1996. "Nos hablamos amado tanto: crisis del estado y organizacion feminina." In John Friedmann et al., eds. *Emergences: Women's Struggles for Livelihood in Latin America.* Los Angeles: Latin American Studies Program, UCLA.

Batt, Rosemary. 1996. "From bureaucracy to enterprise? The changing jobs and careers of managers in telecommunications services." In P. Osterman, ed. *Broken Ladders: Managerial Careers in Transition.* New York: Oxford University Press.

Becker, Gary. 1981. *A Treatise on the Family.* Cambridge, Mass.: Harvard University Press.

———. 1991. *A Treatise on the Family.* Cambridge, Mass.: Harvard University Press.

Beller, Andrea. 1979. "The impact of equal employment opportunity laws on the male/female earnings differential." In Cynthia B. Lloyd et al., eds. *Women in the Labor Market.* New York: Columbia University Press.

Benería, Lourdes. 1979. "Reproduction, production and the sexual division of labor." *Cambridge Journal of Economics* 3(3): 203–25.

———, ed. 1982. "Accounting for women's work." In L. Benería, ed. *Women and Development: the Sexual Division of Labor in Rural Societies.* New York: Praeger, 161–84.

———. 1987. "Gender and the dynamics of subcontracting in Mexico City." In Clair Brown and Joseph A. Pechman, eds. *Gender in the Workplace*. Washington, D.C.: Brookings Institution, 159–88.

———. 1992. "Accounting for women's work: the progress of two decades." *World Development* 20(11): 1547–60.

———. 1995. "Toward a greater integration of gender and economics." *World Development* 23(11): 1839–50.

———. 1996. "Thou shalt not live by statistics alone but it might help." *Feminist Economics* 2(3): 139–42.

———. 1999. "Globalization, gender, and the Davos Man." *Feminist Economics*. 5(3): 61–84.

Benería, Lourdes, and Shelley Feldman. 1992. *Unequal Burden: Economic Crises, Persistent Poverty, and Women's Work*. Boulder, Colo.: Westview Press.

Benería, Lourdes, and Breny Mendoza. 1995. "Structural adjustment and social emergency funds: the cases of Honduras, Mexico and Nicaragua." Paper prepared for UNRISD's project on Economic Restructuring and New Social Policies. *European Journal of Development Research*, Spring.

Benería, Lourdes, and Martha Roldán. 1987. *The Crossroads of Class & Gender: Industrial Homework, Subcontracting, and Household Dynamics in Mexico City*. Chicago: University of Chicago Press.

Benería, Lourdes, and F. Rosenberg. 1999. "Brazil gender review." Report/evaluation of World Bank projects in Brazil.

Benería, Lourdes, and L. Santiago. 2001. "The impact of industrial relocation on displaced workers: a case study of Cortland, N.Y.," *Economic Development Quarterly*, February.

Benería, Lourdes, and Gita Sen. 1981. "Accumulation, reproduction and women's role in economic development: Boserup revisited." *Signs* 7(2): 279–98.

Benham, Lee. 1974. "Benefits of women's education within marriage." *Journal of Political Economy* 82(2/2): S57–S71.

Bergmann, Barbara. 1995. "Becker's theory of the family: preposterous conclusions." *Feminist Economics* 1(1): 141–50.

———. 2000. *Is Social Security Broke? A Cartoon Guide to the Issues*. University of Michigan Press.

———. 1974. "Occupational Segregation, Wages and Profits When Employers Discriminate by Race and Sex," *Eastern Economic Journal* 1(2): 103–10.

Berik, Gunseli. 2000. "Mature Export-Led Growth and Gender Wage Inequality." *Feminist Economics* 6(3): 1–26.

Bisnath, Savitri. 2002. "WTO, GATS and TPRM: Servicing Liberalization and Eroding Equity Goals?" In L. Benería and S. Bisnath, eds. *Global Tensions: Challenges and Opportunities in the World Economy*. New York: Routledge.

Bittman, Michael, and Jocelyn Pixley. 1997. *The Double Life of the Family. Myth, Hope and Experience*. Sidney: Allen and Unwin.

Blackden, C. Mark, and Elizabeth Morris-Hughes. 1993. "Paradigm postponed: gender and economic adjustment in Sub-Saharan Africa." Washington, D.C.: Technical Department, African Region, The World Bank.

Blades, Derek W. 1975. *Non-Monetary (Subsistence) Activities in the National Accounts of Developing Countries.* Paris: OECD.

Blank, Rebecca. 1993. "What should mainstream economists learn from feminist theory?" In Marianne A. Ferber and Julie A. Nelson, eds. *Beyond Economic Man: Feminist Theory and Economics.* Chicago: The University of Chicago Press, 133–43.

———. 1994. *Social Protection vs. Economic Flexibility. Is There a Trade Off?* The University of Chicago Press.

Blau, Francine. 1976. "Longitudinal patterns of female labor force participation." *Dual Careers*, 4. Washington, D.C.: U.S. Department of Labor.

Blau, Francine, and Marianne Ferber. 1986. *The Economics of Women, Men, and Work.* Englewood Cliffs, N.J.: Prentice-Hall.

Bluestone, Barry, and Bennett Harrison. 1982. *The Deindustrialization of America. Plant Closings, Community Abandonment and the Dismantling of Basic Industry.* New York: Basic Books.

Boris, Eileen, and Elizabeth Prugl, eds. 1996. *Homeworkers in Global Perspective: Invisible No More.* New York: Routledge

Boserup, Ester. 1970. *Women's Role in Economic Development.* New York: St. Martin's Press.

Bridger, Sue, Rebecca Kay, and Kathryn Pinnick. 1996. *No More Heroines? Russia, Women and the Market.* London: Routledge.

Brofenbrenner, K. 2000. "Uneasy terrain: the impact of capital mobility on workers, wages, and union organizing." Submitted to the U.S. Trade Deficit Review Commission, September.

Bromley, R., and C. Gerry, eds. 1979. *Casual Work and Poverty.* London: John Wiley and Sons.

Bruce, Judith, and Daysy Dwyer. 1988. *A Home Divided: Women and Income in the Third World.* Stanford, Calif.: Stanford University Press.

Bruegel, Irene, and Jane Humphries. 1998. "Introduction: equal opportunities and employment change in West European economies." *Feminist Economics* 4(1), Spring: 51–52.

Bruegel, Irene, and Diane Perrons. 1998. "Deregulation and women's employment: the diverse experience of women in Britain." *Feminist Economics.* 4(1), Spring: 103–25.

Butler, Judith. 1993. *Bodies that Matter: On the Discoursive Limits of "Sex."* New York: Routledge.

Buviniç, Mayra. 1986. "Projects for women in the Third World: explaining their misbehavior." *World Development* 14(5), May: 653–64.

Çagatay, Nilufer. 2001. "Trade, Gender and Poverty," UNDP, New York. Background Paper for UNDP's report on Trade and Sustainable Human Development, October 2001.

Çagatay, Nilufer, Diane Elson, and Caren Grown. 1996. "Introduction." Special issue on Gender, Adjustment and Macroeconomics. *World Development* 23(11), November: 1827–1938.

Capelli, P. 1999. *The New Deal at Work*. Boston: Harvard Business School Press.

Carr, Marilyn, Martha Chen, and Jane Tate. 2000. "Globalization and home-based workers." *Feminist Economics* 3(3), November: 123–42.

Carrasco, Cristina. 1992. *El Trabajo Doméstico y la Reproducción Social*. Madrid: Instituto de la Mujer.

Cassels, Jamie. 1993. "User requirements and data needs." In *Summary of Proceedings, International Conference on the Valuation and Measurement of Unpaid Work*, sponsored by Statistics Canada and Status of Women Canada. Ottawa, Canada, April 18–30.

Chadeau, Ann. 1989. *Measuring Household Production: Conceptual Issues and Results for France*. Paper presented at the Second ECE/INSTRAW Joint Meeting on Statistics on Women. Geneva, November 13–16.

Charmes, Jacques. 2000. "Size, trends and productivity of women's work in the informal sector." Paper presented at the annual IAFFE Conference. Istanbul August 15–17.

Christopherson, Susan. 1997. "The caring gap for caring workers: the restructuring of care and the status of women in OECD countries." Paper presented at the Conference on Revisioning the Welfare State: Feminist Perspectives on the U.S. and Europe. Cornell University, October 3–5.

Cigno, Alessandro. 1994. *Economics of the Family*. New York: Oxford University Press.

Collins, Mary. 1993. "Opening Remarks," *Summary of Proceedings, International Conference on the Valuation and Measurement of Unpaid Work*, sponsored by Statistics Canada and Status of Women Canada. Ottawa, Canada, April 18–30.

Comajuncosa, Josep M., Francisco Loscos, and Ignacio Serrano. 2001. *Prefaci a 'lElaboració dels Comptes Satéllit de la Produccio Domestica per a Catalunya*. Barcelona: Institut Català de la Dona.

Commonwealth Secretariat. 1989. *Engendering Adjustment for the 1990s*. London: Commonwealth Secretariat.

Conseil d'Analyse Economique and The World Bank. 2000. *Governance, Equity and Global Markets. Proceedings of the Annual Bank Conference on Development Economics in Europe, June 21–23, 1999*. Paris: La Documentation Francaise.

Cornia, Giovanni, Richard Jolly, and Francis Stewart, eds. 1987. *Adjustment with a Human Face*, 1. New York: UNICEF/Clarendon Press, 1987.

Cornwall, Richard. 1997. "Deconstructing silence: the queer political economy of the social articulation of desire." *Review of Radical Political Economies* 29(1): 1–130.

Cravey, Altha J. 1998. *Women and Work in Mexico's Maquiladoras*. Rowan & Littlefield.

Croson, Susan. 1999. "Using experiments in the classroom." *CWEP Newsletter*, Winter.

Daly, Mary, ed. 2001. *Care Work. The Quest for Security.* Geneva: ILO.

Dangler, Jamie. 1994. *Hidden in the Home: The Role of Waged Homework in the Modern World Economy.* Albany, N.Y.: State University of New York Press.

DAW (Division for the Advancement of Women). 1999. *World Survey on the Role of Women in Development, Globalization, Gender and Work,* New York: United Nations.

Deere, Carmen Diana. 1976. "Rural women's subsistence production in the capitalist periphery." *RRPE* 8(1): 9–17.

———. 1990. *Household and Class Relations: Peasants and Landlords in Northern Peru.* Berkeley, Calif.: University of California Press.

Deere, Carmen Diana, and Magdelena León. 2001. *Empowering Women: Land and Property Rights in Latin America.* Pittsburgh: University of Pittsburgh Press.

De Soto, Hernando, 2000. *El Misterio del Capital.* Lima: Empresa Editoria El Comercio.

Dicken, P. 1998. *Global Shift: Transforming the World Economy.* New York: The Guildford Press.

Dijkstra, A. Geske, and Lucia Hammer. 2000. "Measuring socio-economic gender inequality: toward an alternative to the UNDP gender-related development index." *Feminist Economics* 6(2): 41–75.

Doezema, J., and K. Kempadoo, eds. 1998. *Global Sex Workers: Rights, Resistance and Redefinitions,* New York: Routledge.

Dollar, David, and Roberta Gatti. 1999. "Gender inequality, income, and growth: are good times good for women?" Washington, D.C.: The World Bank, Policy Research Group on Gender and Development, Working Paper Series, No. 1.

Drèze, Jean, and Amartya Sen. 1989. *Hunger and Public Action.* Oxford: Clarendon Press.

———. 1995. *India: Economic Development and Social Opportunity.* Oxford University Press.

Duggan, Lynn. 1994. "A gender theory of family policy: on the relevance of equal fallback positions." Paper presented at URPE/ASSA meetings. Boston.

Dussell Peters, Enrique. 2000. *Polarizing Mexico: The Impact of Liberalization Strategy.* Boulder and London: Lynne Rienner Publishers.

ECA (Economic Commission for Africa). 1989. *Adjustment with Transformation.* ECA/CM, 15/6 Rev. 3. Addis Ababa: United Nations.

ECLAC (Economic Commission for Latin America and the Caribbean). 1990. *Transformación Productiva con Equidad.* Santiago, Chile.

———. 1995. *Social Panorama of Latin America.* Santiago, Chile.

Edwards, Richard, Michael Reich, and David Gordon, eds. 1973. *Labor Market Segmentation.* Lexington, Mass.: D.C. Heath and Co.

Ehrenreich, Barbara, and Arlie Russell Hochschild, eds. 2002. *Global Woman: Nannies, Maids, and Sex Workers in the New Economy.* New York: Metropolitican Books.

Elson, Diane, ed. 1979. *Value: the Representation of Labour in Capitalism.* London: CSE/Humanities Press.

———. ed. 1991. *Male Bias in the Development Process*. Manchester: Manchester University Press.

———. 1992. "From survival strategies to transformation strategies: women's needs and structural adjustment." In L. Benería and S. Feldman eds., *Unequal Burden: Economic Crises, Persistent Poverty, and Women's Work*. Boulder, Colo.: Westview Press: 26–48.

———. 1993. "Gender-aware analysis and development economics." *Journal of International Development* 5(2): 237–47.

———. 1995. "Gender awareness in modeling structural adjustment." *World Development* 23(11), November: 1851–68.

———. 1999. "Theories of Development." In J. Peterson and M. Lewis, eds. *The Elgar Companion to Feminist Economics*. Cheltenham: Edward Elgar: 95–107.

Elson, Diane, and Ruth Pearson, eds. 1989. *Women's Employment and Multinationals in Europe*. London: Macmillan Press.

England, Paula. 1993. "The separate self: androcentric bias in neoclassical assumptions." In Marian Ferber and Julie Nelson, eds. *Beyond Economic Man*. Chicago: University of Chicago Press, 37–53.

Epstein, Gerald, Julie Graham, and Jessica Nembhard, eds. 1990. *Creating a New World Economy*. Philadelphia: Temple University Press.

Escobar, Arturo. 1995. *Encountering Development: The Making and Unmaking of the Third World*. Princeton, N.J.: Princeton University Press.

Feldman, Shelley. 1992. "Crisis, Islam and gender in Bangladesh: the social construction of a female labor force." In Lourdes Benería and Shelley Feldman, eds. *Unequal Burden: Economic Crises, Persistent Poverty, and Women's Work*. Boulder, Colo.: Westview Press, 105–30.

———. 2001. "Exploring theories of patriarchy: a perspective from contemporary Bangladesh." *Signs: Journal of Women, Culture and Society* 26(4): 1,097–27.

Ferber, Marianne, and Bonnie Birnbaum. 1977. "The 'new home economic': retrospects and prospects." *Journal of Consumer Research* 4, June: 19–28.

———. 1980. "Housework: priceless or valueless?" *Review of Income and Wealth* 26(4), December: 387–400.

Ferber, Marianne, and Julie Nelson, eds. 1993. *Beyond Economic Man*. Chicago: University of Chicago Press.

Ferguson, Anne. 2001. "Practical and strategic gender interests: Discourse and identity in women's movements in Latin America." Paper presented at the XXIII Latin American Studies Association Conference. Washington, D.C., September 6–8.

Figart, Deborah, and Ellen Mutari. 1998. "Degendering worktime in comparative perspective: alternative policy frameworks." Paper prepared for the Symposium on Work Time. *Review of Social Economy*, Winter: 460–80.

Floro, Maria Sagrario. 1994. "Work intensity and women's time use." In G. Young and B. Dickerson, eds. *Color, Class and Country: Experiences of Gender*. London: Zed Press, 162–81.

———. 1995. "Economic restructuring, gender and the allocation of time." *World Development* 23(11), November: 1,913–30.

———. 1996. "We need new economic indicators to gauge work and well-being." *The Chronicle of Higher Education* 4(15) December 6.

———. 1997. "Time as a numeraire: the institutional and social dimensions of time use." Paper presented at the Rescheduling Time Symposium. University of Manchester, November 6–7.

Floro, Maria, and Kendall Shaffer. 1998. "Restructuring of labor markets in the Philippines and Zambia: the gender dimension." *The Journal of Development Areas* 33, Fall: 73–98.

Floro, Maria, and Gary Dymski. 2000. "Financial Crisis, Gender, and Power: An Analytical Framework," *World Development,* 28(7), July: 1269–1283.

Folbre, Nancy. 1982. "Exploitation comes home: a critique of the Marxian theory of family labour." *Cambridge Journal of Economics* 6: 317–29.

———. 1988. "The black four of hearts: toward a new paradigm of household economics." In J. Bruce and D. Dwyer, eds. *A Home Divided.* Stanford, Calif.: Stanford University Press, 248–64.

———. 1994. *Who Pays for the Kids? Gender and the Structures of Constraint.* New York: Routledge.

———. 1995a. "Economic restructuring, gender and the allocation of time." *World Development* 23(11), November: 1,913–30.

———. 1995b. "Holding hands at midnight: the paradox of caring labor." *Feminist Economics* 1(1), Spring: 73–92.

———. 2000. *The Invisible Heart, Economics and Family Values.* New York: The New Press.

Fontana, Marzia, Susan Joekes, and Rachel Masika. 1998. "Global trade expansion and liberalisation: gender issues and impacts." Institute of Development Studies, University of Sussex, UK.

Fontana, Marzia, and Adrian Wood. 2000. "Modeling the effects of trade on women, at work and at home." *World Development* 28(7), July: 1,173–90.

Frank, Robert, Thomas Golovich, and Dennis Regan. 1993. "Does studying economics inhibit cooperation?" *Journal of Economic Perspectives* 7(2): 159–71.

Fraser, Nancy. 1997. *Justice Interruptus: Critical Reflections on the Postsocialist Condition.* New York: Routledge.

Fraumeni, Barbara. 1998. "Expanding economic accounts for productivity analysis: A nonmarket and human capital perspective." Paper presented at the Conference on Income and Wealth, National Bureau for Economic Research (NBER), March 20–21.

Freeman, Richard B. 1996. *The New Inequality.* Boston: *Boston Review,* December/ January, 1996–1997.

Froebel, F., J. Heinrichs, and O. Kreye. 1980. *The New International Division of Labor.* Cambridge: Cambridge University Press.

Fussel, M. E. 2000. "Making labor flexible: the recomposition of Tijuana's maquiladora female labor force." *Feminist Economics* 6(3): 59–80.

García-Linera, A. 1999. *Reproletarizacion: Nueva clase obrera y desarrollo del capital industrial en Bolivia (1952–1998)*. La Paz: Muela del Diablo Editores.

Gardiner, Jean. 1975. "Women's domestic labor." *New Left Review*. 89, January/February: 47–58.

Geisler, Gisela, and Karen Tranberg Hansen. 1994. "Structural adjustment, the rural-urban interface and gender relations in Zambia." In N. Aslanbeigui, S. Pressman, and G. Summerfield, eds. *Women in the Age of Economic Transformation*. London and New York: Routledge, 95–112.

Gilligan, Carol. 1982. *In a Different Voice*. Cambridge: Harvard University Press.

Giménez, Martha E. 1990. "The dialectics of waged and unwaged work: waged work, domestic labor and household survival in the United States." In Jane L. Collins and Martha Giménez, eds. *Work without Wages: Domestic Labor and Self-Employment within Capitalism*. Albany, N.Y.: State University of New York Press, 25–46.

Goldschmidt-Clermont, Luisella. 1982. *Unpaid Work in the Household: A Review of Economic Evaluation Methods*. Geneva: ILO.

———. 1987. *Economic Evaluations of Unpaid Household Work: Africa, Asia, Oceania*. Geneva: ILO.

González de la Rocha, M. 2000. "Private adjustments: household responses to the erosion of work." UNDP/SEPED Conference Paper Series.

Gora, Ann, and Gloria Nemerowicz. 1991. "Volunteers: initial and sustaining motivations in service to the community." *Research in the Sociology of Health Care* 9: 233–46.

Gordon, David, Richard Edwards, and Michael Reich. 1982. *Segmented Work, Divided Workers: The Historical Transformation of Labor in the United States*. Cambridge: Cambridge University Press.

Grapard, Ulla. 1995. "Robinson Crusoe: the quintessential economic man?" *Feminist Economics* 1(1): 33–52.

Grown, Caren, Diane Elson, and Nilufer Çagatay. 2000. "Introduction" to special issue on Growth, Trade, Finance, and Gender Inequality." *World Development*, 28(7), July: 1,145–56.

Gutmann, Matthew. 1996. *The Meanings of Macho: Being a Man in Mexico City*. Berkeley /Los Angeles/London: University of California Press.

Guyer, Jane. 1980. "Households, budgets and women's incomes." Boston University, Africana Studies Center Working Paper No. 28.

Hacker, Andrew. 1997. "Good or bad, greed is often beside the point." *The New York Times*, June 8.

Haney, Lynne. 2000. "Global discourse of need: mythologizing and pathologizing welfare in Hungary." In M. Burawoy et al. *Global Ethnography: Forces, Connections, and Imaginations in a Post-Modern World*. Berkeley: University of California Press.

Harding, Sandra, ed. 1987. *Feminism and Methodology*. Bloomington, Ind.: Indiana University Press.

———. 1995. "Can feminist thought make economics more objective?" *Feminist Economics* 1(1), Spring: 7–32.

Harris, Rachel. 1997. "Where have all the majors gone?" *Athena*, Spring: 18–19.

Harriss-White, Barbara. 1998. "Female and male grain marketing systems: analytical and policy issues for West Africa and India." In Cecile Jackson and Ruth Pearson, eds. *Feminist Visions of Development: Gender, Analysis and Policy.* London and New York: Routledge, 189–213.

———. 2002. "Development and productive deprivation: male patriarchal relations in business families and their implications for women in South India." Forthcoming in L. Benería and Savitri Bisnath, eds. *Global Tensions: Challenges and Opportunities in the World Economy.* New York: Routledge.

Harrison, Ben. 1994. *Lean and Mean: The Changing Landscape of Corporate Power in the Age of Flexibility.* New York: Basic Books.

Harrison, Ben, and Barry Bluestone. 1988. *The Great U-Turn: Corporate Restructuring and the Polarization of America.* New York: Basic Books.

Hart, Gillian. 1992. "Household production reconsidered: gender, labor conflict, and technological change in Malaysia's Muda region." *World Development* 20(6), June: 809–23.

Hart, Keith. 1972. *Employment, Income and Inequality: A Strategy for Increasing Productive Employment in Kenya.* Geneva: ILO.

Hartmann, Heidi. 1976a. "The family as the locus of gender, class and political struggle: the example of housework." In Sandra Harding, ed. *Feminism and Methodology.* Bloomington, Ind.: Indiana University Press, 109–34.

———. 1976b. "Capitalism, patriarchy, and job segregation by sex." In M. Blaxall and B. Reagan, eds. *Women and the Workplace.* Chicago: University of Chicago Press, 137–69.

———. 1979. "The unhappy marriage of Marxism and feminism: toward a more progressive union." *Capital and Class,* Summer: 1–33.

———. 1981. "The family as the locus of gender, class and political struggle: the example of housework." *Signs: Journal of Women, Culture and Society* 6(3): 366–94.

Heilbroner, Robert, and William Milberg. 1995. *The Crisis of Vision in Modern Economic Thought.* Cambridge University Press.

Himmelweit, Susan. 1995. "The discovery of unpaid work: the social consequences of the expansion of work." *Feminist Economics* 1(2) Summer: 1–19.

Himmelweit, Susan, and Simon Mohun. 1977. "Domestic labor and capital." *Cambridge Journal of Economics* 1, March: 15–31.

Hsiung, Ping-Chun. 1995. *Living Rooms as Factories: Class, Gender, and the Satellite Factory System in Taiwan.* Philadelphia: Temple University Press.

ILO (International Labor Office). 1972. *Employment, Incomes, and Equality: Strategy for Increasing Productive Employment in Kenya.* Geneva: ILO.

———. 1976. *International Recommendations on Labour Statistics.* Geneva: ILO.

———. 1977. *Labour force estimates and projections, 1950–2000.* Geneva: ILO.

———. 1997. *The ILO, Standard Setting, and Globalization,* report of the Director General. 85th Session, Geneva.

———. 1999. *Panorama Laboral 99.* Lima: OIT.

Independent Commission on Population and Quality of Life. 1996. *Caring for the Future: Making the Next Decades Provide a Life Worth Living.* Oxford: Oxford University Press.

INSTRAW (United Nations International Research and Training Institute for the Advancement of Women). 1991. *Methods of Collecting and Analysing Statistics on Women in the Informal Sector and Their Contributions to National Product: Results of Regional Workshops.* INSTRAW/BT/CRP.1. Santo Domingo: United Nations.

Ironmonger, Duncan. 1996. "Counting outputs, capital inputs and caring labor: estimating gross household product." *Feminist Economics* 2(3), Fall: 37–64.

Itoh, Makoto, and Nobuharu Yokokawa. 1979. "Marx's theory of market-value." In D. Elson, ed. *Value: the Representation of Labour in Capitalism.* London: CSE/Humanities Press, 102–14.

Jaquette, Jane. 2001. "Constructing democracy: feminist theory and the challenges of the post–Cold War world." Paper presented at the XXIII International Congress of the Latin American Studies Association. Washington, D.C., September 6–8.

Jennings, Ann. 1993. "Public or private? institutional economics and feminism." In M. Ferber and J. Nelson, eds., *Beyond Economic Man.* Chicago: University of Chicago Press, 111–29.

Juster, F. Thomas, and Frank P. Stafford. 1991. "The allocation of time: empirical findings, behavioral models, and problems of measurement." *Journal of Economic Literature* XXIX, June: 471–522.

Kabeer, Naila. 2000. *The Power to Choose: Bangladesh Women and Labour Market Decisions in London and Dhaka.* London and New York: Verso.

Katz, Elizabeth. 1991. "Breaking the Myth of Harmony: Theoretical and Methodological Guidelines to the Study of Rural Third World Households." *Review of Radical Political Economics* 23(3&4): 37–56.

———. 1991. "Breaking the Myth of Harmony: Theoretical and Methodological Guidelines to the Study of Rural Third World Households," *Review of Radical Political Economics,* 23(3&4), Fall/Winter: 148–73.

Katz, H. C. 2000. *Converging Divergencies: Worldwide Changes in Employment Systems.* Ithaca, N.Y.: Cornell University Press.

Keck, Margaret, and Kathryn Sikkink. 1998. *Activists Beyond Borders: Advocacy Networks in International Politics.* Ithaca and London: Cornell University Press.

Kohr, Martin. 2000. "North-South Tensions at the WTO: The Need to Rethink Liberalization and Reform the WTO." Paper presented at the Global Tensions Conference. Cornell University, March 8–9.

Koopman, Jeanne. 1991. "Neoclassical household models and modes of household production: problems and analysis of African agricultural households." *Review of Radical Political Economics* 23(3&4), Fall/Winter: 148–73.

Kotz, David. 1995. "Lessons for a future socialism from the Soviet collapse." *Review of Radical Political Economics* 27(3), September: 1–11.

Kruse, T. 2000. "Acaso eres trabajador? Notes on industrial restructuring, labor processes, and social subjects." Presented at the Workshop on Latin American Labor and Globalization, Social Science Research Council. San Jose, Costa Rica, July 11–12.

Kucera, David. 2001. *Gender, Growth and Trade: The Miracle Economies of the Postwar Years*. London and New York: Routledge.

Kucera, David, and William Milberg. 2000. "Gender Segregation and Gender Bias in Manufacturing Trade Expansion: Revisiting the "Wood Asymmetry." *World Development* 28(7): 1,191–1,210.

Langfeldt, Enno. 1987. "Trabajo no remunerado en el contexto familiar," in *Revista de Estudios Económicos* 1: 131–46.

Laufer, Jacqueline. 1998. "Equal opportunities and employment change in West European economies." *Feminist Economics* 4(1), Spring: 53–69.

Lavinas, Lena. 1996. "As mulhares no universo da pobreza: o caso Brasileiro." *Estudoes Feministas* 4(2): 464–79.

Leacock, Eleanor and Helen Safa, eds. 1986. *Women's Work: Development and the Division of Labor by Gender*. South Hadley, Mass.: Bergin and Garvey Publishers.

League of Nations. 1938. *Statistics of the Gainfully Occupied Population: Definitions and Classifications Recommended by the Committees of Statistical Experts*. Studies and Reports on Statistical Methods, No.1. Geneva.

Leigh, Duane. 1995. *Assisting Workers Displaced by Structural Change*. Kalamazoo, Mich.: W.E. Upjohn Institute for Employment Research.

Lim, Lin, ed. 1998. *The Sex Sector. The Economic and Social Basis of Prostitution in South East Asia*. Geneva: ILO.

Lim, Linda. 1983. "Capitalism, imperialism, and patriarchy: the dilemma of third world women workers in multinational factories." In J. Nash and M. Fernandez-Kelly, eds. *Women, Men, and the International Division of Labor*. Albany, N.Y.: State University of New York Press.

Lind, Amy, 1990. "Gender, power and development: popular women's organizations and the politics of needs in Ecuador." In Arturo Escobar and Socia Alvarez, eds. *The Making of Social Movements in Latin America*. Boulder, Colo.: Westview Press, 134–49.

———. 1997. "Gender, development, and urban social change: women's community action in global cities." *World Development* 25(8): 1205–23.

Lloyd, Cynthia, ed. 1975. *Sex, Discrimination, and the Division of Labor*. New York: Columbia University Press.

Lloyd, Cynthia, and Beth Niemi. 1979. *Economics of Sex Differentials*. New York: Columbia University Press.

Lutzel, Heinrich. 1989. "Household production and national accounts." Paper presented at the Second ECE/INSTRAW Joint Meeting on Statistics on Women. Geneva, November 13–16.

———. 1998. "Gender and social security policy: pitfalls and possibilities." *Feminist Economics* 4(1), Spring: 1–26.

MacDonald, Martha. 1998. "Gender and Social Security Policy: Pitfalls and Possibilities," *Feminist Economics,* 4(1), Spring: 1–25.

MacKintosh, Maureen. 1978. "Domestic labor and the household." In Annette Kuhn and Annemarie Wolpe, eds. *Feminism and Materialism.* London: Routledge.

Madden, Janice. 1972. "The development of economic thought on the 'Women Problem.'" Special issue on the Political Economy of Women. *The Review of Radical Political Economics* 4(3):21–38.

Majnoni d'Intignano, Beatrice. 2000. "Equality between women and men: economic aspects." In *Governance, Equity and Global Markets: the Annual Bank Conference on Development Economics.* Paris: La Documentation française.

Marwell, Gerald, and Ruth Ames. 1981. "Economists free ride, does anyone else? (Experiments in the Provision of Public Goods)." *Journal of Public Economics* 15(3): 295–310.

McCloskey, Deidre. 1996. "Love and money: a comment on the market debate." *Feminist Economics.* 2(2), Summer: 137–40.

McCloskey, Don. 1990. *The Rhetoric of Economics.* Chicago: The University of Chicago Press.

———. 1993. "Some consequences of a conjective economics." In B. Nelson and M. Ferber, eds. *Beyond Economic Man.* Chicago: University of Chicago Press, 69–93.

McCrate, E. 1995. "The growing divide among American women." Unpublished paper, University of Vermont, Department of Economics.

McKay, Aisla. 2001. "Rethinking work and income maintenance policy: promoting gender equality through a citizen's basic income." *Feminist Economics* 7(1), March: 97–118.

McMichael, Philip 1999. "The global crisis of wage labor." *Studies in Political Economy* 58: 11–40.

Merchant, Carolyn. 1989. *The Death of Nature: Women, Ecology and the Scientific Revolution.* San Francisco: Harper and Row Publishers.

Meurs, Micke. 1998. "Imagined and imagining equality in East Central Europe: gender and ethnic differences in the economic transformation of Bulgaria." In J. Pickles and A. Smith, eds. *Theorising Transition: The Political Economy of Post-Communist Transformations.* London and New York: Routledge: 330–46.

Milberg, William. 1993. "Natural Order and Postmodernism in Economic Thought." *Social Research* 60–62, Summer: 255–72.

Minnich, Elizabeth Kamarck. 1990. *Transforming Knowledge.* Philadelphia: Temple University Press.

Moghadam, Valentine. 1993. *Democratic Reform and the Position of Women in Transitional Economies.* Oxford: Clarendon Press.

———. 2000. "Gender and economic reforms: a framework for analysis and evidence from Central Asia, the Caucasus and Turkey." In F. Açar and A. Gunes Ayata, eds. *Gender and Identity Construction: Women of Central Asia, the Caucasus and Turkey.* Leiden: Brill: 23–43.

Molyneux, Maxine. 1979. "Beyond the domestic labour debate." *New Left Review*, 115, July/August): 3–28.

———. 1985. "Mobilization without emancipation? women's interests, the state, and revolution in Nicaragua." *Feminist Studies* 11(2): 227–54.

Montecinos, Verónica. 2001. "Feminists and technocrats in the democratization of Latin America: a prolegomenon." In *International Journal of Politics, Culture and Society* 15(1), Fall: 175–99.

Moser, Caroline. 1993. *Gender Planning and Development: Theory, Practice and Training*. London and New York: Routledge.

Nash, June, and Maria Patricia Fernández-Kelly, eds. 1983. *Women, Men, and the International Division of Labor*. Albany, N.Y.: State University of New York Press.

Nelson, Julie. 1993. "Some consequences of conjective economics." In Marianne Ferber and Julie Nelson, eds. *Beyond Economic Man*. Chicago: University of Chicago Press: 69–93.

North, Douglass. 1994. "Economic performance through time." *American Economic Review* 84(3): 359–68.

Nussbaum, Martha. 2001. "Women's capabilities and social justice." Paper presented at the conference on Global Tensions: A Conference in Honor of Ester Boserup. Cornell University, March 9–10.

O'Grady, Mary Anastasia. 1997. "Don't blame the market for Argentina's woes." *Wall Street Journal*, May 30.

Oliveira, O., de. 2000. "Households and families in a context of crisis, adjustment and economic restructuring." Colegio de Mexico, Center for Sociological Studies.

Ong, Aiwa. 1987. *Spirits of Resistance and Capitalist Discipline: Women Factory Workers in Malaysia*. Albany, N.Y.: SUNY Press.

Osterman, Paul., ed. 1996. *Broken Ladders: Managerial Careers in Transition*. New York: Oxford University Press.

———. 1999. *Security Prosperity: The American Labor Market: How It Has Changed and What to Do about It*. Princeton, N.J.: Princeton University Press.

Ozler, S. 2001. "Export led industrialization and gender differences in job creation and destruction: micro evidence from Turkish manufacturing sector. Unpublished paper, Economics Department, University of California at Los Angeles.

Palmer, Ingrid. 1977. "Rural women and the basic-needs approach to development." *International Labour Review*, 115(1), January-February: 97–107.

———. 1991. *Gender and Population in the Adjustment of African Economies: Planning for Change, Women, Work and Development* 19. Geneva: ILO.

Papaglia, A. 1995. *The Relocation of Smith-Corona: An Inside Look at Outplacement Counseling*, Cortland, N.Y.: Cortland Press.

Pearson, Ruth, and C. Jackson, eds. 1998. *Feminist Visions of Development: Gender Analysis and Policy*. London: Routledge.

Pérez-Sáinz, J.P. 2000. "Labor market transformations in Latin America during the 90s: some analytical remarks." FLASCO: Costa Rica.

Perlow, Leslie. 1997. *Finding Time: How Corporations, Individuals, and Families Can Benefit from New Work Practices.* Ithaca, N.Y.: Cornell University Press.

Peterson, Janice, and Margaret Lewis, eds. 1999. *The Elgar Companion to Feminist Economics.* Cheltenham, UK, and Northhampton, Mass.: Edward Elgar Publishers.

Piore, M., and C. Sabel. 1984. *The Second Industrial Divide.* New York: Basic Books.

Polacheck, Solomon. 1995. "Human capital and the gender earnings gap." In E. Kuiper and J. Sap, eds. *Out of the Margins: Feminist Perspectives on Economics.* London and New York: Routledge: 61–79.

Polanyi, Karl. 1957. *The Great Transformation.* Boston: Beacon Press.

Portes, Alejandro, and Manuel Castells. 1989. *The Informal Economy.* Baltimore: The Johns Hopkins University Press.

Power, Marilyn, and Sam Rosenberg. 1995. "Race, class and occupational mobility: black and white women in service work in the United States." *Feminist Economics* 1(3), Fall: 40–59.

Prugl, Elizabeth. 1999. *The Global Construction of Gender: Home-Based Work in the Political Economy of the 20th Century,* New York: Columbia University Press.

Pujol, Michele. 1992. *Feminism and Anti-Feminism in Early Economic Thought.* Edward Elgar.

Pyle, Jean. 1983. "Export-led development and the underemployment of women: the impact of discriminatory employment policy in the Republic of Ireland." In J. Nask and M. P. Fernández-Kelly, eds. *Women, Men and the International Division of Labor.* Albany, N.Y.: SUNY Press: 85–112.

Recio, A. 2000. "Empresa, distribución de la renta y relaciones laborales." Paper presented at the VII Jornada de Economía Crítica. Albacete, Spain, February 3–5.

Reich, Michael, David Gordon, and Richard Edwards. 1980. "A theory of labor market segmentation." In Alice Amsden, ed. *The Economics of Women and Work.* New York: St. Martin's Press, 232–41.

Reid, Margaret. 1934. *Economics of Household Production.* New York: John Wiley.

Rodrik, Dani. 1997. *Has Globalization Gone Too Far?* Washington, D.C.: Institute for International Economics.

Roldán, Martha. 1994. "Flexible specialization, technology and employment in Argentina: critical just-in-time restructuring in a cluster context." Working paper WEP 2–22/WP. 240. Geneva: ILO.

———. 2000. *Globalización o Mundialización Teoría y Práctica de Procesos Productivos y Asimetrias de Género.* Buenos Aires: FLACSO.

Rose-Ackerman, Susan. 1996. "Altruism, Nonprofits, and Economic Theory," *Journal of Economic Literature,* Vol. XXXIV (June): 701–28.

Rubery, Jill, Mark Smith, and Colette Fagan. 1998. "National working-time regimes and equal opportunity." *Feminist Economics* 4(1): 71–102.

Rubery, Jill, Mark Smith, Dominique Anxo, and Lennart Flood. 2001. "The Future of European Labor Supply: The Critical Role of the Family." *Feminist Economics,* 7(3), November: 33–66.

Sachs, Jeffrey. 1991. *The Economic Transformation of Eastern Europe: The Case of Poland.* Memphis, Tennessee: P. K. Seidman Foundation.

———. 1997. *Economies in Transition: Comparing Asia and Eastern Europe.* Cambridge: MIT Press.

Sahn, David, Paul Dorosh, and Stephen Younger. 1994. "Economic reform in Africa: a foundation for poverty alleviation." Cornell Food and Nutrition Policy Program, Working Paper 72, September.

Salazar Parreñas, Rhacel. 2001. "Transgressing the Nation-State: The Partial Citizenship and 'Imagined Iglobal Community' of Migrant Filipina Domestic Workers." *Signs, Journal of Women, Culture and Society* 26(4), Summer: 1,129–53.

Santos, Fredrika Pickford. 1975. "The economics of marital status." In C. Lloyd, ed. *Sex, Discrimination, and the Division of Labor.* New York: Columbia University Press.

Sassen, Saskia, 1998. *Globalization and its Discontents,* New York: The New Press.

Sawhill, Isabel. 1977. "Economic perspectives on the family." *Daedalus* 106(2): 115–25.

Schellhardt, T. 1997. "Talent pool is shallow as corporations seek executives for top jobs." *Wall Street Journal,* June 26.

Scott, J. 1986. "Gender: a useful category of historical analysis." *American Historical Review* 91(5): 1,053–75.

Seguino, Stephanie. 2000. "Accounting for gender in Asian economic growth: adding gender to the equation." In *Feminist Economics* 6(3), November: 27–58.

Seguino, Stephanie, Thomas Stevens, and Mark Lutz. 1996. "Gender and cooperative behavior: economic man rides alone." *Feminist Economics* 2(1), Spring: 195–223.

Seiz, Janet. 1991. "The bargaining approach and feminist methodology." *Review of Radical Political Economics* 23(1&2): 22–29.

Sen, Amartya. 1983. "Economics and the family." *Asian Development Review* 1(20): 14–26.

———. 1987. *On Ethics and Economics.* Oxford, U.K., and Cambridge, U.S.: Blackwell.

———. 1990. "Gender and comparative conflicts." In I. Tinker, ed. *Persistent Inequalities: Women and World Development.* New York: Oxford University Press, 195–223.

Sen, Gita. 1996. "Gender, markets and states: a selective review and research agenda." *World Development* 24(5), May: 821–29.

Sen, Gita, and Caren Grown. 1987. *Development, Crises and Alternative Visions: Third World Women's Perspectives.* New York: Monthly Review Press.

Shivakumar, Sujai. 1996. "The concept of value in the recognition of women's work." Paper prepared for the UNDP symposium on Recognizing and Documenting Women's Work. Seoul, Republic of Korea, May 28–30.

Soros, George. 1998. *Crisis of Global Capitalism.* New York: Public Affairs Press.

Spalter, Ruth, R. 1997. *Downsized, Right-Sized and Out-Sourced: Meeting the Challenges of Corporate Restructuring.* Washington, D.C.: U.S. Department of Labor.

SSP/UCECA (Secretaría de Programación y Presupuesto/Unidad Coordinadora del Empleo, Capacitación y Adiestramiento). 1976. *La Ocupación Informal en Areas Urbanas.* Mexico D.F., December.

Standing, Guy. 1989. "Global feminization through flexible labor." *World Development* 17(7): 1,077–95.

———. 1999. *Global Labour Flexibility: Seeking Distributive Justice.* New York: St. Martin's Press.

———. 2003. "Globalization: The Eight Crises of Social Protection." In L. Benería and Savitri Bisnath, eds. *Global Tensions: Challenges and Opportunities in the Global Economy,* New York: Routledge.

Stiglitz, Josep. 2002. *Globalization and Its Discontents.* New York and London: W. W. Norton.

———. 1994. "Rethinking economics through a feminist lens." *American Economic Review* 84 (2): 143–47.

Stone, Kathy. 2001. "The new psychological contract: implications of the changing workplace for labor and employment law." *UCLA Law Review* 48(3).

Strassmann, Diana. 1993. "Not a free market: the rhetoric of disciplinary authority in economics." In Marianne Ferber and Julie Nelson, eds. *Beyond Economic Man.* Chicago: University of Chicago Press, 54–68.

Strober, Myra. 1984. "Towards a general theory of occupational sex segregation: the case of public school teaching." In B. Raskin, ed. *Sex Segregation in the Workplace: Trends, Explanations, Remedies.* Washington, D.C.: National Academy Press, 144–56.

Taylor, Lance, ed. 1990. *Socially Relevant Policy Analysis: Structuralist Computable General Equilibrium Models for the Developing World.* Cambridge, Mass.: MIT Press.

Tiffany, Jennifer. In progress. "Lives and Livelihoods in Cortland, N.Y." Ph.D. dissertation, Department of City and Regional Planning, Cornell University.

Tilly, Charles, Immanuel Wallerstein, Aristide Zolberg, E. J. Hobsbawm, and Lourdes Benería. 1995. "Scholarly controversy: global flows of labor and capital." *International Labor and Working-Class History* 47 Spring: 1–55.

Tinker, Irene, ed. 1990. *Persistent Inequalities: Women and World Development.* New York: Oxford University Press.

———. 2003. "A Tribute to Ester Boserup: Utilizing Interdisciplinarity to Analyze Global Socio-Economic Change." In L. Benería and Savitri Bisnath, eds. *Global Tensions: Challenges and Opportunities in the Global Economy.* New York: Routledge.

Tohidi, Nayereh. 1996. "Guardians of the nation: women, Islam and Soviet modernization in Azerbaijan." Paper presented at the conference on Women's Identities and Roles in the Course of Change. Ankara, Turkey, October 23–25.

Tripp, Aili Mari. 1987. "The impact of crisis and economic reform on women in Tanzania." In L. Benería and S. Feldman, eds. *Unequal Burden: Economic Crises, Persistent Poverty, and Women's Work.* Westview Press: 159–80.

Trzcinski, Eileen. 2000. "Family Policy in Germany: A Feminist Dilemma." *Feminist Economics* 6(1), March: 21–44.

UNDP (United Nations Development Programme). *Human Development Report.* Various years. New York: Oxford University Press.

UNIFEM (United Nations Development Fund for Women). *Progress of the World's Women 2000,* New York.

United Nations. 1984. *Improving Concepts and Methods for Statistics on the Situation of Women.* Series F, no. 33. New York: United Nations.

———. 1999. *Women Survey on the Role of Women in Development: Globalization, Gender and Work.* New York: United Nations.

United Nations Office at Vienna. 1989. *World Survey on the Role of Women in Development.* New York: United Nations, Centre for Social Development and Humanitarian Affairs.

United Nations Statistical Commission. 1983. *Demographic and Social Statistics: Social Indicators and Links among Social, Demographic and Related Economic and Environmental Statistics.* New York: United Nations.

United Nations Statistical Office/ECA/INSTRAW. 1991a. *Handbook on Compilation of Statistics on Women in the Informal Sector in Industry, Trade and Services in Africa.* Santo Domingo and New York: United Nations.

———. 1991b. *Synthesis of Pilot Studies on Compilation of Statistics on Women in the Informal Sector in Industry, Trade, and Services in African Countries.* Santo Domingo and New York: United Nations.

Waring, Marylin. 1988. *If Women Counted: A New Feminist Economics.* San Francisco: Harper and Row.

WIDE (Network Women and Development Europe). 2001. *Comercio Internacional y Desigualdad de Género. Un analisis de los acuerdoes comerciales entre la Unión Europea y América Latina: El caso de Mexico y del Mercosur.* Brussels: WIDE.

Wiegersma, Nancy. 1991. "Peasant patriarchy and the subversion of the collective in Vietnam." *Review of Radical Political Economics* 23(3 & 4), Fall/Winter: 174–97.

Wood, Adrian. 1991. "North-South trade and female labor in manufacturing: an asymmetry." *Journal of Development Studies* 27(2).

———. 1994. *North-South Trade, Employment and Inequality: Changing Fortunes in a Skill Driven World.* Oxford: Clarendon Press.

Wood, Cynthia. 1997. "The first world/third party criterion: a feminist critique of production boundaries in economics." *Feminist Economics* 3(3), Fall: 47–68.

Woolley, Frances. 2000. "Degrees of connection: a critique of Rawls's theory of mutual disinterest." *Feminist Economics* 6(2), July: 1–21.

World Bank. 1990. *Making Adjustment Work for the Poor: A Framework for Policy Reform in Africa.* Washington, D.C.: The World Bank.

———. 1995. *World Development Report.* New York: Oxford University Press.

———. 1996. *World Development Report: From Plan to Market.* Oxford University Press.

———. 2000a. *Making the Transition Work for Women and Central Asia.* Washington, D.C.

———. 2000b. *World Development Report, 2000-01: Attacking Poverty.* New York: Oxford University Press.

———. 2001. *Engendering Development.* Washington, D.C.: The World Bank and Oxford University Press.

WuDunn, Sheryl. 1998. "Bankruptcy the Asian way." *The New York Times*, September 8.

Ybarra, J. A. 2000. "La informalozación como estrategia productiva. Un analisis del calzado valenciano." *Revista de Estudios Regionales* 57: 199–217.

Young, Kate, Carol Wolkowitz, and Roselyn McCullagh, eds. 1981. *Of Marriage and the Market: Women's Subordination in International Perspective.* London: CSE Books.

# Index